CW00786704

Literary Trauma

SUNY series in Psychoanalysis and Culture

Henry Sussman, editor

LITERARY TRAUMA

Sadism, Memory, and Sexual Violence in American Women's Fiction

DEBORAH M. HORVITZ

STATE UNIVERSITY OF NEW YORK PRESS

Published by
State University of New York Press, Albany

Printed in the United States of America

For information, address State University of New York Press,
State University Plaza, Albany, NY 12246

Production, Laurie Searl
Marketing, Fran Keneston

Library of Congress Cataloging-in-Publication Data

Horvitz, Deborah M., 1951-
Literary trauma : sadism, memory, and sexual violence in American women's fiction / Deborah M. Horvitz.
p. cm—(SUNY series in psychoanalysis and culture)
Includes bibliographical references (p.) and index.
ISBN 0-7914-4711-1 (alk. paper)–ISBN 0-7914-4712-X (pbk. : alk. paper)
1. American fiction–Women authors–History and criticism. 2. Psychological fiction, American–History and criticism. 3. Psychoanalysis and literature–United States. 4. Women and literature–United States. 5. Psychic trauma in literature. 6. Sex crimes in literature. 7. Violence in literature. 8. Sadism in literature. 9. Memory in literature. I. Title. II. Series.

PS374.W6 H68 2000
813.009'353—dc21 99-089796

10 9 8 7 6 5 4 3 2 1

For Elizabeth Ammons
and
In Memory of My Father

Contents

Acknowledgments		ix
Chapter One	Introduction: Bearing Witness	1
Chapter Two	Reading the Unconscious in Leslie Marmon Silko's *Almanac of the Dead*	25
Chapter Three	Freud and Feminism in Gayl Jones's *Corregidora* and Dorothy Allison's *Bastard out of Carolina*	39
Chapter Four	Hysteria and Trauma in Pauline Hopkins's *Of One Blood; Or, the Hidden Self*	57
Chapter Five	Postmodern Realism, Truth and Lies in Joyce Carol Oates's *What I Lived For*	75
Chapter Six	Intertextuality and Poststructural Realism in Margaret Atwood's *Alias Grace* and Charlotte Perkins Gilman's "The Yellow Wallpaper"	99
Chapter Seven	Conclusion: Words Finally Spoken	131
Notes		135
Works Cited		157
Index		169

ACKNOWLEDGMENTS

I am grateful for the help I received from James Peltz and Laurie Searl at SUNY Press, for the suggestions and support of my readers, and to Pam Makie for her cover design. I would also like to thank Linda Bamber and Joycelyn Moody, both of whom read an early version of this book. Their insights, conversations, and humanity will always be with me. And, thank you, Jeanne Smith, for help every step of the way.

Portions of chapter 2 appeared previously in *Studies in American Indian Literature.*

Portions of chapter 3 appeared previously in *Contemporary Literature*, volume 39, no. 2, Summer 1998.

Portions of chapter 4 appeared previously in *African American Review*, volume 33, no. 2, Summer 1999.

CHAPTER ONE

Introduction

Bearing Witness

> It is impossible to separate the text of a culture from the text of an individual.
>
> —Susan S. Lanser

> In 1996, a woman was raped every three minutes in this country; seventy eight per cent of them knew their attackers.
>
> —Bureau of Justice
> National Victim Center

> Take your mouth and make a gun.
>
> —Paule Marshall
> Advice from her mother

This book examines literary representations of psychic trauma provoked by sexual violence. Grouping fiction written by North American women either at the turn into or toward the close of the twentieth century, I focus on writers who assume responsibility for "witnessing" and testifying to traumatic events that are pervasively cultural and, at the same time, experienced and interpreted as personal: Charlotte Perkins Gilman's "The Yellow Wallpaper" (1892), Pauline Hopkins's *Of One Blood; Or the Hidden Self* (1902–1903), Gayl Jones's *Corregidora* (1975), Leslie Marmon Silko's *Almanac of the Dead* (1991), Dorothy Allison's *Bastard Out of Carolina* (1992), Joyce Carol Oates's *What I Lived For* (1994), and Margaret Atwood's *Alias Grace* (1996). Despite the differences and dissonances among these fictions, they unite and, to some extent, engage with each other in their respective attempts to deconstruct the relationship between political power and sexual violence at both institutional and individual levels. Put another way, each text qualifies as trauma literature and performs, though not in every case by authorial intention, one of the early tenets of the second wave of the Women's Movement in the West: the fusion of the political and the personal.

My discussion relies on critical methodologies developed from the discourses of women's studies, feminist theory, African American and Native American literary studies, cultural studies, multiculturalism, and psychoanalytic literary theory—all but the last of which developed from the political activism of the civil rights, the women's, and the anti-war movements of the 1960s and early 1970s. In addition, my own expertise in psychoanalytic theory, particularly trauma theory, as a clinical psychiatric social worker and psychotherapist in Boston for many years, informs my readings of the included texts. Conceptually, Annette Kolodny's well-known concept of literary criticism as "playful pluralism" that is "responsive to the possibilities of multiple critical schools and methods, but captive of none" (161) characterizes my critical approach, which blends intellectual exchange from several fields of study.

The pioneering efforts of feminist scholars who have challenged the criteria establishing the canon of "great" American literary works make it possible for me to group diverse texts, which span a century and cross boundaries of race, ethnicity, social class, sexual orientation, and narrative style.[1] To be sure, had I selected a homogeneous group of writers, say, post-World War II white women in the United States, it would be easier to generalize or draw conclusions about their texts. However, such a study would, in my view, merely reproduce existing hegemonic, usually racist discourse. One premise of this book is that the writers in it, whose races, ethnicities, socioeconomic classes, and sexual orientations simultaneously converge and diverge, reflect (though of course, not thoroughly) those who actually produce American fiction. Furthermore, I am influenced by innovative academicians and clinicians in the social sciences, medicine, and the humanities who have recognized the value of liberating psychoanalytic ideology from its patriarchal roots, and who are reworking and revising Freudian ideas to address women's concerns.[2] In addition, a number of African American literary scholars have recently started to draw upon psychoanalytic theory as a critical framework for textual analysis.[3] Significantly, the work of these scholars has paved the way for my study, which assumes as its starting point the possibility of race-cognizant, feminist, psychoanalytic literary criticism.

My chronology focuses exclusively on two *fin de siècle* periods. The first is the turn into the twentieth century and includes works published in 1892 and 1902–1903; the second is the closing decades of the twentieth century and, with the exception of Jones's 1975 novel, concentrates on the years between 1991 and 1996. The seven texts are thematically linked by intersecting concerns, including political and personal trauma, gender and race politics, male violence against women, and curiosity about intrapsychic processes, particularly memory; and it is not accidental that a number of ideas explored in the fiction coincide with radical concepts occupying the forefront of an extended modern conversation on psychoanalysis. Promising to be emancipatory eras for women, the final decades of both centuries are periods in which investigations into psychic trauma, specifically violence against women, occur; the first inquiry focusing on the etiology of hysteria and the second, on widespread domestic violence. At the end of the 1800s, Freud announced the astoundingly high incidence of rape, incest, physical and emotional abuse against women and children, only to precipitate an effective patriarchal backlash which silenced that discussion and discredited its evidence. Likewise, the late twentieth-century revelation of an epidemic of domestic abuse is fighting a similar reactionary backlash, which attempts to mute the conversation and deny women's reality.

Indispensable to analysis of the sociopolitical conditions restricting women's lives and causing their traumas is a political climate permitting, even encouraging, resistance to entrenched patriarchal power. Known for her theoretical and clinical work with trauma and its survivors, contemporary psychiatrist, Judith Herman, believes that "in the absence of strong political movements for human rights, the active process of bearing witness inevitably gives way to the active process of forgetting" (9), which, of course, serves to thwart the battle against sexual abuse. Correspondently, literary critic, Elizabeth Ammons maintains that a reformist feminist "political climate ha[s] the effect of empowering women, including writers," thus enabling them to challenge their "historically assigned inferior status" (*CS* vii) at both cultural and personal levels. Ammons indicates that "women writers at the beginning of the twentieth century flourished in large part—as they do . . . in the 1980s—because of an intensified and pervasive feminist political climate" (*CS* vii). Still, turn-of-the-century fiction by women, like the inquiry into trauma, was followed by a censoring backlash. Similarly, at the turn into the twenty-first century, we find women-authored fiction prospering; yet, an unmistakable anti-feminist backlash trails close behind. Parallel social dynamics underlie both trauma and literary studies. The emergence of ingenious intellectual work, in either (or any) field, depends upon the existence of an introspective, broad-minded, cultural environment. On the subject of trauma research, Herman reminds us:

> To hold traumatic reality in consciousness requires a social context that affirms and protects the victim and that joins victim and witness in a common alliance. For the individual victim, this social context is created by relationships with friends, lovers, and family. For the larger society, the social context is created by political movements that give voice to the disempowered. (9)

In the same vein, Ammons observes that "it is no accident . . . that the second great wave of the women's movement in the United States and the second great burgeoning of women writers as a group occurred at the same time" (*CS* viii). In yoking together these two highly politicized turns of the century, including their backlash, I wish to raise the stakes on Silence. I emphasize the fact that silence is *not* a neutral act; rather, it is a politically regressive one that passively permits the continuation of violence against women and children.

In the following chapters, I argue that each novel in this study examines a repressive sociopolitical ideology of empowerment and disempowerment and, in so doing, confronts the intensely destructive dynamic of sadomasochism. Sadism, as I define it, is a psychological mechanism in which the sadist enacts and gratifies unconscious erotic fantasies by inflicting pain and violence. Masochism, sometimes mistakenly understood to mean the enjoyment of pain, is, in fact, a complex psychodynamic in which powerlessness becomes eroticized, then entrenched within the victim's self-identity. For the sake of clarity, I discuss sadomasochism as it specifically appears in each text, such as organized genocide in Silko's novel or child abuse and incestuous rape in Allison's, as though it were *either* political/cultural *or* personal/psychological. But I am constructing an artificially sharp "difference" for analytical specificity and discursive purposes only, bearing in mind that in *trauma*, the borders separating "political" from "psychological" become blurred, penetrable, and eventually disappear. Indeed, in these novels, the convergence of political and psychological sadomasochism marks the occurrence of trauma. For example: Mutt, in Gayl Jones's *Corregidora*, is provoked to beat his wife both by his jealousy toward men who he believes leer at her *and* his rage at slavery. By probing how legally sanctioned and institutionally promulgated atrocities subjugate not only individuals, but also entire cultures, the writers I discuss recognize that frequently, if not always, the phenomenon of trauma conflates political and psychological processes.

Just as these authors share an interest in representing political ideologies of power in realist fiction, they also document how these ideologies, when enacted, permeate their protagonists' conscious and unconscious intrapsychic lives. That a fictional character may remain unaware of either the political or psychological dimension of her or his trauma does not impede a literary critic from recognizing such meaning. For example: While a victim of domestic abuse may fail to recognize that a component of her abuser's behavior is motivated by institutionalized misogyny, the reader's capacity to perceive such meaning remains. Each writer, in command of her creative production, asserts that the impact of major traumatic events is never identical on any two people, and that trauma manifests where political and psychological forces fuse. On this point, literary theorist, Cathy Caruth, who has written extensively on psychoanalytic and trauma theories, states: "If Freud turns to literature to describe traumatic experience, it is because literature, like psychoanalysis, is interested in the complex relation between knowing and not knowing. And it is, indeed at the specific point at which knowing and not knowing intersect that the language of literature and the psychoanalytic theory of traumatic experience precisely meet" (*UE* 3). At this site of fusion, in other words, story originates.

To comprehend the magnitude of trauma, it is necessary to focus on the individualized nuances and textures of each victim's narrative. Although certain events outside ordinary experience—such as forced relocation and incarceration in a concentration camp or reservation, a Japanese internment camp, or a slave ship—are universally and indisputably considered horrific, they are not unidimensional phenomena that are experienced identically by each victim. Toni Morrison emphasizes the importance of humanizing victims whose experiences are frequently represented as indistinguishable. Therefore, she develops each of *Beloved*'s characters uniquely to differentiate among the "great lump of slaves" (Darling 7) and avoid what Hortense J. Spillers calls "totalizing narratives" (140). Similarly, in the work of the writers I discuss, trauma and the sadomasochism which foments it are carefully contextualized within identifiable, political, historical, and cultural constructions; for instance, Aubrey's incestuous rape of Dianthe in Hopkins's *Of One Blood* has distinctly different meanings from Glen's of Ruth Anne in Allison's *Bastard out of Carolina*.

My concern in this book is to examine how individuals internalize the material conditions of their lives, by which I mean their social and economic realities, through symbols, fantasies, and metaphors in order to build a unique and personalized interpretation of the world. Indeed, this is Claudia Tate's focus when, in her recent book, *Psychoanalysis and Black Novels: Desire and the Protocols of Race* (1998), she thinks about how individuals create internal representations of "the material and the psychical . . . so as to construct personal meaning" (15). Conversely, my book also explores how personal meaning is either consciously or unconsciously projected onto materialist culture by intrapsychic representations. For the protagonists in this study whose lives have been irreversibly disrupted by both an internalization of violent sadomasochistic events and an externalized projection of these events, the borders between their "inner" and "outer" worlds dissolve, leaving them feeling lost and fragmented.

Psychologist Elizabeth Waites explains trauma as "an injury to mind or body that requires *structural repair*." According to Waites, "a main effect of trauma is disorganization, a physical and/or mental disorganization that may be circumscribed or widespread," and this disorganization causes "*fragmentation of self, shattering of social relationships, erosion of social supports*" (22, 92; emphasis added). Similarly, in *Worlds of Hurt: Reading the Literatures of Trauma*, Kalí Tal defines trauma as "a life-threatening event that displaces [one's] preconceived notions about the world" (15). Tal stresses that the event must be experienced first-hand, and not vicariously perceived or mediated through any textual conduit, such as a book or a movie. Likewise, Judith Herman conceptualizes trauma as a "threat to life or bodily integrity, or a close personal encounter with violence and death" (33), a view that is especially relevant to my discussion on "The Yellow Wallpaper" in chapter 6. Chaim Shatan, a psychiatrist who works with Vietnam combat veterans, describes trauma as a psychic state in which "reality is torn asunder leaving no boundaries and no guideposts" (qtd. in Tal 15). Thus, the question for both the writer and the literary critic becomes: How can such a lost, indefinable state of existence be narratively represented? Can narrative, itself, by compelling victim-survivors to remember and to repeat stories suffused with terror, panic, and pain, serve a palliative role in the healing process? Certainly, psychoanalysis believes that crucial to recovering from an experience of trauma is the capacity and willingness to incorporate that traumatic event *inside* one's self as an indispensable piece of personal history and identity. Since, in the fiction in this study, narrative is inextricably entwined with memory and the process of remembering, the greater one's ability to "make story" out of trauma, which is defined differently for each protagonist, the more likely s/he is to regain control of her or his life after that trauma.

While the process of psychoanalysis provides useful paradigms for thinking about these questions and decoding the language(s) of rupture, fragmentation, and even psychosis, for a political analysis of trauma literature by women writers, I am informed by feminism's challenge to patriarchal power, especially to the artificial rupture between the political and the personal. As an example of that challenge, Jane P. Tompkins' well-known, early essay "Sentimental Power: *Uncle Tom's Cabin* and the Politics of Literary History" (1978), confronts "the male-dominated scholarly tradition that controls both the canon of American literature . . . and the critical perspective that interprets the canon for society" (82). Likewise, Nina Baym, in her important early book, *Woman's Fiction: A Guide to Novels by and about Women in America, 1820–1870*, also published in 1978, analyzes the work of women writers whose novels, though widely read at the time of publication, have subsequently been neglected. Explaining that these forgotten texts are disparaged for, among other reasons, their sentimentality, a term linking gender and genre, Baym wishes "to correct such a bias" (14) by taking seriously narratives that "interpreted experience within models of personal relations, rather than classes, castes, or other institutional structures" (18). Similarly, focusing on texts by white men, including Henry James's *The Bostonians* and Ernest Hemingway's *A Farewell to Arms*, Judith Fetterley, in another early study, *The Resisting Reader: A Feminist Approach to American Literature* (1978), points out that because "classical" American literature assumes the universal American experience is male, the reader of these works must either identify as male or endure a sense of alienation from the text. To expose this issue, Fetterley sets out to "examine American fictions in light of how attitudes toward women shape their form and content . . . and thus . . . change our understanding of these fictions, our relations to them, and their effect on us" (xi). However, formative as such early feminist literary scholarship was, it focused solely on white writers and white women readers, a deficiency in much feminist literary criticism that continues to require repair.[4]

Barbara Smith's 1977 landmark essay, "Toward a Black Feminist Criticism," was rightfully "filled with rage" (169) at white feminist critics who were (re)defining feminist literary theory without even a cursory glance toward the work of black women writers. Responding to white scholars who seemed to be advocating the creation of a new canon, yet promised one as elitist and racist as the existing patriarchal one, Smith wrote: "A Black feminist approach to literature that embodies the realization that the politics of sex as well as the politics of race and class are crucially interlocking factors in the works of Black women writers is an absolute necessity" (170). Along with Smith, critics such as Hazel Carby, Barbara Christian, Trudier Harris, Deborah McDowell, Hortense J. Spillers, Claudia Tate, and Cheryl Wall, working individually or collaborating on anthologies, contributed to the development of a diverse, race-attentive body of feminist theory; and literary scholarship written by and focused on women writers of color flourished in the 1980s. In a 1990 essay, Smith notes the positive changes and cites this impressive critical undertaking by and about women of color.[5] Yet, she cautions that although "the personal isolation [Black feminist critics] face and the ignorance and hostility with which [their] work is met have diminished in some quarters, [that ignorance and hostility] have by no means disappeared" (784). I am reviewing this familiar territory in literary history because my study brings together theories and concepts that have not been united under one roof before. Thus, a brief clarification of how trauma studies, psychoanalysis, and feminist theory converge with African American, Native American, and European American literary theories and multiculturalism may be useful.

Like Barbara Smith, David Theo Goldberg articulates the necessity for political analyses of the relationships among power, race, and the literary canon. He advocates multiculturalism describing it as an investigation of "the body of political relations" (9). Central to Goldberg's view is the concept of "incorporation" which, unlike ideas of assimilation and integration,

> does not involve extension of established values and protections over the formerly excluded group. . . . [Instead,] the body politic becomes a medium for transformative incorporation, a political arena of contestation, rather than a base from which exclusions can be more or less silently extended, managed, and manipulated. . . . Incorporation . . . empowers those once marginalized in relation to the dominant and forceful of the body politic. (9)[6]

Focusing on multiculturalism and addressing the necessity of a more equitable distribution of power to include disenfranchised ethnic groups, Goldberg simultaneously, if coincidentally, articulates the primary aim of the women's movement when he endorses access to power for "those once marginalized in relation to the dominant and forceful of the body politic."

Running parallel to literary critical revision and reconstruction during the 1970s, 1980s, and 1990s, scholars in philosophy, history, clinical psychiatry and the social sciences have attempted to extricate psychoanalysis from its gender-determined and race-bound hierarchies. In the United States, since the mid-1970s, white psychoanalytic feminists involved in this project have included Jessica Benjamin, Phyllis Chesler, Nancy Chodorow, Dorothy Dinnerstein, Jane Flax, and Carol Gilligan.[7] As philosopher Diana Tietjens Meyers writes, "Freud's hidebound conservatism regarding gender has not deterred feminists from capitalizing on the emancipatory potential of psychoanalysis that is embedded in its rich account of intrapsychic forces and interpersonal dynamics" (9). Because psychoanalytic theory relies upon an exquisitely detailed, sophisticated framework which locates the onset of psychological growth and development in infancy, it is unparalleled in its focused attention on individual and interpersonal as well as intrapsychic conflicts that emphasize the unconscious. Interested in both gender and racial issues, Elizabeth Abel, Judith Butler, Jennifer Fleischner, Mae G. Henderson, Marianne Hirsch, Barbara Johnson, Toni Morrison, Nell Irvin Painter, Arnold Rampersad, Hortense J. Spillers, Claudia Tate, and Michele Wallace are among the theorists who recognize the multifaceted potential of psychoanalytic theory when it is employed for textual criticism.

Today, the collaboration between psychoanalytic theory and literary criticism tends to focus on poststructuralist analyses, particularly on Lacan's antihumanist deconstruction of Freudian theory in which Lacan emphasizes Saussure's work on semiotics. But critics who predated poststructuralism by decades, such as Edmund Wilson in *The Wound and the Bow* (1941), Leslie Fiedler in *Love and Death in the American Novel* (1960), Kenneth Burke, and Lionel Trillings, had been applying Freudian concepts to interpret literary works. Emory Elliot explains that "it was Freud's career and vision of man, rather than the details of the psychoanalytic method, that . . . fired the critical imaginations" (1013) of Wilson, Burke, and Trilling. Also, between the late 1950s and the early 1970s, psychologists were writing very reductive biographies of writers, including Thomas Wolfe, Emily Dickinson, Sylvia Plath, and Herman Melville, in which the author's "psychopathology" was the vantage point from which they examined the work.[8] Elizabeth Wright and Peter Brooks join Elliot in pointing out that "psychoanalytic criticism . . . was slow to shift out of [this] cumbersomely biographical mode" (E. Elliot 1004). Still, by the mid-1970s, influenced by Lacan and Derrida, textual psychoanalytic criticism began to change; a 1977 essay by Shoshana Felman "inaugurat[ed] a dialectical exchange between psychoanalysis and literature. . . . In challenging the assumption of the authority of psychoanalysis over literature, Felman paved the way, via a Lacanian notion of transference, for a psychoanalytic reading practice" (Wright, *Feminism* 224).[9] By the 1980s, psychoanalytic and feminist scholars began to collaborate in literary studies; presently, in the 1990s, literary critics focusing on issues of race and multiculturalism are deepening that collaboration.

That the paradigm for psychoanalytic theory originated with white, western European, male physicians who envisioned its praxis as a clinical treatment for white bourgeoisie has not prevented some scholars of color from finding aspects of it useful as tools for biography and literary analysis.[10] Hortense J. Spillers, for one, goes so far as to say that "little or nothing in the intellectual history of African Americans within the social and political context of the United States [provides as] effective [a tool as] . . . psychoanalytic discourse, revised or classical, in illuminating the problematic of 'race'" (135). While almost all scholars agree that psychoanalysis is meaningless (despite its advanced feminist revisions) unless it is contextualized within detailed and sophisticated political/cultural analyses, several critics concur with Michele Wallace who argues "that the general failure [of Freudian theory] to take into account the impact of 'race' or cultural diversity is not necessarily owing to anything intrinsic to psychoanalysis but, rather, it has to do with who uses psychoanalysis and what it is generally used for" (Goldberg 261). Indeed, in *Psychoanalysis and Black Novels*, Claudia Tate explains that she seeks to:

> demonstrate the analytical possibilities of psychoanalysis for articulating-complicated conflicts of narrative desire in African American literary texts. . . . Psychoanalytic theory can inform African American literary scholarship by revealing how the material and cultural paradigms of race and gender that typically frame this scholarship do not entirely address the complex textuality of this literature. While such paradigms can effectively describe the external conditions that produce personal experience, they cannot explain how individuals internalize or represent those conditions so as to construct personal meaning. It is precisely this process of internalization—the dialectical engagement of the material and the psychical—that I am attempting to analyze in black textuality. (15)

In this landmark study, Tate (re)interprets and thus stakes an authoritative claim in psychoanalytic theory. She narrows the gap between it and black feminist literary criticism by demonstrating indisputably that individualized constructions of emotional and mental or psychic life are crucial to African American literary scholarship.

Preceding Tate, in the opening paragraph of *Playing in the Dark: Whiteness and the Literary Imagination* (1992), Toni Morrison similarly observes that "the narrative into which life seems to cast itself surfaces most forcefully in certain kinds of psychoanalysis" (v). She describes her experience of reading the "autobiographical novel" of white French feminist scholar, Marie Cardinal, in which Cardinal "document[s] her madness, her therapy, and the complicated process of healing" (v) in *The Words to Say It* (1975).[11] If the work of Algerian born Cardinal is not pertinent to my study, Morrison's illuminating interpretations of Cardinal's "autobiographical novel" are, and I will employ them to argue that psychoanalysis can be used and/or misused as an instrument for literary analysis. First, it can satisfy the need for what Spillers calls "a concept of the 'one' . . . missing in African American cultural analysis" (140). In addition, psychoanalysis can provide, as it did for Cardinal, a relationship within which one reimagines, reconfigures or rewrites her narrative while simultaneously recognizing that self-loathing (almost invariably a symptom of depression) is neither a "fixed" nor an essential entity of one's self. Rather, self-hatred is usually comprised of culturally biased views forcefully imposed from the *outside.* Unconsciously, as if by osmosis, one identifies with these psychologically damaging projections, especially if they are repeatedly enforced. Psychoanalysis facilitates the loosening of the Gordian knot that self-loathing becomes, which, in turn, permits self-hatred to be understood and, ultimately, shed. One of my arguments throughout this book is that an analogous process occurs in literature. Fictional characters experience trauma and, subsequently, as a self-protective response, repress its memories. And, it is within the discourse of healing that the operative dynamics among memory, remembering, and narrative converge. Then they may find both the capacity to remember and "the words to say it," making healing possible.

Problematically, as Morrison points out, issues of race are almost always ignored in psychoanalytic theory, as they are, most frequently, in literary texts by white writers, even when their presence is manifest and obvious. Illustrating this, Morrison spotlights Marie Cardinal's elaborate account of the Louis Armstrong concert she was attending when her initial anxiety attack occurred. That she was listening to Louis Armstrong, a fact which, from her detailed description of the music, was clearly paramount to Cardinal, "goes unremarked—by her, by her analyst, and by the eminent doctor, Bruno Bettelheim, who wrote both the Preface and the Afterword" to *The Words to Say It* (Morrison vii). Only Morrison wonders: "What on earth was Louie playing that night?" (vii). How one "manages *not* to see meaning in the . . . presence of black surrogacy" (13) is a question that *Playing in the Dark* addresses, and it is a question relevant to my study as well. Considering Morrison's analysis, I suggest that the absence of racialized discourse from psychoanalytic theory can motivate interested critics to adapt the methodology of psychoanalysis, *itself*, as a tool with which to analyze, deconstruct, and even repair its own "lack," thus, enhancing its applicability to literary analysis.[12] In other words, in the same way that feminism and psychoanalysis are not necessarily but are potentially compatible, as Benjamin and Gilligan show us, so, too, race awareness and psychoanalysis inform each other as Tate and Morrison demonstrate. A psychoanalytic perspective that is committed to being both feminist and race-cognizant informs the following pages.

Research on psychic trauma, which has been historically entwined with psychoanalytic theory, has increased in the past decade. In the progressive political climate of the most recent women's movement starting in the 1960s, feminists have successfully raised public awareness about sexual and domestic violence against women and children. In a long overdue attempt to encourage women to bring legal charges against men who have raped and abused them, even when the crimes occurred several years earlier, the court systems in several states have adopted reforms that extend the statutes of limitations on prosecuting perpetrators of sexual crimes against children. Additionally, the growing body of literature by and about survivors of the Nazi Holocaust, the Vietnam War, and childhood abuse/incest significantly broadens perspectives on traumatic experience.[13] Recent work on trauma by psychoanalytic feminist theorists, most notably Laura S. Brown, Cathy Caruth, Shoshana Felman, Judith Herman, Kalí Tal, and Elizabeth Waites, focuses as well on what I am calling cultural or political trauma, that is: an officially sanctioned, sadomasochistic system of oppression in which a targeted group, perceived by the dominant culture as an obstacle to the goals of the existing hegemony, are tortured, imprisoned, or killed. In this country, slavery, genocide of American Indians, and the witch hunts of the seventeenth century are examples of cultural and political trauma. In contrast, by using the terms "individual," "personal," or "psychological" trauma, I refer to sadomasochistic violence against a *designated* victim, who is personally known by her assailant; victims of domestic abuse and incest are examples.[14] Michele Wallace emphasizes this convergence of political and personal trauma when she points out that "large numbers of African-Americans (as well as other peoples [sic] of color) continue to be traumatized by the American experience." Furthering this connection, she adds a psychoanalytic perspective when she asks: "What is the role of fantasy and the unconscious in the experience, recollection, or memory of trauma? Moreover, what kind of psychological damage does trauma cause and can such victims be reached by psychoanalysis?" (Goldberg 263, 262). Still, having distinguished here between "psychological" and "political" processes, I want to emphasize once again that, in the experience of trauma, such distinctions fall apart, and, as Wallace's inquiry demonstrates, the categories merge.

According to Judith Herman, "the systematic study of psychological trauma . . . depends on the support of a political movement. Indeed, whether such study can be pursued or discussed in public is itself a political question" (9). Only when political action in North America and Western Europe has focused public attention on the need for social change has research on psychic trauma gained legitimacy. Over the past one hundred and twenty-five years, three unique forms of trauma have emerged into public consciousness: hysteria in the late Victorian era, combat neurosis following World War I, and violence against women and children in our era. Each time public attention to trauma was precipitated and contextualized by political activism. While symptoms of hysteria among middle- and upper-class women prompted the first extended study into trauma, as I will discuss shortly, it was seriously investigated for the second time in response to symptoms of "shell-shock" presented by soldiers returning from the First World War. Research on combat trauma stopped shortly after that war, but resumed following World War II; it reached a peak during and immediately following the Vietnam War, but became a casualty of conservative backlash after the Gulf War when large numbers of soldiers, returning ill from the Mideast, displaying clusters of physiological symptoms, which were eventually classified as Gulf War Syndrome, were pejoratively labeled "hysterics" and "malingerers." It was not until 1980, in the third edition of the American Psychiatric Association's *Diagnostic and Statistical Manual of Mental Disorders* (DSM III), that "Post Traumatic Stress Disorder" became a recognized diagnostic entity; PTSD includes the previous diagnoses of "shell-shock," "combat neurosis," "combat fatigue," and "traumatic neurosis."

To return to the first serious study of trauma, nowhere was the enabling relationship between progressive political activism and psychoanalysis more apparent than in the story of hysteria. Still, the subsequent effort to suppress Freud's announcement in 1896 of his revelation that "at the bottom of every case of hysteria there are one or more occurrences of premature sexual experience, occurrences which belong to the earliest years of childhood" (Gay 103), uncannily resonates with a contemporary attempt to silence the same conversation.

Even for an abbreviated summary of the history of hysteria, one must begin in France at the end of the eighteenth century. The French Revolution of 1789 established a secular, republican government, but one so unstable, it was overthrown seven times between 1789 and 1870. When the secular Third Republic was established in 1870, its leaders were committed to undermining the power base of its chief opponent, the Catholic Church. Overnight, women and hysteria were in the spotlight. How hysteria's symptoms would be interpreted—as demonic possession or medical illness—became a focus of this prolonged political conflict, because, as one of the Third Republic's founding fathers remarked, "women must belong to science, or they will belong to the church" (Jules Ferry qtd. in Herman, 15). French neurologist, Jean-Martin Charcot, a strong supporter of the anti-clerical state, and committed to revolutionizing and humanizing the care of hysterics, was determined to elevate hysteria to the status of a neurological disorder meriting serious medical inquiry. Toward this end, he modernized the Salpêtrière Hospital for the purpose of studying and providing refuge for hysterics. By 1880, he had succeeded in "his mission . . . to claim hysterical women for science" (Herman 15). Though Charcot concentrated on its symptomatology, he did not pursue hysteria's unconscious symbolic meaning; it was left to Freud and Pierre Janet, to expand upon William James's early work with hypnosis to determine its etiology.[15] The result was Freud's publication of "The Neuro-Psychoses of Defense" (1894), in which he recognizes trauma as the source of hysteria. (All three—Freud, Janet, and James studied with Charcot at the Salpêtrière, though not at the same time). Two years later in 1896, Freud published *The Aetiology of Hysteria*, wherein he explains that the exact kind of trauma to which he refers is "premature sexual occurrences . . . which belong to the earliest years of childhood" (103). With this declaration, Freud explicitly ascribes the origins of hysteria to child rape or incest. Given Victorian values, it is not surprising that this revolutionary theory of childhood sexual abuse met with a "notably unfriendly reception" in Vienna (Gay xxxvi).

In his enthusiasm to announce the seduction theory to the Viennese Society for Psychiatry and Neurology in late April 1896, Freud failed to anticipate his audience's predictable contempt. Hysteria was prevalent; moreover, his analysands in Vienna, as well as the women in Paris whom he interviewed and studied, were the daughters, sisters, and wives of distinguished bourgeois families. With his public disclosure that hysterical symptoms were the pathological expression of sexual abuse, Freud was identifying the very men he was addressing as guilty of child rape and incest. Many, if not most, in his audience abruptly walked out, signaling the end of this line of inquiry into sexual trauma almost as soon as it began. Unsurprisingly, the Society for Psychiatry and Neurology, a supremely patriarchal body, refused to relinquish its authority over women's lives; indeed, an open admission that its most respectable men were committing "perverted acts against children" (Freud's letters to Fliess) would indicate nothing less.[16] Herman writes that although sexuality continued to be Freud's focus, "the exploitative social context in which sexual relations actually occur became utterly invisible. Psychoanalysis became a study of the internal vicissitudes of fantasy and desire, dissociated from the reality of experience" (14). Perhaps, the repudiation of the whole of psychoanalysis by many contemporary feminists can be attributed to an understandable, but erroneous, residual fear that accepting a

Freudian theoretical framework is tantamount to ignoring women's material lives. In other words, a Manichean dualism is unnecessarily assumed in which fantasies, dreams, and the creations of the unconscious are analyzed at the expense of, rather than in complementary conjunction with, the social and economic realities of women's lives.

Freud's well-known and much debated rejection of his own seduction theory shortly after he announced and published it in 1896 destructively altered the course of psychoanalysis.[17] Herman holds his renunciation responsible for the fact that psychoanalysis, "the dominant psychological theory of the next century was founded in the denial of women's reality" (14). Yet, it is a mistake to hold Freud solely responsible for ending the investigation into sexual trauma. If, as I argue, a progressive political context is necessary for radical theories to be accepted, or even explored, as was the case when Charcot modernized the treatment of hysteria in the 1880s, then perhaps Freud underestimated or remained unaware of the changes in the political climate that had been supporting his work. In France, the enlightened effort to understand traumatized women was contextualized by the struggle for secular rule. But, when the clerical forces were finally defeated in the 1890s, women were no longer needed to showcase the superiority of scientific expertise over religious ideology. Later, by the turn of the century, as women began to organize and speak out for themselves, it became inexpedient for any man with political ambitions to champion them. "As long as the study of hysteria was part of [a] . . . crusade, discoveries in the field were widely applauded and scientific investigators were esteemed for their humanity and courage. . . . The study of hysteria had lured [psychoanalysts] into a netherworld of trance, emotionality, and sex" (Herman 17), from which they were eager to escape. Suffering women themselves, unattached to any other cause, provided inadequate motivation for professionals to continue the psychological investigation into their trauma; discussion of sexual violence was, once again, silenced by the late 1890s.

Yet, another possibility must be considered. Perhaps the issue of sexual violation, especially incest, evokes feelings so profoundly disconcerting that no matter how progressively politicized or socially transformed the public consciousness is, when incestuous rape becomes part of public discourse, we can expect an almost immediate and very powerful backlash. There is something uniquely "unspeakable" about incest, as if discussing its existence exacerbates it. Consequently, I think we must ask: Is it possible that incest is so widespread, its incidence so high, that just the mention of the word reflexively summons fear, rage, guilt, denial in any era? At the very end of the nineteenth century, when public momentum for an exploration of sexual trauma waned, physicians studying it felt animosity directed toward them, similar to that experienced by those who work with sexual trauma victims now. Where incest is widespread, backlash is unavoidable when public attention is focused on it, regardless of century, continent, or level of enlightenment.

If the horror of incest overrides even the most sophisticated culture's capacity for openness, the resultant silencing of women is certainly political. That women developed hysterical symptoms in response to earlier incidents of sexual violence helps to explain their traumas psychologically. But, the counterpart to this notion is political: Only in a culture that sanctions heterosexual misogyny can sexual violence proliferate. If there is an enabling aspect to the relationship between the personal and the political, there is also a destructive one in which patriarchy, itself, traumatizes women. Herman notes that "violence is a routine part of women's sexual and domestic lives" (28)—a comment which brings to mind Wallace's statement that "large numbers of African-Americans . . . continue to be traumatized by the American experience." Both Herman and Wallace are implying that violence may be an assimilated facet of ordinary life for everyone, except heterosexual white men. In fact, when Pauline Hopkins closes her novel, *Of One Blood*, she seems to be suggesting as much.

That the dialectic of trauma includes denial and repression is readily apparent. We encounter now, at the end of this millennium, an anti-feminist backlash which seeks to disempower women by judging them "hysterical" (read "mentally unstable liars") when they speak of their own trauma. This wave of backlash, which targets psychoanalysis as well as feminism, resonates with the cultural repression that has followed every period of intense public debate on trauma over the past one hundred years. Backlash against Charcot's work with hysteria began around 1893 and included accusations that he staged and scripted the hospitalized women's "performances" for his famous Tuesday lectures. Even before Freud asserted that incestuous sexual abuse was epidemic, Charcot regretted commencing a medical inquiry that focused almost entirely on women's symptoms. Interest in hysteria diminished in France when women were no longer needed to aid the anti-clerical campaign. In a parallel fashion, the contemporary public's indifference to large numbers of veterans seeking medical care for Gulf War Syndrome assures that little, if any, research on combat trauma, such as that which followed the Vietnam War, will occur now. Women's liberation groups brought to public consciousness the high incidence of domestic violence, the need to investigate its psychological ramifications, and the urgency of legal reforms favoring victims' rights, but sadly these advances may not be permanent, and must be vigilantly safeguarded against counteraction.

An example of contemporary backlash, the False Memory Syndrome Foundation (FMSF) is an organization comprised primarily of parents, who, from their standpoint, have been erroneously accused of sexual abuse by their own adult children. Through the psychotherapeutic process of free association, the self-identified victims slowly uncover incidents of rape and molestation committed against them, sometimes years earlier. Because of the severity and nature of the trauma, however, the survivors evoke the defense/coping mechanisms of denial or repression in which the memories are avoided or "forgotten" and, under ordinary circumstances, not accessible to cognition. FMSF members, claiming that repressing and recovering memories of traumatic events are impossible, address virulent criticism, not to their accusers, but to the psychotherapists whom they believe have confabulated these concepts. In fact, the "false memory" group accuses the therapists of brainwashing their patients into believing in the veracity of fantasized recollections.

Uncanny similarities exist between this contemporary shift toward suppressing the discussion of sexual violence against women and children and the nineteenth-century movement to silence that same discussion. Today, articles in both scholarly journals and popular magazines caution women who seek psychotherapy to beware of monomaniacal zealots, disguised as trustworthy psychotherapists, whose mission is to convince naive patients that they were incest victims when they were not.[18] Such accusations that therapists brainwash their patients into recalling repressed memories of sexual abuse reflect backlash in several ways. Representing female psychotherapists as witches hunting for young girls as prey to convert into their "man-hating" cults in a culture that has, lest we forget, a less than tolerant history regarding witches, FMSF members and their supporters portray women therapy patients as mindless zombies who can be manipulated into believing whatever they are told. They also warn therapists against deceitful patients who either fabricate entire stories of child rape or confuse their fantasies with reality.[19] Such propaganda clearly perpetuates the misogynistic objectification of women, while protecting both individual sexual abusers and a patriarchal system that views its women as gullible and spineless, so that it can continue to deny that men rape them. In spite of the unwavering efforts of the women's movement over the last twenty-five years to resist and deconstruct patriarchy's lies in which women are depicted as more apt to beguile, exaggerate, or become crazy than to be authentic victims of sexual violence, a backlash similar to the one at the close of the last century has not been preempted.[20]

Cathy Caruth explains that the victim's capacity to recover repressed memories long after the life-threatening event is inherent in the traumatic experience, and can enable healing. She points out that to assimilate completely the full impact of trauma contemporaneous with its occurrence defies its very nature.

> Traumatic experience . . . suggests a certain paradox: that the most direct seeing of a violent event may occur as an absolute inability to know it; that *immediacy, paradoxically, may take the form of belatedness*. The repetitions of the traumatic event—which remain unavailable to consciousness but intrude repeatedly on sight—thus suggest a larger relation to the event that extends beyond what can simply be seen or what can be known, and is inextricably tied up with the belatedness and incomprehensibility that remain at the heart of this repetitive seeing" (*UE* 91, 92; emphasis added).

If Caruth is right, then, portions, at least, of trauma will be denied upon impact. Still, trauma's reverberations persist. Echoing in the victim's mind, intermingled with her everyday thoughts, the memories turn up in the form of symptoms, including anxiety, depression, and "conversion symptoms," wherein psychological pain is converted into physiological disorders, just as it was in hysteria a century ago. "Conversion reactions . . . can now be understood as the body's way of remembering trauma. The so-called 'belle indifference' classically associated with hysteria can be seen as a direct consequence of the dissociation between mind and body" (Waites 15). If the victim-survivor seeks psychotherapy for her symptoms, it is possible that she will, through the process of free association, regain or recover repressed memories of an earlier trauma.

On what do I base my belief that psychoanalysis provides a reliable—indeed, an indispensable—lens through which to see sexual trauma? First, unlike an ideology such as Marxism, which is predicated on fixed and uniform interpretations of oppression, psychoanalysis is based on individual, hence unique, perceptions and representations of cultural experiences and intrapsychic conflicts. In its most basic sense, psychoanalysis presumes that a patient, whose seemingly irreconcilable feelings and fears have been unconsciously repressed, will reveal what has been buried over time through the process of free association if the analytic dyad is a stable, trusting relationship. Focused on individual personality development, psychoanalytic theory suggests a framework in which a constantly shifting, never static complexity of unconscious structures, influenced by interaction among one's desires, drives, wishes, childhood experiences, physiology, neurobiology, and the totality of one's environment, struggle toward attaining pleasure in "love and work." When applied to literary criticism, this theoretical system, which is sometimes criticized for the intensity of its focus on the self, offers an enhanced perspective not provided by any other theoretical framework, because intrapsychic dynamics, like fingerprints, are impossible to duplicate. Of course, this is not to disavow Jung's concept of a "universal unconscious" or what Wright calls a "trans-individual unconscious" (*Feminism* 224); psyches *do* share symbolic representations. Yet, and this is my point, each remains a unique construction.

Reminiscent of Freud's initial theory that sexual exploitation is at the root of hysteria, the psychodynamic of heterosexual sadomasochism operates as an axis around which my selected novels revolve. Specifically, I show that within each narrative, the male protagonist experiences sexual excitement when he inflicts pain upon or forcibly induces helplessness in a woman. Each writer configures a sexual relationship embedded in this Western hegemonic script of male-subject abuser or oppressor of a female-object. As a psychological phenomenon, this sexual sadomasochism moves across and through racial and ethnic boundaries. At the same time, it is contextualized by the various constructs of race, class, and ethnicity that are uniquely elaborated within each of the seven texts. Heterosexual sadomasochism, a forceful and repeated trope that extends throughout and beyond the fiction in my study, is taken up by these writers as a serious political and intrapsychic liminal event, because it is a widespread, ongoing societal problem. Although it receives a lot of attention in psychoanalytic literature, and although it is contextualized differently in each novel, this psychodynamic cries out for more critical work by literary scholars.

That past experiences of trauma must be consciously acknowledged in order for personal and political relationships to be reconstituted is the connecting assumption between psychoanalysis and the texts under discussion. The authors I study are, above all, *artists* committed to bearing witness to oppression. They understand that true political change is impossible without a metamorphosis in which those desires and wishes considered unspeakable—certain sexual, aggressive, even sadistic feelings—become a deliberate part of public, as well as private, discourse. Their narrative representations of trauma expose the need for social transformation; they target for disruption such bureaucratic institutions as the legal and medical systems or the ways in which capitalism and consumerism comprise the engine of the "democratic" political vehicle.

One recurrent trope in the books I investigate concentrates on the protagonists' varying capacities to use art, especially narrative, as a method of "working through" or healing from trauma. I consider how sexual and artistic passion is expressed in each text when it is developed within a matrix of violence and oppression, and I seek to understand how memories of torture and stories of brutality can be preserved, even transformed into art, without reproducing oppression. Contrary to the American myth of "leave the past behind/begin life anew," neither individuals nor civilizations can survive severance from their familial and historical ancestries, despite the sadomasochistic relationships within them. Indeed, as the chapters which follow show, rupture with the past precipitates trauma. Each novel traces a course parallel to that of the process of psychoanalysis in that individual characters (as well as entire cultures) experience crises when they unintentionally thwart the possibility of a future in order to avoid a confrontation with a painful past. As if mimicking the "talking cure," each text functions as an analyst.[21] The rhetorical structure or analyst provides for the character or patient a framework wherein repressed memories can surface into consciousness. And the latter finds, to varying degrees, that hysterical symptoms diminish when repressed memories and their accompanying feelings are recalled and verbalized.

Theodor Adorno believed that no meaningful poetry could be written after Auschwitz because, in his view, post-holocaust art automatically attempts to make sense of that event and, by that very act, insults and invalidates the ordeal of survivors. Countering Adorno, I agree with Kalí Tal who believes that "literature of trauma is written from the need to tell and retell the story of the traumatic experience, to make it 'real' both to the victim and to the community" (21). The need to be listened to, in addition to the "need to tell," is a trope that appears and reappears in the written and oral testimony of victims. According to Peter Brooks, "the desire to *captivate* a possible listener" (*RP* 54) is fundamental to each of us. (Interestingly, "captivate" can be read as having sadistic overtones.) In reference to sexual abuse, repetitive "retelling" emanates, at least in part, from the surrounding guilt and shame that rape and incest victims almost invariably report. My chapter that discusses Jones's *Corregidora* and Allison's *Bastard out of Carolina*, proposes a political-psychological analysis of this humiliation and self-imposed blame that plagues abuse victims.

While five of the seven texts in my grouping are contemporary, none is formally postmodern. Though Oates is considered a neo-realist and her work, like Silko's and Atwood's, incorporates characteristics of postmodernism, none would be appropriately categorized with postmodern authors such as Kathy Acker, John Barth, Donald Barthelme, William Gaddis, William Gass, Don DeLillo, Tama Janowitz, and Thomas Pynchon.[22] Under the rubric of postmodernism, a "thoroughly" deconstructed, non-hierarchical framework in which every subjective utterance has equal value and no voice has more "author"ity than any other, anyone's assertion that s/he is a victim because s/he feels victimized must be considered legitimate. On the subject of postmodern critics, Tal asserts:

> The approach of most postmodern critics is inappropriate when applied to reading the literature of trauma. Postmodern critics have been concerned with the problematics of *reading*. As professional readers, it is in their interest to put forward the argument that any text, properly read, can be "understood." Those among them who do not claim to be able to divine the author's intent simply claim that an author's intent is irrelevant. It's obvious that this approach won't work for the literatures of trauma. The act of *writing*, perhaps less accessible to the critic, is as important as the act of reading. (17)

Competing tensions exist between an aspect of postmodernism—that which privileges one's subjective perspective over all else—and the need for a consensual definition of trauma. Certainly, it makes sense for the sufferer to determine the presence of trauma. Yet, the following example emphasizes how a survivor's *right* to a narrative may be co-opted by inappropriately applying the diagnosis of "trauma."

Literary theorist Shoshana Felman and psychoanalyst and co-founder of the Video Archive for Holocaust Testimonies at Yale, Dori Laub, collaborated to produce the book, *Testimony: Crisis in Witnessing in Literature, Psychoanalysis, and History* (1992). In it, Felman discusses a crisis of "critical dimensions . . . gathering momentum" (48) that broke out in a graduate seminar she taught at Yale entitled "Literature and Testimony." After the class watched videotaped interviews with holocaust survivors, "there was a sort of *panic* that consisted in both emotional and intellectual disorientation, *loss of direction.* One person [felt] that he literally 'lost the whole class,' everything . . . got somehow 'disconnected.' The videotape viewing was described [by students] as 'a shattering experience' . . . 'not just painful, but very powerful'; [Felman named their feelings] '*anxiety of fragmentation*'" (49). Undoubtedly, viewing the survivors' testimony evoked myriad profoundly disturbing feelings in Felman's students, but such reactions are warranted and fitting; indeed, they are noteworthy only if absent. Rather than perceive the class's distress as normative and help her students integrate the emotions quite naturally evoked from the excruciating testimonial videotapes, Felman interpreted their responses as expressions of *their* trauma, features of which she compared to what is experienced by actual survivors. In Felman's reworked definition, one participates in the victim's trauma, *and is oneself a victim*, simply by coming into contact with a survivor's testimony.

Felman addressed her class: "I will suggest that the significance of the event of your viewing of the first Holocaust videotape was, not unlike [Paul] Celan's own Holocaust experience, something akin to *a loss of language*. . . . It is this *loss* Celan precisely talks about. . . . You can now, perhaps, relate to this loss more immediately, more viscerally, when you hear the poet say that *language was 'all that remained'*" (50). Felman interprets the fact that the "obsessed" (48) seminar members shared their emotions with each other outside rather than within the classroom as evidence of their need to "*break the very framework of the class* (and thus emerge outside it), in much the same way as the writers [the class] examined somehow all *broke through the framework* of what they had initially set out to write" (48). In my view, her "knowledge" of *their* feelings is highly problematic, as is her manipulation of Celan's (and other survivors') experience in a concentration camp.[23] Significantly, according to Felman, one need not experience trauma to be a trauma victim; to feel "something akin" to, in this case, the pain of a holocaust survivor, it is sufficient to watch videotapes of survivors and listen to their stories. Clearly, I differ. Trauma victims and survivors have experienced *first-hand* a "life-threatening event that displaces [their] preconceived notions about the world" (Tal 15). Second-hand or vicarious perception of trauma is not tantamount to experiencing it.

Emphasizing the specifically individualized or "first-hand" dynamics of trauma in each text in this study, I examine a particular facet of women's subjugation, which includes not just the sadism forced upon them, but also how powerlessness becomes eroticized, then entrenched within the victim's self-identity. In a recent essay, Mae Henderson argues that women "participate in the eroticization of dominance and submission. . . . [This] complicity on the part of women . . . reflect[s] the extent to which the sexual fantasies and practices of women have been conditioned by an ideology of female submission, thereby perpetuating patriarchal violence and domination" (286). Additionally, psychoanalytic feminist Jessica Benjamin, in describing her own work, states that she "seeks to understand how domination is anchored in the hearts of the dominated" (*BL* 5). I believe that unless or until we illuminate and understand this dynamic, instead of denying it, we will unwittingly collude with malicious violence against women.

In "Power, Sexuality, and Intimacy" (1986), Muriel Dimen writes that there is "a missing link in the theory of patriarchy. . . . Although theories of mind and society abound, no present theory puts psyche and society together so that the whole story of patriarchy, including women's experience and its contradictions can be told" (35). My aim is to address the disjuncture Dimen identifies with trauma as an overt site of convergence. The power of the unconscious, the depth and persistence of desires and wishes that entrap people within repetition compulsions that can determine entire courses of lives are evident tropes repeated within many fictional texts and are beginning to receive deserved attention in literary scholarship.

My Introduction is weighted in the direction of theory. Still, all of the authors I have grouped employ innovative narrative form, characterized by ambiguity, paradox, alternating narrators, fluidity of time, and a facade of chaos, which, in turn, creates politically radical parallel- or subtexts formally. Each one challenges the post-Enlightenment concept of a "grand narrative." For example, Gilman's and Hopkins's works, published in 1892 and 1902–1903 respectively, are early expressions of modernism. Gilman gives voice to the "madwoman in the attic," rewriting her story seventy-five years before Jean Rhys did the same for Bronte's Bertha Rochester. Eliminating the omniscient (read male) narrator, Gilman breaks with tradition by authorizing the subjective, marginalized voice of an unnamed woman descending irretrievably into madness to write her own story, while she simultaneously challenges the prevalent cultural practices on defining and treating madness, hysteria, and depression. Hopkins, whose work Elizabeth Ammons calls "profoundly experimental" (Greusser 211), blends existing genres to invent her own hybrid narrative style. Three of the five contemporary novels—those written by Jones, Silko, and Allison between 1975 and 1994—overtly discuss taboo, suppressed subjects, including heterosexual and homosexual sadomasochism.

Oates experiments with narrative form to bring together what most critics consider to be an oxymoronic pairing: the tradition of realism with the project of postmodernism. Her fully developed, psychologically complex and accurate characters are geographically and historically rooted in time and place (New York in the early 1990s). Deliberately, she writes herself into the tradition of American realism that includes Charles Chesnutt, Theodore Dreiser, Ellen Glasgow, William Dean Howells, Sinclair Lewis, Upton Sinclair, and Edith Wharton; in fact, I argue that she models her protagonist, Corky Corcoran, on Sinclair Lewis's George Babbitt, a fictional character clearly identified with realism. Yet, her book's title adumbrates the ambiguity surrounding the novel. As in Gilman's story, the reader is gradually ensconced in the narrator's increasingly depressed and deluded mind, and it is only from his perspective that we can experience the narrative.

Atwood also experiments at a formal level, producing *Alias Grace* in an original form I call poststructural realism. Though she insists that "truth" is an ephemeral, sociolinguistic construction, she does so in the context of a life-and-death double murder trial in which discovering "what really happened" is the primary objective. Like Oates, Atwood draws her characters with exquisite, anti-minimalist delineation consistent with realism's tradition; in fact, reviewers have commented on the nuanced details with which she represents Grace Marks's work life.[24] But as soon as we begin to feel comfortable with Grace's version of her narrative, she reminds us that "perhaps [she] will tell [us] lies" (*AG* 41). Atwood further blurs the border between inside and outside the text by interspersing authentic historical figures with fictional characters, without revealing which is which. Likewise, she combines imagined reports of the murders with actual newspaper accounts from 1842. She confronts and undermines the concept of truth by contradicting every assertion of it with an equally plausible, yet conflicting, version of the same event.

The chapter immediately following this Introduction, "Reading the Unconscious in Leslie Marmon Silko's *Almanac of the Dead*," focuses on intersecting political and psychological trauma in the aftermath of the European invasion of the Americas resulting in the dislocation and genocide of Native Americans. Silko probes the inter- and intra-generational repetition of sexual violence, specifically sexual sadomasochism, from both cultural and psychological perspectives. She asserts that a heretofore unexamined, though lethal, repercussion of the European conquest is a perverse and pervasive sexual dynamic in which erotic pleasure is experienced only when physical pain is inflicted on the "other." Sexuality, as well as art and literature, has been contaminated. In this anti-capitalist novel, Silko redefines what it means to "consume" or be "consumed."

In chapter 3, "Freud and Feminism in Gayl Jones's *Corregidora* and Dorothy Allison's *Bastard out of Carolina*," I propose a new paradigm for thinking about certain aspects of a girl's so-called Oedipal conflict, a paradigm reflective of the pleasure and "author"ity of "story-making" as opposed to the failure and masochism of "penis envy." Experiencing sexual desire, intellectual curiosity, and the need or drive for knowledge at around the same time, the child interweaves sexuality and narrative, using the latter to explain the former. Focusing on the conflation of psychological trauma and culturally sanctioned violence, I discuss the shame that *Corregidora*'s Ursa and *Bastard*'s Ruth Anne share regarding their sadomasochistic sexual fantasies.

Chapter 4, "Hysteria and Trauma in Pauline Hopkins's *Of One Blood; Or the Hidden Self*," argues that Hopkins represents her central female character, Dianthe Lusk, as suffering from hysteria's conversion symptoms, including trances, dissociative states, and amnesia, in order to explore the politics underlying that diagnosis, particularly race and gender issues. Since a psychological diagnosis is always a personal matter, and hysteria, in particular, implies earlier, repressed, sexual trauma, Hopkins is entwining the political with the personal by racializing Dianthe's sexual trauma and, in so doing, placing it in the historical context of slavery. In addition, Hopkins's indictment of racist patriarchy, represented by its agent, Aubrey, introduces a trope linking that novel with those of Atwood and Gilman, which I discuss together in chapter 6. The three share an interest in the intellectual and popular discourse at the turn into the twentieth century on the "new psychology," particularly hysteria.

"'Honesty is an art': Postmodern Realism, Truth and Lies in Joyce Carol Oates's *What I Lived For*," chapter 5, discusses Oates's analysis of the hypocrisies of democracy and liberalism, and demonstrates that "forgetting" one's past can be fatal. Formally linking trauma, political/"masculine" power, and sexual desire, Oates examines her male protagonist's intricate way of alienating and isolating his memories. As they conflate, his mind collapses, which Oates rhetorically imitates by shifting between literary devices of American realism and postmodernism, a structural approach that links this text with several others in my discussion. For example, both Oates and Atwood raise important existential questions about "truth," "certainty," and "knowledge" by yoking realism with its theoretical "opposite," postmodernism. In addition, I adapt Lacan's use of Saussure's semiotic theory to discuss the rupture and trauma that result when one's wishes and desires, as well as one's memories, are repressed.

Chapter 6, "Intertextuality and Poststructural Realism in Margaret Atwood's *Alias Grace* and Charlotte Perkins Gilman's 'The Yellow Wallpaper,'" emphasizes the "dialogue" that takes place between these two texts regarding the mistreatment of women in the nineteenth century by the medical profession. While Atwood discusses the evolution of psychiatry by interlacing actual historical figures with fictional characters who converse about the latest developments in psychology and neurology, Gilman exposes the sadism inflicted upon women by the institution of medicine. Both books bear witness to and warn against the traumatic "double-bind" entrapping women whose stories are manipulated or repressed. Knowing that if she missteps, she can be sentenced indefinitely to a "lunatic asylum" (at which point she will lose her money, property, and children), a privileged woman's daily existence can be a life-and-death struggle to hide her depression and hold onto her sanity. Both protagonists are imprisoned: Gilman's narrator by the "treatment" she barely survives as a patient of S. Weir Mitchell, and Grace by her sentence of life imprisonment. Atwood mocks, as well as imputes, the legal system that judged Grace, showing that her verdict was based more upon her status as an orphaned, adolescent, Irish immigrant and domestic servant than on the weight of the evidence against her.

In the conclusion, chapter 7, "Words Finally Spoken," I return to a consideration of the relationships among race, psychoanalysis, feminism, and trauma within the different cultural/historical contexts presented in the texts, all of which render complex political-psychological dynamics of repeated intergenerational abuse in which a victim becomes an oppressor. For women who are abused, the novels in this study contend that telling the story, which inevitably is a psycho-political one, can bring coherence to chaos.

CHAPTER TWO

Reading the Unconscious in Leslie Marmon Silko's *Almanac of the Dead*

> In trying to become "objective," Western culture made "objects" of things and people when it distanced itself from them, thereby losing "touch" with them. This dichotomy is the root of all violence.
>
> —Gloria Anzaldúa

> Somebody has to tell the truth.
>
> —Leslie Marmon Silko

In her second novel, *Almanac of the Dead* (1991), Native American writer Leslie Marmon Silko warns Western civilization to avoid the earth's destruction by finally heeding the important message that native people have been trying to communicate for at least five hundred years: bear witness to past and current oppression, and return stolen land. Committed to social change, Silko understands that cultural and political trends in history as well as individual psychological patterns of behavior will repeat unless victims and perpetrators alike consciously acknowledge and internalize their meanings. Silko moves simultaneously in several narrative directions to emphasize her mandate that the past no matter how painful, must be recognized and remembered. Interweaving Native American spiritual beliefs, Freudian psychoanalytic theory, and aspects of Marxian ideology, *Almanac of the Dead* creates an encoded vision of destruction and liberation.[1]

Silko presents us with the formidable task of deciphering and interpreting her almanac's camouflaged, encrypted, and predictive stories in order to avoid the fatal consequences of ignorance. Raising the stakes of this ultimatum so that its violation results in civilization's demise, she suggests that the textual process of decoding her narrative parallels that of untangling the disguised content of the unconscious, for the actual manifestation of each code is the same. That is, both appear through dreams, symbols, stories, and repetitive, frequently surreal, imagery. Through her manipulation of the concept of repetition, she blends diverse ideas into a synchronous text designed to expose the emptiness and arbitrariness of categories and divisions. In her recently published interview with Silko, Ellen Arnold refers to *Almanac* when she remarks to its author: "Your writing itself really models the kinds of things you are talking about. . . . You take so many different ideas, you take what you like and what's useable [*sic*] out of it all, and don't reject things outright" (25). Silko responds in kind, pointing out that "that's what's so special about the Americas and about the tribal people of the Americas. . . . What matters about human beings, and that's what the old folks knew, what matters is how you feel and how you are and how you see things, and not how you are on the outside" (26).

Integrating a broad array of seemingly paradoxical ideologies into her narrative, as a ceremony does through dance, Silko reveals a non-Western, indigenous, whole view of the world in which greed and consumption are anathema. Political and literary theories, tribal customs, and psychoanalysis come together to illuminate the text's unique style. As Silko, herself, explains, "just because everyone wants to fall in and draw lines and exclude, well, that's the behavior of Europeans." "People aren't aware of how much they've internalized these European attitudes" (Arnold 11). Of course, it makes sense that most, if not all, of the literary criticism on *Almanac* focuses on its life-and-death, anti-capitalistic political message and contextualizes the book within issues specifically relevant to Native American culture.[2] My reading is from a psychoanalytic perspective, an approach I suggest Silko invites when she links sexual sadomasochism with Freudian theory. Through Lecha, a central female character in the novel, Silko explains that "Freud had been one of the first to appreciate the Western European appetite for the sadistic eroticism and masochism of modern war."[3] Due to its length and complexity, perhaps any reading of *Almanac* is bound to be a partial one. I offer mine focused in large part on the Destroyers' sexual sadism, as complementary to the rich and variegated interpretations of this very important book. As in Oates's novel, which I will discuss in a later chapter, I call this form postmodern realism. While "truth" and "meaning" exist within the stories, they are multivocal truths. Serving as *Almanac*'s touchstone is a quality embedded within American Indian culture that believes in harmonious blending and coexisting of disparate and discordant ideas.

Silko invents the Destroyers, also known as Gunadeeyahs, an evil clan whose destruction and cannibalism span thousands of years on at least three continents. Acting individually and collectively, passing on their sadistic sexual perversions to each new generation, the Destroyers are the first to develop a hunger for the taste of human flesh. Enacting their conflated desires for sex and violence, which make them, in *Almanac*'s world, the originators of sexual sado-masochism, the Gunadeeyahs contaminate humanity until sexual greed becomes so prevalent, it appears normative. Silko traces the expanding fictional clan for centuries as they branch out, establish themselves in every level of American culture and government and, thus erode every remnant of the continent's native soul. She renders the process by which political and personal sado-masochism merge by imagining how the Destroyers access power; and this, I will argue, leads to the present tense of the novel where the reader immediately encounters a planet whose cultures and people are indisputably in the midst of traumatic events. That most, if not all, of the text's non-native characters are oblivious to the explosive conditions surrounding them serves to exacerbate the emerging violence and to emphasize the concept of "repetition," a central trope in *Almanac*, which I will discuss later in the contexts of literary and psychoanalytic theories, and Silko's interpretation of Marx's stories.

Readily apparent in *Almanac* is Silko's hatred of capitalism, capitalistic greed, and consumerism. In order to create an historical context for late twentieth-century capitalism, she investigates greed's cultural and psychological history by anthropomorphizing it in the form of the Gunadeeyahs. In so doing, Silko discloses her version of what underlies capitalistic greed. At its source, she discovers not a desire for money and private property, but rather "appetites whetted for disembowelment and blood" (*A* 760). Hence, the predilection for power and money that we encounter in the present-day Destroyers, such as Menardo and Max Blue, is nothing less than a modernized version of Greed's sexualized cannibalism. Ironically, in *Almanac*, contemporary capitalism reflects social "progress." Originating as barbaric passion for "more death and more dead bodies to open and consume" (*A* 760), it has evolved *into* socially sanctioned avarice for more land and more material objects to consume. Indeed, Silko poses this fascinating question: Is there any difference between the primitive Gunadeeyahs who delight in the taste of human organs, and the contemporary ones who, like Beaufrey and Trigg, profit economically by killing babies and selling their organs? Not only did the child Beaufrey feel that he and Albert Fish, the Long Island *Mayflower* descendant, who murdered and cannibalized children for nineteen years, were "kindred spirits because they shared not only social rank, but complete indifference about the life or death of other human beings" (*A* 534), but the adult Beaufrey murders baby Monte, then harvests and sells his organs. And, Trigg pays homeless men to donate blood to his profit-earning plasma center; then, as *all* of the victims' blood drain from their unaware bodies, he performs fellatio on them.

In Silko's history, the original Destroyers were sorcerers who first appeared in Mexico thousands of years before the Europeans; it is they who first eroticized violence. Their obvious "appetite for blood and sexual arousal from killing" (*A* 759) forced the native people to escape north into the Arizona and New Mexico desert. But the sorcerers "wanted to continue the sacrifices. They had been excited by the sacrifice victim's feeble struggle; they had lapped up the first rich spurts of hot blood." They conquered, killed, and "robbed graves for human flesh and bones" as they followed the fleeing people north (*A* 760). Two hundred pages earlier, Yoemi tells her granddaughters, Lecha and Zeta, the same story from the old almanacs. "The people who hated sorcery and bloodshed had fled north to escape the cataclysm prophecied when the 'blood worshipers' of Europe met the 'blood worshipers' of the Americas" (*A* 570). Each tribe (and, to some extent, each person) has its own version of the sorcerers' arrival and the ancestors' escape north. But, as I will argue later, only Menardo's grandfather has a story that *explains* the genesis of the original Destroyers.

Linking sexual excitement with murder, the original Destroyers perpetuated sexual sadism until it was irresistible and contagious; they created social/cultural trauma and circulated it through centuries. In this traumatized environment, the Destroyers experienced sexuality only when they were inflicting pain. Intending to warn future generations of the early Gunadeeyahs' sadism, the original almanacs record story after story of their savagery; but eroticized violence only increased, and in her *Almanac*, Silko continues the stories of the Destroyers' sadism. Furthermore, she imagines all the sadism that we encounter throughout her text derives from the same source—the original Gunadeeyah clan. Not until the text ends do we understand the concentricity of these sadistic stories, which link a long line of Destroyers from Montezuma to Trigg, and many in between.

Sadistic imagery replaces artistic beauty in a culture that is so consumed with corruption, greed, and individual hedonism that no community for art exists. Controversially, Silko chooses pornography for the rhetorical strategy with which to represent sadism. In so doing, she reclaims for her text and for women's writing, enraged and sexually violent language, a political as well as a narrative maneuver that expresses how a culture injecting sadism into sex and sexuality will destroy itself. While such discourse is used more frequently by male writers, many feminists as well as non-feminists will consider it no victory for women that Silko has broken a gender barrier to include material historically taboo. However, because the language mimics the dehumanizing story it tells—as Bernard Hirsch writes, "for Silko, how a story is told is inseparable from the story itself" (158), pornography is the deliberate and perfect discourse with which to write the histories as well as the contemporary stories of the Destroyers.

The con-fusion of beauty with bloody violence—I use "con-fusion" to mean both the merging and conflating of the two as well as the mistaking of one for the other—is a trope throughout *Almanac*. Silko explores the insidious corruption of aesthetic beauty, underscoring the mummification of human life and culture during the Destroyer's reign, by narratively linking exquisite, floral images with pain, sadism and death. The "Eric Series," an explicit example of this con-fusion, is a photography montage taken by David, a contemporary Destroyer, of his former lover Eric, who commits suicide by shooting himself in the head because of his unrequited love for David. Violence motivates art when David finds and then spends several (for him) delicious hours photographing Eric's mutilated body. Seese discovers the developing prints but does not immediately identify them as pictures of Eric's suicide. She sees a beautiful "field of *peonies and poppies—cherry, ruby, deep purple, black . . . [a] nude nearly buried in blossoms of bright reds and purples.* The nude human body innocent and lovely as a field of flowers" (*A* 106; emphasis added). As she looks closer she realizes the innocent nude is Eric's dead body, the beautiful flowers his blood and brains—"blood thick, black tar pooled and spattered across the bright white of the chenille bedspread" (*A* 106). When the "Eric Series" is exhibited at an elegant gallery, we meet Seese's exact words in those of an art critic, who draws attention to the "pictorial irony of a field of red shapes which might be *peonies—cherry, ruby, deep purple, black—and the nude human figure nearly buried in these 'blossoms' of bright red*" (*A* 108; emphasis added).

Two very different perspectives produce identical descriptions of the photographs. By recognizing that the photograph is neither Eric nor an artistic representation of him, Seese "sees" through the presentation; and the chapter, named from her perspective, is called "Suicide." Unlike her, the art critic knows precisely what s/he is looking at, but does not see in the sense that Seese does. The Destroyer critic is reviewing Destroyer art and loves it. The photographic fusion of sadism, blood, and suicide shows David's creative brilliance, according to the review, and he is highly praised both for his artistic expression and for his "clinical detachment" (*A* 107). This chapter, from the reviewer's standpoint, is called "Art."[4]

The flowery metaphors—buds and blossoms—simultaneously undermine and expand "feminine" symbols by combining them with violent and violating imagery. This fusion is radical both in the literal meaning of radical (change from the root) and in the political, revolutionary sense. The resplendent yet torturous representations in the photographs warn, as do the ancient almanacs, of imminent destruction. Lecha's tip to Seese—that "Freud had sensed the approach of the Jewish holocaust in the dreams and jokes of his patients" (*A* 174)—reminds us that the process of deciphering the symbols of the unconscious converges with that of decoding the stories from the old almanacs.

And Seese, the first Caucasian to read the almanacs, represents the possibility of hope or redemption for white people through her unfeigned interest in the ancient pages. However, despite the significance of Seese's transformation, the rescue of white people is certainly not *Almanac*'s central worry. [5]

The pleasure-pain nexus repeats intergenerationally in *Almanac*. "Violence begat violence, but if the Destroyers were not stopped, the human race was finished" (*A* 739) is an echoing and haunting trope throughout this text. Individual and organized Destroyers seek sexual pleasure through sadism. In so doing the wish to hurt, abuse or violate recruits the oppressor into objectifying victims. In *America without Violence*, Michael Nagler notes that dominators "dehumanize their intended victims and look on them not as people but as inanimate objects" (qtd. in Tanner 33), permitting the Destroyer to hurt and kill without acknowledging the victim's subjectivity. In a remarkable explanation of genocide, highlighting Nagler's point, Silko explains that if the oppressor cannot annihilate his targeted race entirely, he can infect it with the sadistic, even eroticized urge to become an oppressor and then watch it destroy itself over generations.

Silko suggests a superb example of cultural, intergenerational sadomasochism which, at the same time, exemplifies, in psychoanalytic language, the "repetition compulsion": "The most persuasive evidence of the Third Reich's success could be seen in Israel, where Palestinians kept in prison camps were tortured and killed by descendants of Jewish holocaust survivors. The Jews might have escaped the Third Reich, but now they had been possessed by the urge to inflict suffering and death. Hitler had triumphed" (*A* 546). Certainly, Hitler deserves his place in the line of well-known Destroyers who, like Montezuma, accessed his powers of sorcery to make sadism contagious. In addition, from a psychoanalytic perspective, Silko observes the defense mechanism of "identification with the aggressor": an intersubjective means of coping with trauma in which victims feel compelled to enact the reverse of their own experience, so that they become the sadists and persecute their own victims. In Silko's example of this dynamic—the oppression of Palestinians by Jewish holocaust survivors—the victim-turned-sadist obsessively repeats the behavior and, in so doing, expands the dynamic of "identifying with the aggressor" into a very specific repetition compulsion. While this is a well-known psychodynamic process, it is discussed more widely as a phenomenon occurring between individuals rather than within cultures, even though its implications for cultural analysis seem clear.[6]

In *Unexplained Experience: Trauma, Narrative, and History*, Cathy Caruth explains that "the repetition at the heart of catastrophe—the experience that Freud will call 'traumatic neurosis'—emerges as the unwitting reenactment of an event that one cannot simply leave behind" (2). The performance of the repetition compulsion simultaneously at both the psychological and cultural levels is precisely what *Almanac*'s character, Tacho, refers to when he remembers "the killing and devouring [that] occurred behind bedroom doors, inflicted by parents and relatives; and the village of sorcerers continues generation after generation without interruption" (*A* 478). Tacho's thoughts clearly fuse personal and cultural sadomasochism. "Personal" or domestic violence is what "occurred behind bedroom doors"; yet, this violence takes place in a hegemonic culture wherein "entire villages [were] populated by sorcerers, all living together" (*A* 478). If, in Silko's words, "Hitler had triumphed," he did so for two reasons: his Destroyer sorcery enabled him to dominate his culture and, also, because he understood the victim's unconscious need to repeat traumatic events.

I believe that Silko is inviting readers to explore, even play with, manifold meanings, readings, interpretations of repetition in order to introduce an important non-Western possibility: opposing ideas can and must exist simultaneously side by side. She emphasizes the concept of repetition in her use of Marx's stories, as well as in her reliance upon the original Mayan almanacs for her novel's prototype. She expresses her point regarding repetition and Marx in this way: Angelita, a disciple of Marx and leader of the people's revolution, imagines him "as a storyteller who *worked feverishly to gather together a magical assembly of stories* to cure the suffering and evils of the world by the *retelling* of the stories" (*A* 316; emphasis added). Two hundred pages later, Silko tells us again that Marx was "*feverishly working to bring together a powerful, even magical, assembly of stories.* In the *repetition* of the workers' stories lay great power . . . power to move millions of people" (*A* 520; emphasis added). Undoubtedly and emphatically, Silko is calling attention to the concept of repetition. First, she actually repeats, almost word for word, identical images; then she underscores, in both passages, the enormous power residing within the retelling and the repetition of the stories.

Repetition is not only a trope in *Almanac*; it is a meta-narrative device contouring the novel's structure. Paula Gunn Allen explains that repetition is central to aspects of Native American literary theory, and within ceremony,

> repetition operates like the chorus in Western drama, serving to reinforce the theme and to focus the participants' attention on central concerns while intensifying their involvement with the enactment. One suits one's words and movements (if one is a dancer) to the repetitive pattern. Soon breath, heartbeat, thought, emotion, and word are one. The repetition integrates or fuses, allowing thought and word to coalesce into one rhythmic whole. (63)

Understanding repetition differently, Freud discusses the "compulsion to repeat" in *Beyond the Pleasure Principle* (1920), in which he writes that the traumatized person is "obliged to *repeat* the repressed material as a contemporary experience instead of . . . *remembering* it as something belonging to the past" (12). Recall Silko's example of the subjugation of Palestinians by holocaust survivors, fifty years after Hitler. Perhaps she attributes the Destroyers' intergenerational evil to the fact that they have repressed all histories, stories, or memories from their ancestors and, as a result, have absolutely no link to their pasts. Thus they blindly and unceasingly repeat the violence of their predecessors.

Although Freud and Allen read repetition quite differently—Freud suggests one uses it to "change the ending" of an unhappy or traumatic event, while Allen describes it as a method used during ceremony to induce an "hypnotic state of consciousness" that allows the ceremonial participant to devote his/her complete attention to "becom[ing] literally one with the universe" (62)—*Almanac*'s capacity to contain such an unconventional blending of views exemplifies, actually enacts, Silko's view of storytelling.

Silko recognizes repetition's presence in the original, ancient almanacs.[7] In fact, she invokes it as she points it out: "the Mayan almanacs had really strong images that are often repeated. . . . A lot of the remnants covered war, destruction, politics, war, destruction, politics" (Perry 326). I suggest one reason the images and stories were repeated both in the original almanacs and in Silko's contemporary one is that, in American Indian culture, the "stories are alive. . . . There's a kind of living spirit in [them] that can't be seen," but they must be told and retold as "whole" because the living spirit is only "there when the story is all together. . . . If you break the words apart and say, 'Where is the spirit?' . . . it is like pulling a human apart and saying, 'Does this make you alive, does this make you alive?'" (Silko in Perry 324). If the stories are alive only when they are "whole," then the same must be true for the body. *Almanac* is very concerned with the separation of the "part" from the "whole," regardless of subject—stories, human beings, or land.

Linking cannibalism and capitalism through her descriptions of the original Destroyers' driving need for human bodies with the contemporary one for money, Silko redefines what it means to be a "consumer" or "consumed." Quests for money and flesh originate in the same primitive urge for power; economic greed merely camouflages the primeval drive to devour human beings. Capitalism, by definition in this text, irreparably ruptures the human soul, literally separating body from mind, heart from soul, past from present, mother/earth from child. Silko's stories about Beaufrey, Trigg, Albert Fish, Hitler, and Jeffrey Dahmer interlock on dismemberment to show what happens when people are severed from Indian ways.[8] Cannibalism may be psychotic, but it is, according to Silko, an inevitable outgrowth of trying to get "around the fact that you have to share" (Silko qtd. in Arnold 23). Put another way, Beaufrey's decision to murder Monte mimics Leah Blue's plan to irrigate the desert, and vice versa, because what is inherently bizarre in both these schemes is the notion that such surgical invasions can be made on and to what is alive, both the human body and the earth.

Clearly anathema to Indian life and culture is the notion that one could survive a complete severance from the land. Unsurprisingly, the white geologist searching for uranium "had violated the Mother Earth, and he had been stricken with the sensation of a gaping emptiness between his throat and his heart" (*A* 121); essentially, he committed suicide by making the Earth incapable of caring for her children.[9] (Lecha and Zeta's father was one such geologist.) Personifying this European mentality that parts can exist on their own, that is, separate from their whole and their foundation, the character of Menardo abandons his Indian grandfather who nourishes him with stories, in order to "pass" for white. Menardo's self-imposed detachment from his past is lethal.

In a dramatic departure from every section of this text both preceding and succeeding it—and itself comprising fewer than two full pages—Silko gives the *only* first person narrative voice to Menardo, which he gives to his Indian grandfather, fondly called "the old man," who told stories of how his ancestors saw "it" coming.[10] Menardo tells the reader directly: "*I* was a young child, *I* felt frightened. . . . *I* interrupted to ask what 'it' was" (*A* 257; emphasis added). "It" is the reign of "Death-Eye Dog" or "Fire-Eye Macaw," stories about the five hundred year domination by Evil. What is Silko encoding in Menardo's first person account of the old man's story of the Europeans? In the story (excerpted below), she delves beneath capitalism to investigate *its* origins, and emerges with a psychoanalytic explanation: traumatized people wishing to feel well and "whole," like the metaphoric "orphans" in the story, may express that wish in disguised form as an unstoppable, narcissistic and sexualized demand for power.[11]

According to the old man, the Europeans were abandoned and betrayed by their god, causing them to become sadistic toward people and indifferent toward the earth. His story links Adam and Eve, the Judeo-Christian first persons with the narrative or grammatical first person. Although the story itself is in the third person, it is discussed from the perspective of the listening child, Menardo, not that of the omniscient narrator.

> Their God had created them but was soon furious with them, throwing them out of their birthplace, driving them away. The ancestors had called Europeans "the orphan people" and had noted that as with orphans taken in by selfish or coldhearted clanspeople, few Europeans had remained whole. They failed to recognize the earth was their mother. Europeans were like their first parents, Adam and Eve, wandering aimlessly because the insane God who had sired them had abandoned them. (*A* 258)

The old man would probably agree with Lecha's sardonic view of Christianity, which is that Jesus Christ *embodies* sexual sadomasochism. In the grandfather's story, the Destroyers are traumatized clans enraged at their god and seeking vengeance. The Gunadeeyahs' big mistake, however, is to project that hatred onto other peaceful civilizations whom they arbitrarily identify as enemies, then, conquer and kill them. But, of course, having misunderstood their own unconscious messages and dreams in the first place, this savagery does not bring satisfaction, only more hatred and a growing need to kill. According to the old man, the Gunadeeyah clan may have started out as victims of their god, but they evolved into monsters. From monsters, they gradually became sadistic, civilized "consumers," and have, by now, objectified the world.

Significantly, the old man's story offers the missing link between the original Gunadeeyahs and the contemporary Destroyers and, to exhibit its importance, he alone is given first-person narrative status. Silko's point, and certainly my argument throughout this book, is that when cultural and psychological sadomasochism(s) converge, trauma will inevitably result; the abandoned orphans-turned-Destroyers illustrate this. Attributing the Europeans' anger to their "flimsy attachments to one another and their children [as well as] their abandonment of the land where they had been born" (*A* 258), Menardo's visionary grandfather "recognized evil, whatever name you called it" (*A* 259), and sensed Menardo's vulnerability to the Destroyers. Just as his ancestors, knew Death-Eye Dog was coming in their generation, the old man felt "it" in his grandson and used the force of the story to warn him. But Menardo's fatal flaw is his inability to translate messages; in Gloria Anzaldúa's words, he has no "awareness of the part of the psyche that . . . communicates in images and symbols" (38). Unable to decipher the old man's stories, he then refuses to heed the snake's warning of death in his dreams. Betraying his history, Menardo loses access to the "ancestors' spirits [which] were summoned by the stories" (*A* 316), and he is "lost" like the aimless Adam and Eve in his grandfather's story.

If the old man's tale is cautionary, then so is the one Silko tells to punctuate the moment in Menardo's childhood when he discovers that the taunts of "flat nose," hurled at him by other children, stem from the fact that his grandfather is Indian. Since this means that all of the adored stories about his ancestors must also be about Indians, Menardo abandons his grandfather because, if it were not for the child's nose, he could pass for *sangre limpia*. Following the old man's death, he makes up the story that his nose never healed from a boxing injury and, from then on, Menardo "passes" for white. The myopia he exhibits by "erasing" his past in adolescence foreshadows the disasters he will mastermind in adulthood as an influential and rich Destroyer. His estrangement from him"self" and his ancestry culminates in his crazy, arrogant invasion of the jungle in order to construct a mansion architecturally imitating the Mayan pyramid found today in the ruins at Chichén Itzá.[12] Neither Menardo nor Alegría, the mansion's architect, realize that they are blatantly disrespecting a sacred temple, nor do they know that during the spring and autumn equinoxes, a great stone serpent appears on the staircase of the original Mayan pyramid. "A series of triangles on the north staircase becomes an undulating serpent as the shadows fall upon it!"[13] Judith Sanders explains that "Alegría's creation is a temple not to a god and to time, like its Mayan prototype, but to money. It is a temple to Capitalism" (3). Perhaps the paragraphs in Menardo's voice, the opening page of the "Mexico" section of *Almanac*, emphasize the profound crossroads when the child abandons his grandfather, his mother—the earth—and is reborn a Destroyer, a critical and pernicious moment for him and for everyone. He pays for his betrayal with his life in a bizarre murder-suicide—among the most insane deaths in the book—because he betrays not only his grandfather, his nation and the earth, but himself.[14]

Surprisingly, and certainly in contrast to Menardo, Seese—See-er/Seer/Cease, joins with native characters who possess what Anzaldúa calls "*la facultdad*—the capacity to see in surface phenomena the meaning of deeper realities, to see the deep structure below the surface" (38). Seese shuns the perverted merger of loveliness and sadism that comprise Destroyer "art." When she is pregnant with Monte, she has a nightmare about a previous pregnancy ending in an abortion, arranged and paid for by Beaufrey. Her nightmare produces images of blood, surgery and numbness, until "dozens of yellow rosebuds have been scattered over a hospital bed with white sheets. The rosebuds have wilted, and the edges of the petals have dried up" (*A* 52). Among the Europeans, Seese alone does not embrace torture, blood or murder. Death and pain do not seduce her even when they come packaged in superficial beauty—a clue from Silko that Seese "sees" and "understand[s] more than you think" (*A* 24). Her flower buds wilt and dry before they blossom, reflecting her feelings about her aborted or "ceased" fetus. Although she starts out a Destroyer, even naming her murdered baby after Montezuma, she evolves through her relationships with Lecha and the almanacs. Revolting against and revolted by Destroyer demands, she helps cease the reign of Death-Eye Dog, first unconsciously through her inability to mother the next generation of Montes, and then consciously when she casts in her lot with Lecha and the revolution.

Early in the novel, Lecha warns Seese that "nothing happens by accident here" (*A* 21). In fact, Lecha's advice to Seese performs as Silko's identical warning to the reader to pay close attention to everything. Life on the ranch is encrypted, and it is incumbent upon the reader, as it is on Seese, to carefully decipher it. For example: the reader learns on page forty-three that Seese has a special ability to understand math. But what we do not know for another seven hundred pages is that this tiny clue into her personality adumbrates her metamorphosis: "She got lost in the lines and equations; she could imagine any number of possibilities from all the signs and symbols. She read many things into them, many more than mathematicians had anticipated. Now she knows that all of it is a code anyway" (*A* 43).[15] Seese's capacity to understand codes places her immediately in harmony with the ancient almanacs—a potential that perhaps Lecha, with or without the help of her psychic powers, recognized in Seese—and would explain the unlikely choice of a young, white woman as the almanacs' transcriber. Additionally, that she interprets symbolic codes recalls the language of the unconscious as well as the first description we have of the Mayan almanacs: "Through the decipherment of ancient tribal texts of the Americas the Almanac of the Dead foretells the future of all Americas. The future is encoded in arcane symbols and old narratives" (*A* n. pag.). In fact, an encrypted passage opens *Almanac.*

Tipping over the stereotype of "women's workplace," the book introduces Lecha and Zeta in their kitchen which, "because of recent developments" (*A* 20), is piled high not with food and simmering soup, but with guns, drugs and boiling dye. Zeta "has been dyeing everything she wears dark brown. No reason, Zeta claims, just a whim" (*A* 21). The implications of this are endless until, toward the novel's close, we understand that the sisters' kitchen is one of many headquarters for the war preparations undertaken by the people's armies. Since Silko's characters and stories do "not run in a line for the horizon but circle and spiral instead like the red-tailed hawk" (*A* 224), readers may not realize that *Almanac*'s centripetal force is political-military revolution: the native peoples' retaking of the continent has been the novel's propeller all along.[16] Uncannily, three years after Silko's imaginary insurrection begins in Chiapas, the Zapatista's actual revolt originates in the identical site in southern Mexico on January 1, 1994.[17]

Although a detailed discussion of the Zapatista rebellion is beyond the purview of this study, it must be mentioned.[18] Silko's belief that the energy of words motivates political, personal, and social transformations is a sanguine assumption underlying *Almanac.* For example, her depiction of Marx's work describes her own. "Word by word, [his] stories of suffering, injury, and death had transformed the present moment, seizing listeners' or readers' imaginations so that for an instant, they were present and felt the suffering of sisters and brothers long past. The words of the stories filled rooms with an immense energy that aroused the living with fierce passion and determination for justice" (*A* 520). Elizabeth Cook-Lynn points out that Silko "obviously clings to the idea that the imagination plays a functional role in political and social life" (89); and Paula Gunn Allen writes that, in Native American literary theory, a story "contains the power to transform something (or someone) from one state or condition to another" (103). Perhaps the Zapatista uprising represents just such a transformation; that is, political action in southern Mexico summoned by Silko's words, symbols, and images.

Before the Europeans came to this continent, the warning snake brings the essential final message: *"what I have to tell you now is that this world is about to end"* (*A* 135). Now, several hundred years and pages later, the stone serpent has reappeared. People make sacrifices to it, "but none had understood the meaning of the snake's reappearance; no one had got the message" (*A* 703). Still, Lecha and Zeta, warned by Yoemi, knew the serpent's return signified more brutality from the Destroyers and, for the twin sisters, it was time to make the final preparations for war.

Almanac of the Dead is a war novel. Calling it her "seven-hundred-sixty-three page indictment for five-hundred years of theft, murder, pillage, and rape" (Perry 327), Silko records over three hundred years of insurrections by black and Indian slaves, revealing a cruelly, imperialistic history that most white people prefer to ignore. The Destroyers' sadomasochistic construction of human relationships, their commodification of art, their objectification of sex, and, in Marxist terms, their alienation from the work they produced leads to "America's fascination with blood and violent death" (Silko qtd. Perry 327). The solution, warns Silko, lies in a recognition that the center of Western civilization will not hold; we must remember and return to the ways of native ancestors who understood that *real* power resides in stories.

CHAPTER THREE

Freud and Feminism in Gayl Jones's *Corregidora* and Dorothy Allison's *Bastard out of Carolina*

> Every mention of her past life hurt . . . like a tender place in the corner of her mouth that the bit left. . . . It was not a story to pass on.
>
> —Toni Morrison *Beloved*

Written nearly a century after *Of One Blood*, Gayl Jones's *Corregidora* (1975) and Dorothy Allison's *Bastard out of Carolina* (1992), both first novels, explore complex, commingled relationships among sexual trauma, its repression, and its potential healing through narration or narrative. Within these "hysterical" texts, in which trauma is forcibly and violently enacted upon a female body, political or historical factors merge with personal and psychological ones to induce experiences so devastating that we wonder how, or if, they can be endured. In *Corregidora* and *Bastard*, culturally instituted, legally sanctioned sadomasochism—slavery in the first text, class prejudice resulting in poverty in the second—becomes inseparably entwined with individual and psychological sadomasochism—domestic violence and incest in both texts, which situates each traumatized protagonist within a concatenation of circumstances unique to her social, historical, geographical, familial, and psychological experiences.[1] For *Corregidora*'s Ursa, whose mind and spirit reside within the sociopolitical institution of slavery, although slavery ended one hundred years earlier, "ordinary" daily life is traumatic. *Bastard*'s Ruth Anne, victimized by systematic sadism in the form of poverty, is physically and socially deteriorating from hunger, beatings, and humiliation because of her family's "low" class status. Contextualized by and inextricably linked with these "external" traumas are "internal," personal, and domestic ones: Ursa is physically and emotionally abused by two husbands, and Ruth Anne is raped and repeatedly beaten by her stepfather.

Still, both novels emphasize the crucial need to understand and integrate one's past especially when that story derives from and is embedded in sexual/violent trauma. In *What I Lived For* (1994), Joyce Carol Oates warns that "the past never yields to the future but in fact directs it, determines it, and is in turn preserved in it" (17). If this proves true in Oates's text, Jones and Allison, who are less fatalistic than Oates, believe that with memory and narrative, Ursa and Ruth Anne (also known as Bone) are capable of moving forward into their futures without repressing or recreating the sadism of their pasts. Judith Herman asserts that "remembering and telling the truth about terrible events are prerequisites both for the restoration of the social order and for the healing of individual victims" (1). Interpreting what Herman calls "remembering and telling the truth" to mean communicating the constructed story of the trauma without violently reenacting it, I suggest that narrative offers a unique possibility for healing. Not until the victim encounters and translates her "unspeakable" tragedy into "her"story can she envision a future devoid of violence. However, pivotal to the formal structure of these two novels is the fact that trauma works to subvert, if not entirely prevent, precisely this rehabilitative process, especially when its victims are traumatized again by being silenced. Thus, each text becomes a meta-story centered upon the protagonist's search for and acquisition of story.

In Jones's *Corregidora*, Ursa literally journeys home to learn the heretofore secret story of her past from her mother. Significantly, she discovers that Mama's sexual life, like her own, has been ruined by slavery. The daughter and granddaughter of slaves, Mama is thwarted by her own grandmother's mandate that the women in the family bear children to whom they must repeat and pass on the story of slavery. Over the generations, this high-minded edict has deteriorated into robotic procreation devoid of sexual pleasure, and lost is the wish to preserve the past. At risk for Ursa is her identity as an artist, without which her physical survival is meaningless. For *Bastard*'s Ruth Anne, whose rape and ongoing beatings by her stepfather destroy her self-image and cause her to feel alienated or detached from her body, emotional survival depends upon salvaging her creative/sexual capacities and pleasures. Only if she unites her wounded and fragmented "selves"—her ravaged and, according to her, "ruined" body with her "other self" who wishes for love, sex, and artistic expression—can she have a future.

Psychoanalytic theory provides a useful framework with which to approach the discursive nexus of trauma, repression, healing, and narrative. The first part of this chapter suggests a paradigm for discussing an aspect of a girl's psychosexual development, which both converges with and diverges from

Freud's theory that sexual difference and epistemology are linked. While Freud attributes the genesis of intellectual curiosity and the drive for knowledge, termed "epistemophilia" to the moment when a child becomes consciously aware of sexual differences, I do not believe that *any* single event exists as the site or the root of "original" or "primary" curiosity. When the little girl notices anatomical distinctions, her curiosity, in its drive to solve this mystery, can work to deepen her capacity for narrative. Rather than the trauma that, according to Freud, results when she discovers that she does not have a penis, I think that her awareness of difference leads to still another rewarding realization: a new or different use of narrative. Relying on *story* to satisfy her curiosity, and motivated by the ecstasy of "knowing," she resourcefully designs a plot to solve a confusing puzzle.[2] The second part of my argument examines Jones's text in the context of contemporary black feminist scholarship.

That "castration anxiety" and "penis envy" have disappeared as subjects of serious discourse does not mean that their resonance has evaporated from our culture's consciousness. Deconstructing aspects of Freud's assumptions regarding sexual difference and epistemology forces a head-on collision with his damaging conclusion that women's "lack" of a penis evokes in them irreparable depression. According to Freud, the girl's first foray into the intellectual world, provoked by her wish to explain biological gender differences, is a traumatic confrontation with the fact that she does not have a penis. From this perspective, women's intellect and creativity are forever inhibited. Even more disturbing is that, without explanation, Freud yokes a woman's depression regarding her body's "lack" of a penis with her discovery or *knowledge* of that "lack." He writes that "the impression caused by this failure in the first attempt at intellectual independence appears to be of a lasting and deeply depressing kind" ("Leonardo da Vinci" 453); but is the "failure" her missing penis, her desire for "intellectual independence," or are they, to Freud, one and the same, meaning that anatomy is both biological and intellectual destiny?

To some extent, I rework Freud's erroneous idea that sexual difference is, for girls, a trauma. Instead, I think that it fascinates and evokes curiosity in children of both genders. That narrative has aesthetic form suggests a child expresses the conundrum of "difference" artistically through story. The urge for a satisfying explanation of "difference," which, for an assortment of reasons, is not forthcoming from adults, inspires the little girl to imagine and narrate her own clarifying script. Indeed, as a puzzle, sexual difference stirs creativity, inviting children to use art in the form of stories to solve the incomparable mystery. Still, the ability to summon stories from within oneself presumes psychological freedom, an internalization of what object relations theorist D. W. Winnicott calls a "good enough mother," which allows the little girl to move unencumbered between fantasy and reality. Such is not the case in either *Corregidora* or

Bastard. For Ursa and Ruth Anne, the stories they ultimately come to "know" are buried in sexual sadomasochism.

At around age two, according to current psychoanalytic thinking, children recognize biological sexual difference in new ways.[3] Most likely, a young girl has seen the naked bodies of boys or men before but, cognitively, was not sufficiently mature for the dissimilarities to have explicit meaning in her conscious mind. That she can now translate earlier images into words evokes myriad feelings, including pleasure, desire, astonishment and, most significant, curiosity. Reacting to her new observations, the child "invents" narratives to demystify "difference." In this sense, fantasy/story—artistic creation—is inextricably encoded with her perception of bodily differences. Of course anatomical gender distinctions are "real," but the narratives that children conceive in order to understand those differences, unique to each girl's psychology, are constructed within her particular cultural context. Inspired by an urge to "know," her mind shifts into high gear, working hard at elaborating fantasies, imagining scenarios, and constructing plots so that she produces explicatory dramas from her confusion. She embarks upon an inquiry into "sexual difference" which will evolve and deepen as she grows, but it is a search with no clear find and its vicissitudes may engage her forever. Sexual difference is *both* the symbolic representation for all difference as well as the impetus for examining that particular one.

From the perspective of object-relations theory, Jessica Benjamin revises Freud's theory that the unconscious source of girls' desire is readily understood as penis envy. She emphasizes the child's conflicting yet simultaneous needs for mutuality and independence *within* intimate relationships. Benjamin links this wish with an acknowledgment of gender difference:

> At this very point, where desire becomes an issue, the realizations of gender difference first begin to take hold in the psyche. . . . What is really wanted at this point in life is recognition of one's desire; what is wanted is recognition that one is a subject, an agent who can will things and make them happen. . . . Desire is intrinsically linked, at this point, to the striving for freedom, for autonomy, but this striving is realized in the context of a powerful connection. (*BL* 102, 105)

Underlining a critical distinction between Freudian psychoanalytic theory and object-relations theory, Benjamin points out that it is impossible for one's subjectivity to be recognized without a "recognizer"; hence independence requires intimacy.[4] Informed by Benjamin's model, I add the dimension of story-making, which functions in response to desire in two ways. First, as a direct result of acknowledging gender distinctions, the child designs a narrative strategy that works in conjunction with the epistemological drive to make sense of new information. And second, narrative facilitates expression of the child's unique identity and individual feelings. Similar to how imagined stories work for adults, the child realizes that her story is like no other and marks her separateness.

Feminist scholars have rewritten crucial aspects of psychoanalysis so that it operates as a theoretical construct that is responsive to women's development. And several contemporary critics are now reworking it into a useful paradigm for cultural analyses; yet, few, if any, changes have enhanced the theory's hypothesis regarding "intellectual awakening" and curiosity; these remain relatively static since Freud's framework, in which, for women, curiosity is (at best) devoid of pleasure.[5] However, film theorist Laura Mulvey infuses it with passion and excitement. She maintains:

> Curiosity describes a desire to know something secret so strongly that it is experienced like a drive. It is a source of danger and pleasure and knowledge. Its pleasure is derived from the fulfillment of a desire to know, either by seeing with one's own eyes or through the intellectual exercise of puzzle or riddle solving. (x)

In *Corregidora*, Ursa's "desire to know something secret" is inhibited by her mother's silence; *Bastard's* Ruth Anne, on the other hand, all too aware of her "secret" of Glen's abuse, is the one keeping silent. She attempts to transform her nightmare into narrative as a means of coping with what she considers to be her "damaged" and "ruined" body, but that proves impossible since her stories themselves, along with her desires, wishes, and passions are entrenched in sadomasochism.

In fact, Bone's erotic fantasies reveal that her sexual desire is actually shaped or constructed by violence.

> My fantasies got more violent and more complicated as Daddy Glen continued to beat me. . . . I was ashamed of myself for the things I thought about when I put my hands between my legs . . . ashamed for masturbating to the fantasy of being beaten. . . . I couldn't stop my stepfather from beating me, but *I* was the one who masturbated. . . . How could I explain to anyone that I hated being beaten but still masturbated to the story I told myself about it? [6]

Bastard represents oppressed female sexuality formed on and from violence. A powerful indictment of men, marriage, and heterosexuality, this text yokes male-female intimacy with the potential denial and destruction of women. No heterosexual relationship in this novel (and many are portrayed) offers anything desirable or appealing. The best ones are dull and unreliable; the worst are potentially lethal. All the Boatwright men are philandering, alcoholic, ineffective husbands and fathers, and Granny tells Bone that her own great-grandfather left them several times for other women.

In her rendering of Ruth Anne's sexual identity, Allison reveals the secret that her protagonist shares with Jones's Ursa: a link between physical pain and sexual pleasure. Unable to imagine anything but horror associated with sex or sexuality because her physical torture invades and pervades her thoughts as well as her body, Bone con-fuses—conflates as well as mistakes one for the other—sex with violent victimization. She has orgasms while fantasizing that she is tied to a blazing haystack, or left to starve to death as blackbirds peck at her body.

Similar to her experience of erotic desire, Ruth Anne suffuses her passion for music with her extreme self-loathing when she awakens to the pleasure of art in the form of live gospel music. Interestingly, both she and Ursa recognize in gospel music and blues, respectively, the possibility of transformation and transcendence; in both texts, artistic passion represents escape.

> The night seemed to wrap all around me like a blanket. My insides felt as if they had melted . . . The sweet gospel music poured through me . . . I knew I was the most disgusting person on earth. I didn't deserve to live another day . . . The music was a river trying to wash me clean. . . . That was what gospel was meant to do—*make you hate and love yourself at the same time, make you ashamed and glorified.* (*B* 135; emphasis added)

By enjambing Bone's sensual attraction to and intense excitement about the music with her powerful hatred toward herself, Allison constructs violence as the site of convergence for art, sexual desire, and sexual sadomasochism. Trapped by pain and helplessness, Bone continues to be beaten as she enters puberty, embedding her even deeper in chaos while entwining her experiences of sexual desire with feelings of pain. Shame underlies and underlines her sexuality, growing as the beatings from Glen become more frequent and more severe. On this point, Herman explains that:

> The child entrapped in this kind of horror develops the belief that she is somehow responsible for the crimes of her abusers. Simply by virtue of her existence on earth, she believes that she has driven the most powerful people in her world to do terrible things. . . . Her nature must be thoroughly evil. The language of the self becomes a language of abomination. (105)

Bone confides "I lived in a world of shame. I hid my bruises as if they were evidence of crimes I had committed. I knew I was a sick disgusting person" (*B* 113). The more Glen hurts her, the more she feels "bad, evil, nasty, willful, stupid, [and] ugly" (*B* 252).

Western culture's erotic objectification of the female, intrinsic to Mulvey's theory of the "male gaze" as well as to Freud's concept of scopophilia (sexual pleasure in looking), offers a useful framework with which to view the sexual violence in *Bastard* and *Corregidora*. While Freud "associated scopophilia with taking other people as objects, subjecting them to a controlling and curious gaze" (Mulvey 16), Mulvey explains that

> in a world ordered by sexual imbalance, pleasure in looking has been split between active/male and passive/female. The determining male gaze projects its fantasy onto the female figure, which is styled accordingly. In their traditional exhibitionist role women are simultaneously looked at and displayed, with their appearance coded for strong visual and erotic impact so that they can be said to connote *to-be-looked-at-ness*. Woman displayed as sexual object is the *leit-motif* of erotic spectacle. (19)

Within these two novels, violence is the result of collusion between the projection of the male gaze and the eroticization of the female. Although Mulvey focuses on the cinematic gaze where the male is either another character in the film or a spectator, I apply her idea to Ursa who is a blues singer on stage, and I will think about the gaze cast upon her by the male spectators, including her husbands Mutt and Tadpole. In contrast, *Bastard*'s Ruth Anne inverts the more usual configuration of scopophilia in which a male "gaze" is directed toward a woman, and she imagines herself the *enviable* focus of the objectification.

> I imagined people watching while Daddy Glen beat me. . . . Someone had to watch—some girl I admired. . . . Sometimes a whole group of them would be trapped into watching. . . . In my imagination I was proud and defiant. . . .Those who watched admired me and hated him. I pictured it that way and put my hands between my legs. It was scary, but it was thrilling too. Those who watched me, loved me. It was as if I was being beaten for them. (*B* 112)

She reverses the terror that she actually experiences when attacked by Glen, and "nobly" and stoically accepts her beating. Although she is a proud, defiant heroine to her fictitious audience, her daydreams reveal how the masochistic side of her sexuality becomes structured.[7] In this fantasy, she is important and admired while Glen is despised, but her price for love is to be sadistically brutalized.

Scopophilia operates differently in *Corregidora*. According to Freud, the source of the voyeuristic gaze is the child's wish to view the private and forbidden—the parents' genitals and the primal scene—but in ordinary development, the urge to look is overridden by shame. Staring at his wife as she performs on stage, Mutt can neither avert his eyes nor deny her "difference," and his objectifying gaze nearly costs her her life. He projects his own fears onto the other men in her audience, then blames her for attracting sexual attention. Right before Mutt throws her down a flight of stairs, causing a miscarriage and rendering her sterile, he tells her that he is angry because men stare at her when she sings:

> "'I don't like those mens messing with you,' he said.
> 'Don't nobody mess with me.'
> 'Mess with they eyes.'"[8]

Crucial to my argument is that Jones's novel literally opens with this excruciatingly violent act which determines the circuitous and variegated course of the entire book. In other words, sadism, objectification, tyranny, loss, and castration anxiety formally structure *Corregidora*, including Ursa's emancipatory reunion with her mother. In *Intimate Violence* (1994), Laura Tanner asserts that there is an inextricable "connection between the scopophilic gaze and the objectifying force of violence. The power of the gaze to master and control is forced to its inevitable culmination as the body that was the object of erotic pleasure becomes the object of violence" (33)—precisely the dynamic we see operating between Mutt and Ursa.

Four generations of sadistic, sexual secrets intersect Ursa's rapprochement with her mother to finally uncover the "truth" about her foremothers and Corregidora. In order to understand how I theorize "sadism," I will briefly summarize the story that Ursa and the reader learn of her past. Corregidora, the Portuguese slavemaster who owned Ursa's great grandmother, makes her his concubine, forcing her to sleep with his white wife also. When Great Gram's daughter by him is barely out of childhood, he rapes her, impregnating her too, then sells her into prostitution, making Corregidora the father of both Ursa's grandmother and mother. When slavery is abolished in Brazil, all official documents attesting to its existence are burned, leaving no written records of Ursa's maternal ancestry. Great Gram pronounces that the Corregidora women (they all keep his name) must "make generations" to orally pass down the story of their enslavement, meaning that the women's bodies are again used as the site of history's inscription. That is, their commodification is continued by the women themselves, not for money this time, but for history. Great Gram's mandate to "make generations" might have gone unchallenged into a fifth generation, but Ursa's hysterectomy forces her to confront the subjugating forces in her life for the first time. Without the opportunity to inscribe her own story, Ursa, like Sophocles' Oedipus, acts from her unconscious; she is propelled and compelled by "the inner necessity or drive of the [family] drama" (de Lauretis, *Alice* 125) that she inherits as a Corregidora woman: to mechanically "make generations."[9] Written on her body, Ursa's story exemplifies Peter Brooks's point that the represented body may become "a site of signification—the place for the inscription of stories—and itself a signifier, a prime agent in narrative plot and meaning" (*BW* 5).

Replete with cruelty, *Corregidora* is a text that illustrates Mulvey's contention that "sadism demands a story, [it] depends on making something happen, forcing a change in another person, a battle of will and strength, victory/defeat" (22). In *Alice Doesn't* (1984), Teresa de Lauretis takes Mulvey's connection between sadism and story one step further by suggesting a "*structural* connection between sadism and narrative . . . that may presuppose the agency of desire." She wants to consider "the possibility of an integral relationship, a mutual structural implication of narrative with desire and *a fortiori* sadism" (104), distinguished from a thematic connection. Using Sophocles' Oedipus, as well as Freud's emblematic adoption of the drama, deLauretis argues that historically "story" has been male with the female characterized as "other," or "non-man": certainly the object, not the subject, of desire. She argues that sadism, defined in male myth and story by heroes who "slay," "penetrate," "attack," "overcome," and do "battle," needs narrative. In Jones's text, sadism is interwoven and synthesized within the characters. Certainly all the Corregidora women are victims of men, but also they act unwittingly as oppressors; and the end of the novel (to which I will return) undermines the assumptions that connect sadomasochism with gender.

Jones, exploring the sadism that Ursa's story "demands," reveals the question that haunts Ursa: "What is it a woman can do to a man that make him hate her so bad he wont to kill her one minute and keep thinking about her and can't get her out of his mind the next"? (*C* 184).[10] The answer is that she can eroticize pain. Ursa thinks "about pleasure mixed in the pain" (*C* 50); she questions the sexuality of her foremothers and tells Mutt: "I wonder about their desire" (*C* 102). Earlier Ursa thinks "of the girl who had to sleep with her master and mistress. Her father, the master" (*C* 59). Her every thought regarding sex or sexuality is suffused with stories about slavery, Corregidora, prostitution, humiliation, and pain. But Jones's most radical and political question is why the women remain so psychologically attached to Corregidora—"How much was hate for Corregidora and how much was love"? (*C* 131). Although this remains unanswerable, Ursa offers the possibility that hate and desire, like pain and pleasure, are one and the same. "Two humps on the same camel. Hate and desire both riding [her maternal ancestors]" (*C* 102). Perceptively understanding the intermingling or nexus of hate and pain with desire and pleasure, Ursa begins to comprehend the nature of her foremothers' attachment to Corregidora.

If Jones's novel deals directly with the links between sexual pleasure and pain, and love and hate, and does so by (re)constructing the master/slave relationship, then Benjamin's theory on the dialectic of control addresses the same link, also by considering the master/slave dyad. Her Hegelian model of recognition, at work, too, in Hopkins's *Of One Blood*, states that in order for one to know that s/he exists, one has to be recognized as an independent being by another. The human condition presupposes intersubjectivity. Both Benjamin and Herman write about the slavemaster's need for acknowledgment, even affirmation from the slave, because without it "the master is actually alone . . . the person he is with is no person at all" (Benjamin, *BL* 65). Therefore, if the master or dominator reduces his victim to non-person status, he defeats his own purpose. From the perspective of the slave, the more alone and isolated she is, the more she becomes dependent on the "master." Herman observes, "the more frightened [the captive] is, the more she is tempted to cling to the one relationship that is permitted: the relationship with the perpetrator" (81). If Hegel is right—that one's deepest longing is to be "known" and recognized as a separate self—then the slave will grasp at that identity because, as a prisoner, she has no other. For Hegel and Benjamin, identity or recognition is tantamount to survival. And this is an adult reworking of Benjamin's analysis discussed earlier regarding the young child's need for mutual recognition. Similarly, Hegel would ally himself with object-relations as opposed to drive theorists because he views developmental projects as taking place within a dyad. Likewise, when Adam Phillips notes that "hell is not other people but one's need for other people" (45), he could be referring to Hegel's and Corregidora's master-slave relationships.

When Martin, Ursa's father, contemptuously asks his wife and her mother—"how much was hate and how much was love"—for Corregidora, he is prompted by his disgust for their obsession with the white slaveholder. But perhaps what he mistakes for their love is their definition of themselves as "slaves." Psychologically, they are of course still dominated and oppressed; they do not lose that self-perception just because abolition becomes law. And that identity, in order to have meaning, requires its counterpart, "master." Ironically, Corregidora *must* live on, so that Ursa, Mama and Grandmama feel recognized as independent and willful agents in their own destinies. They keep his violent authority alive through husbands Mutt, Tadpole, and Martin who beat, humiliate and commodify them.[11] Additionally, the women, including Ursa, keep the slaveholder alive through the unconscious tyranny that precludes free-will, which they learn from their mothers and pass on to their daughters. When Mutt tells Ursa "we ain't them" meaning their enslaved great grandparents, "[Ursa] didn't answer that, because the way [she'd] been brought up, it was almost as if [she] was" (*C* 151). Before Ursa remaps the family terrain, the Corregidora women were unconsciously replicating their exploitation by passing on and silently demanding a pre-scripted story. Like Sophocles' Oedipus, who is governed by his own repressed psyche until catastrophe hits his kingdom, Ursa walks blindly into Great Gram's plan (don't forget she is pregnant at the time of her fall). When Ursa discovers that her familial and sexual histories are inseparable from each other as well as linked with those of her maternal ancestors, she constructs her own story, which finally puts an end to this sadomasochistic cycle. Like Marie Cardinal, Ursa finds "the words to say it," and, in so doing, remembers and reclaims her violent legacy without needing to repeat it.

Hearing "the same story over and over again" (*C* 11) from her foremothers renders it "sterile" for Ursa. As they narrate the stories that dominate their memories, the women's voices merge into one reducing the once valuable histories to recitations in which Corregidora remains the master. His story still rules and obliterates theirs. While listening to Great Gram tell the story, Ursa thinks "it was as if the words were helping her, as if the words repeated again and again could be a substitute for memory. . . . As if it were only the words that kept her anger" (*C* 11). Even for Great Gram the feelings are divorced from the story and only skeletal words remain. Remarkably, when Ursa listens to Mama talk about Corregidora, the daughter stares at her mother "because she wasn't Mama now, she was Great Gram" (*C* 124). Ursa notices that "it was as if their memory, the memory of all the Corregidora women, was her memory too, as strong with her as her own private memory, or almost as strong" (*C* 129). Although Ursa did not experience slavery and Corregidora first-hand, his is the only story she knows, and she has been raised to believe that her very existence is to "give evidence" of his.

Culminating in Ursa's journey home to hear the truth from her mother, Jones's text again parallels that of Sophocles' *Oedipus*, revealing that if past secrets are not reckoned with, they, like Corregidora, will remain the masters of the text and determine its outcome. Ursa's trip is precipitated by a conflation of memories or fantasies in which her frustrated wish to share her past with Mutt and her inability to experience sexual feelings converge with memories of Corregidora as "whoremonger." When Mutt tells Ursa "long as a woman got a hole, she can fuck" (*C* 100), she immediately thinks of Corregidora who made his money selling women's bodies, including those of her mother and grandmother. She becomes aware of Mama as a woman full of unrequited "desire and loneliness . . . closed up like a fist" (*C* 101). Betrayed by her mother who hated men, yet tells Ursa she has no choice but to "make generations," Ursa will "reproduce" her foremothers' despair unless Mama gives her the story from which she can form a separate, sexual identity. Jones makes the point that the evolution of a woman's sexuality is predicated upon (re)union with the maternal world, mimicking psychological thought that adult sexual identity requires an intersubjective relationship with the mother or maternal figure.

Like Oedipus, Ursa is given the story of a murderous father and a mother who can only reveal the family plot-line, not her own thoughts and memories. Mama could "bear witness to what she'd never lived, and refuse me what she had lived" (*C* 103). Ursa needs Mama's truth, which is that Mama, too, has no sexual desire; she was beaten and treated like a "whore," and is driven toward Martin by the family repetition compulsion—to "bear generations." She tells Ursa "it was like my whole body knew it wanted you," but she desires no man and feels as though her body, which she refers to as "it," is divorced from her mind and her emotions, and "it" bore Ursa. Both women's lack of desire drives men to hate them, but with the frightening realization that her life shadows her mother's, Ursa claims the presence of her own sexuality by reclaiming the past. Learning Mama's story empowers her to inscribe her own; if Oedipus is blinded by the truth, Ursa is illuminated. And, when she next sees Mutt, she temporarily transforms the power structure. Conscious of her past, Ursa no longer needs to compulsively repeat it; she can abandon the mandate and, to a greater extent, *choose* her future.

Unlike *Bastard out of Carolina*, *Corregidora* loudly declares itself a heterosexual text, rejecting lesbianism even though it appears to represent a logical choice for Ursa, who considers all men "slavemasters," and does not want to (and later cannot) have children. But from an economic as well as a psychological standpoint, *Corregidora* is a critique of the marriage bond as a form of slavery, and therefore no option such as lesbianism can exist; there is no exit from either institution.

Turning now to Allison's text, I will think about Ruth Anne's artistic inspiration—the intense sensations heretofore associated only with gospel music—when she stays with her lesbian aunt Raylene who earns a living fishing garbage out of the river and transforming it into utensils and trinkets. Tentatively and temporarily relieved from her despair, and intrigued with Raylene's art, Ruth Anne begins to collect garbage herself while her aunt informs her: "trash rises . . . out here where no one can mess with it, trash rises all the time" (*B* 180). As she considers how rage forms and informs sexual and artistic passions, Allison provides lesbianism as a life-saving alternative to the dangers of heterosexuality. Raylene's metaphor (and her actual work) of making beauty out of trash resonates deeply within Bone, connecting her own and Raylene's lesbianism and artistic creativity with comfort and safety.[12]

While *Bastard* and *Corregidora* are very different texts, both explore the dynamics of dominance and submission, linking pain to pleasure and hate to desire, with violence forming the background. If Mulvey is right that "sadism demands a story," Laura Tanner, who emphasizes that "pain destroys narrative, shatters referential realities, and challenges the very power of [representative] language," (29) is also right. Ruth Anne and Ursa document their abusive "masters'" stories on and in their bodies, but they subvert the imposed inscriptions by telling their stories in their own words.[13] Written in the first person, both texts raise the stakes involved in the process of reading violence, because neither aesthetic form nor literary convention (though both are present) protects the reader from the victim's unrelenting, excruciatingly detailed account of her pain. Yet, if the woman's beaten and battered body represents the dominator's story, then how does the oppressed and bruised woman speak?

Just as the master is only empowered by the existence of the slave, the abuser is only validated by the exposed bloody body of his victim. Tanner explains that "coopted by the rapist's [or abuser's] story, the victim's body—violated, damaged, and discarded—is introduced as authorization for the very brutality that has destroyed it" (33). She suggests that if the victim cannot make her story understood, the responsibility lies with the reader. Readers may lapse into intellectualized, scholarly postures serving as defense mechanisms to distance them from painful narrative, but Tanner's point is even more subtle. She urges a reading strategy in which

> *seeing into* violence . . . becomes a form of resistance when what is exposed before the eyes of the reader/viewer is not his or her own helplessness but the dynamics of violation; the critical reader in the scene of violence uncovers not just the vulnerability of the victim or the observer but the very power dynamics upon which the violator's force depends. The power of the reader to resist [feeling helpless] . . . often parallels, in the representation of intimate violence, the power of the reader to resist complicity . . . through unconscious participationin the act of violation represented therein. (15, 16)

Tanner's mandate to the reader is that s/he must examine the dynamics of power structures that allow, perhaps even promote, the continuation of violence.

Corregidora and *Bastard*, like a number of contemporary novels authored by women, are domestic war stories, calling for analyses of culture-specific, familial and sexual relationships within a capitalistic patriarchy.[14] I have discussed the sadomasochism between Ursa and Mutt which opens and formally structures Jones's novel. Denial and self-deception, subtler manifestations of sadomasochism, underlie the violence permeating Allison's book. For example, look at how *Bastard* begins. Sound asleep in the back seat of her brother's truck when it smashes into another car, Anney, who is nine months pregnant with Ruth Anne, is thrown through the windshield, landing on the pavement unharmed and still asleep. She is rushed to the hospital, delivers the baby without awakening, and continues to sleep for the next three days. According to Bone, her mother was, "strictly speaking," (*B* 1) not at her birth.[15] Significantly, this event foreshadows Anney's inability to confront the fact that her husband Glen tortures her child. When her sister tries to discuss it, Anney defends him: "He does love [Bone]. I know he does. . . . [A]ll Glen really needs is to know himself loved, to get out from under his daddy's meanness" (*B* 132). Silence, fear, obsession, and trauma narratively structure *Bastard* and the text, like Ruth Anne, is haunted and invaded by more than Glen's viciousness. Anney's need to camouflage her family's secret proves almost fatal for Bone, who is of course wrong that, "strictly speaking," her mother was not at her birth, but right that her mother was unconscious, just as she remains metaphorically "unconscious" to Glen's abuse until the brutal rape that closes the text. We know this book raises the horrible dilemma of Anney's need to choose between her husband and her child, both of whom she loves desperately, but equally it addresses the potentially cataclysmic repercussions of lying to oneself and refusing to bear witness to one's own story.[16] At the close of the novel, Ruth Anne, though far from happy, is finally safe. Anney "wakes up" to the truth regarding Glen's cruelty, and simultaneously confronts her own inability to leave him. Only then can she leave Bone safely within Raylene's protection.[17]

Ursa, too, has an epiphanous moment at the close of Jones's text, in which hate and love, sadism and masochism join in her final meeting with Mutt. While performing fellatio on Mutt, Ursa realizes

> what it is a woman can do to a man that make him hate her . . . one minute . . . and can't get her out of his mind the next. . . . It had to be sexual. . . . In a split second of hate and love [she] knew what it was. . . . A moment of pleasure and excruciating pain at the same time, a moment of broken skin . . . that stops just before sexlessness, a moment that stops before it breaks the skin: 'I could kill you.' (*C* 184)

At the end of this novel, a woman is the subject, not the object, of her own rage and she maintains control of her wish for revenge. Despite her perceptive recognition that Corregidora, not Mutt, was the true slavemaster and is the real enemy, Ursa was nearly killed by her former husband and she sought vengeance. In the same instant, she confronts *and* suppresses her sadistic urges to dominate, subjugate, and "enslave" her male oppressor, thereby underlining the fact that executed behavior, not images and impulses, defines a sadist. Liberating violent desires from rigid, stereotypic gender alignments, Jones stakes out and claims those feelings for women's purview. Reversing the existing power structure by making a woman the sadist/oppressor is neither a desired nor a useful solution to racist, sexist political systems. But Jones's strategy in simply suggesting it is revolutionary.

Equally important and simultaneous is Ursa's momentary blurring of the borders that define her existence as separate from that of Mama and Great Gram, and keeps the past distinct from the present. During the same sexual encounter, Ursa realizes she "didn't know how much was me and Mutt and how much was Great Gram and Corregidora . . . but was what Corregidora had done to *her*, *to them,* any worse than what Mutt had done to me . . . than what Mama had done to Daddy, or what he had done to her in return?" (*C* 184).[18] Aware of the fact that she can sexually control a man through sadomasochism, she identifies herself as a Corregidora woman; at the same time, her choice not to exploit that power is her declaration of independence from her "mothers." If she wonders "how much was me and Mutt and how much was Great Gram and Corregidora," then she is consciously working to understand and assimilate her history, rather than mindlessly perpetuating a destructive, "inherited" repetition compulsion.

This psychoanalytic reading, in which Ursa transforms her sexual wishes into a desire for knowledge, and then, from that desire, creates her own narrative, complements or even mirrors issues raised in black feminist scholarship. Emphasizing both the protagonist's and the writer's need to resist silence and to write honestly and accurately about black women, Patricia Hill Collins, Hortense Spillers and Barbara Christian (among others) discuss the politics of creating personal narrative in fiction by and about black women. Deborah McDowell observes that "the result is not only greater complexity and possibility for [black women writers'] heroines, but also greater complexity and artistic possibility for themselves as writers" (Gates, *RB* 99).

By salvaging her voice from silence, Ursa is the first Corregidora woman to disrupt Gram's prescription for her body—to "make generations"—thus, to render the flesh made word, reversing the pattern of her foremothers; she anticipates Audre Lorde's comment that "the transformation of silence into language and action" (Collins 98) is politically resistant and stands at the heart of deconstructing and disturbing our culture's hegemonic discourse and racist representations of black women. When the silenced speak, the inner world becomes a source of power. Psychoanalytic theory evolves into a radical politics, thereby dismantling the misperception that concern with one's intrapsychic and interpsychic life conflicts with a commitment to social activism. "The personal is political" in Jones's text because Ursa's private or personal story includes a brilliant critique of the relationship between domestic abuse and sexist, racist oppression as well as an examination of the relentless trauma of slavery one hundred years and four generations later. Additionally, by formally structuring this novel as a psychological journey, Jones undermines stereotypic and racist representations of black women by rendering a quite specific, complex character whose desires and urges intersect one hundred years of African American history.

Like many contemporary women writers, Jones and Allison are interested in artistic passion and how it can be rescued and retrieved from the domain of cruelty. For Ursa, this is a life and death question and her answer lies in music. She is a blues singer whose passion is evoked by singing and nothing else; returning to the stage is her only motive for recuperating from her "accident." She tells Mutt: "I sang because it was something I had to do" (*C* 3). Barbara Christian reminds white literary critics that African American women's fiction struggles constantly with the relationship between racism and sexism, and while much is written about this from the perspectives of economics and social status, the prices black women pay in terms of self-expression, identity and empowerment are too often forgotten. Christian maintains: "To be able to use the range of one's voice, to attempt to express the totality of self, is a recurring struggle in the tradition of [black women] writers from the nineteenth century to the present" (234).[19] She is talking about writers, using "voice" metaphorically, but Jones makes Ursa a blues singer because of the importance of "Black women's music as a site of the expression of Black women's self-definitions. These recordings represented the first permanent documents expressing a Black women's [*sic*] standpoint" (Collins 100). Ann duCille writes that, "in its treatment of erotic coupling and marriage, *Corregidora* is 'dearly beloved blues'—[duCille's] name for a particular variety of art that focuses (often as a lament) on the problems of married life and romantic relations" (*Skin Trade* 73). Ursa speaks the unspeakable by "writing," actually singing, her own story in the margins of the "master text."

Of course, Ursa cannot render Corregidora's story obsolete; after all, it is her family history. But by seriously inquiring into the questions that plague her (and haunt the text), she exposes a deep secret: love and hate, as well as pain and desire, *are* "two humps on the same camel." Radical in its sexual explicitness, dealing directly with the power of sex, the novel's final scene reveals Ursa's own sadomasochism. Not only does she frankly recognize her wish for violent revenge, but by uncovering this insight during sex, she links erotic pleasure with the violence in herself, which enables her, finally, to reclaim her own desire. In other words, only when Ursa comprehends that her passions for sexuality and vengeance are "two humps of the same camel," can she disentangle them; courageous enough to confront her psychological truths, Ursa can "diffuse" her feelings and, thus, experience sexuality without the burden of her rage. Jones understands that Ursa's sexual desire is repressed until she liberates herself by accepting her sadistic urges. Knowledge frees her in the same way it does Oedipus—to consciously *know* one's personal and political history is to have more command over one's life.

Jones knows full well that she is transgressing the edges of "acceptable" or "appropriate" characters and content. In an essay entitled "About My Work," she asks: "Should a black writer ignore [characters with a 'negative image,' such as her own Eva], refuse to enter 'such territory' because of the 'negative image' . . . or should one try to reclaim such complex, contradictory characters?" (Evans 233, 234).

Exploring the sexual violence of rape and incest, Allison and Jones highlight the fact that trauma is rooted simultaneously and inextricably within cultural, historical, domestic, and psychological forces. Fiction persistently offers the acquisition of story as a means by which the repetitive cycle of violence or pain and its repression can be stopped. American women writers such as Willa Cather, Frances Ellen Harper, Zora Neale Hurston, Maxine Hong Kingston, Toni Morrison, Gloria Naylor, and Edith Wharton present varied, complex, straightforward and encrypted views of individuals struggling against the convergence of political and cultural as well as personal and psychological victimization.

Locating the sites in selected American literature where "external" and "internal" trauma—slavery and rape, poverty and incest, genocide and domestic murder—intersect offers the possibility of understanding more about the intricate dynamics that operate between the psyche and society. For Ursa, reconstructing the past by bringing to consciousness repressed or "lost" traumatic memories that are steeped in sexual sadomasochism makes possible her artistic and sexual expression. In order to appreciate the importance of Bones's "re-member"ing her past, one must read her story within the context of Allison's life as, in her other work, she encourages us to do. (See Allison's *Two or Three Things I Know for Sure* [1995] and *Skin* [1994].) If fictional Raylene reconfigures trash into utensils, Allison transforms actual and remembered trauma into art.

CHAPTER FOUR

Hysteria and Trauma in Pauline Hopkins's *Of One Blood; Or, The Hidden Self*

I hadn't so much forgot as I couldn't bring myself to remember.
—Maya Angelou *I Know Why the Caged Bird Sings*

Throughout this book, I note similarities between the process of psychotherapy and the "real," metaphorical, or allegorical journeys of specific protagonists in my selected texts. Early psychological and neurological studies of the relationship between trauma and hysteria from which modern psychoanalytic psychotherapy evolved show that hysterical symptoms diminished when repressed traumatic memories were recovered and, along with their accompanying feelings, put into words. In other words, in psychotherapy, as in these texts, only when the stories of the past are remembered, told, and comprehended can the future be imagined. The works I examine share an imperative close to the heart (and backbone) of psychotherapy: Without emotional and cerebral recognition of wounded and ravaged pasts, personal and political change is impossible.

Though the medical and psychological literature contemporaneous with Pauline Hopkins might lead one to suspect that only white, middle-class women were vulnerable to the medical diagnosis of hysteria, my thesis is that Hopkins, in her novel *Of One Blood; Or, the Hidden Self* (serialized in the *Colored American Magazine*, 1902–1903), deliberately represents Dianthe as suffering from hysteria to emphasize that this is not the case.[1] She attributes to Dianthe several of hysteria's classic conversion or somatic symptoms, including trances, amnesia, fainting spells, lethargy, passivity, and dissociative states of consciousness, in order to investigate the politics of this illness. Although I will briefly discuss *Of One Blood* as an "hysterical" text, my primary foci are the ways in which Hopkins racializes the turn of the century discourse on hysteria by considering its relevance to African American women and girls who were sexually traumatized during and after slavery. She interprets the behaviors and symptomatology of hysteria as expressions of the very specific trauma inherent in the political and familial histories of black women: rape and incest perpetrated by white men.

As an hysteric, Dianthe represents, or more precisely, her body represents the site of the convergence of violence, racism, and misogyny. Most obviously, she is sexually coerced by Aubrey, but also her "light" skin color testifies to miscegenation resulting from two additional rapes—those of her mother and grandmother by their white "master," Aubrey Livingston's father. Hopkins imbues the intriguing ideas of the "new psychology" at the turn of the century with significance for black women by using them to explore racially motivated sexual sadism: slavery's eroticization of cruelty. Incorporating the aspect of Freud's controversial view on hysteria which considers repressed sexual trauma its source, Hopkins calls attention to the confluence of intrapsychic and political forces that results in sexual and political domination, specifically Aubrey's oppression of Dianthe. And, from what I can determine, *Of One Blood* is the first, possibly the only, text by a black woman at the beginning of the twentieth century to do so.

In her chapter in *Bonds of Love* titled "Master and Slave," Jessica Benjamin argues that within the "master's" fantasy of erotic domination lies his wish for independence and his wish for recognition. For complex reasons based on early disturbances in the infant-mother relationship, the child cannot satisfy his ordinary and expected desire for differentiation—an identity separate from that of the mother—intersubjectively through "mutual recognition." Hence, his wish to be independent is perverted into his need to be dominant. Influenced by Hegel, Benjamin defines a dialectic of control like this: "If I completely control the other, then the other ceases to exist, and if the other completely controls me, then I cease to exist" (53). In this paradigm, in which dependence becomes synonymous with annihilation, existence itself is at stake. Domination is eroticized when the "master" forcibly takes control of the slave's body. Benjamin asserts that the master's "sadistic pleasure consists not in direct enjoyment of [the slave's] pain, but in the knowledge of [his] power over her—the fact that [his] power is visible, that it is manifested by outward signs, that it leaves marks" (57).[2] Psychologically, Aubrey, who personifies white Western patriarchal dominance, quite literally appropriates the identity and body of Dianthe in order to assert his own "self." But this psychodynamic, compelling as it is, could not have been so blatantly and publicly promulgated in this way if racism were not an institutionalized part of the culture.

In order to link Benjamin's ideas regarding the literal or figurative "master/slave" relationship, and Dianthe's hysterical symptoms, particularly her somatic disorders, dissociative trances, and passivity, with the literary concept of the hysterical text, I consider Claire Kahane's description of the latter. She reminds us that Freud considered the origin of female hysteria to be the traumatic "scene of passive submission to another's desire" (34). Furthermore, Freud insists that female sexual pleasure always derives from eroticized submission—"being done to rather than doing" (Kahane 34). Thus, there is no room, in Freud's view, for active female sexuality. According to Kahane, this double-bind dynamic expresses itself narratively in the hysterical text, which

> exhibits features of a discourse in crisis: excessive splittings and displacements off the subject of the story, frequent paralyses of plot, phonemic rather than semantic continuities, and seemingly gratuitous and often bizarre disruptions of narrative sequence. . . . The narrative voice struggles . . . against these textual instabilities . . . to find a form that will contain the confusions of its utterance. (xiv)

While *Of One Blood* combines disparate, even incongruous or paradoxical, narrative forms and styles, and moves simultaneously in different directions, both geographically—Ethiopia and the United States—and rhetorically, intermingling traditions, such as historical romance, realism, allegory, fantasy, science fiction, and mystery, it does so not because the novel is struggling "to find a form that will contain the confusions of its utterance" or because it is a "discourse . . . [in] crisis." Rather, Hopkins's text imitates the unique, mutable, often incomprehensible activity of the psyche's unconscious. At the same time, the novel remains logical and synchronous, a blending of narrative styles that previews modernism, if not postmodernism.

Crucial to my reading of *Of One Blood* as an hysterical text is recognizing that the "cure" for its hysteria is encrypted within the novel's narrative structure. The trope that "contain[s] the confusions of [the text's] utterance" is the mysterious, coded communication from Luke 12 that Mira's spirit sends to her two children, Reuel and Dianthe: "There is nothing covered that shall not be revealed."[3] Anticipating their traumas, Mira tries to warn them to retrieve their forgotten African identities, which underlie nearly every aspect of their stories. Like the native ancestors in *Almanac of the Dead* who send warning messages to their descendants, Mira urges Reuel and Dianthe to recall their repressed memories and watch for clues in symbols and imagery. Contextualized by Mira's message, Hopkins refers to Du Bois when she portrays Reuel, lonely and isolated by the secret of his "passing," "wanting for strength to rend the *veil*" (*OOB*

442; emphasis added; see n.8). Formally accentuating Mira's admonition, *Of One Blood* emphasizes that survival depends upon exposing what is psychologically buried.

When Reuel understands that he is truly King Ergamenes, he remembers the story from his childhood "that he was descended from a race of African kings. He remembered his mother well. From her he had inherited his mysticism and his occult powers. The nature of the mystic within him was, then, but a dreamlike devotion to the spirit that had swayed his ancestors; it was the shadow of Ethiopia's power" (*OOB* 558). In the language of Du Bois, that nature was a link to his "black soul" and, also, to his mother. Through this memory, Reuel realizes what is perhaps the most important aspect of his mysticism; not only is spiritualism a part of his identity, but it unites him with the larger world which includes a new understanding and appreciation of his racial, familial, and maternal histories. What we assumed was exclusively his intellectual passion regarding the preternatural actually derives from deeper sources as well. As his remembered story indicates, Reuel identifies his mysticism as his mother's legacy to him and yokes it with Ethiopianism.

Yet my analysis emphasizes the immediacy with which his thoughts turn toward his mother when he discovers his "other" identity. Certainly she represents a recuperated piece of African ancestry connecting him, through his inherited mysticism, to Ethiopia. Additionally, the fact that Mira occupies a place in Reuel's memories at the precise moment in which he recovers his lost personality mimics a well-established observation in the psychotherapeutic process. As the therapy patient participates in intrapsychic change, s/he almost invariably evokes memories of her/his mother, perhaps as a touchstone or talisman of the past. Reminiscent of developmental phases in childhood and adolescence when issues of autonomy and dependence are negotiated, the wish to "revisit" the familiarity of the past, denoted by the mother, accompanies periods of self-discovery and growth. Reuel "remembers" Mira as he is suddenly struck by the enormity of the changes that he is about to undergo. Similarly and significantly, Dianthe's memory is entirely restored when she learns her true identity from her maternal grandmother, accentuating the notion that recovering one's familial and racial ancestry illuminates the past as well as the present.

Situating Hopkins—journalist, senior editor of the *Colored American Magazine*, and writer of fiction—within the early psychological/philosophical/political discourse on hysteria begins with the fact that she was writing in Boston, an intellectual mecca for anyone interested in the study of the human mind at the turn into the twentieth century. In her study of the evolution of psychiatric thought and practice in that era, Elizabeth Lunbeck notes that "Boston Psychopathic Hospital became the leading mental hospital in the United States" (329), and she describes Boston as "the nation's psychiatric capital throughout the first twenty years of the [twentieth] century. . . . In any account of American psychiatry's progress, Boston and Massachusetts figured prominently" (12).[4] Furthermore, as Cynthia Schrager's essay on Hopkins explains, information about the "new psychology" was readily accessible outside of academic/medical circles.[5]

> The distance between academic and popular psychologies in American-culture has always been relatively small, and the new psychology was reported widely in the popular press at the turn of the century. One survey of popular magazines of the period reveals widespread interest in such subjects as mental healing, hypnosis, and multiple personality, beginning in 1890. (Greusser 189)

But Hopkins's *specific* knowledge of Freud's theory that repressed sexual trauma underlies hysteria can be established through her relationship with psychologist and philosopher William James, her contemporary, who also was teaching and writing in Boston. That she followed his work closely is evidenced in *Of One Blood* and suggests strongly, if not affirms, that she knew about the exciting and disturbing developments in the research on hysteria.

Aspects of James contribute to the prototype for Reuel Briggs, the protagonist of *Of One Blood*. An African American medical student "passing" for white, Reuel demonstrates his alliance with James in that both are physicians at Harvard with special interests in mesmerism, metaphysical phenomena, and unusual states of consciousness. While most commonly referred to as *Of One Blood*, this text's subtitle, *The Hidden Self*, immediately introduces James, who wrote an essay by that name, first published in *Scribner's Magazine* in 1890; indeed, the title of the book that Reuel is reading when the narrative opens, *The Unclassified Residuum*, is a phrase borrowed from that essay. Although he feels depressed, even suicidal, Reuel's mind engages passionately with the book "just published and eagerly sought by students of mysticism, and dealing with *the great field of new discoveries* in psychology" (*OOB* 442; emphasis added). James's piece opens: "*The great field for new discoveries . . . is always the Unclassified Residuum*," meaning scientific data that belong to no clearly delineated category or "the mass of phenomena generally called *mystical*" (James 247, 248; emphasis added). Specifically, James's article discusses Pierre Janet's new work, which reveals the success of hypnosis with people, almost all of whom are women, suffering from hysteria and multiple personalities—results which confirmed James's own clinical experience.

James's pre-Freudian theory of the "hidden self" hypothesizes that every conscious mind contains layers of "buried" or "secondary" selves, each one replete with its own memories and emotions. That hypnosis could successfully bring repressed or "hidden" personalities to the surface in hysterics allowed James to take his ideas further and speculate that perhaps hypnosis could actually induce telepathic communication between the selves.[6] Though unconscious, the well of memories within the "other" selves greatly influences the thought processes and behavior of the "primary" self, and these memories are sometimes expressed in instances of automatic writing. Additionally, Alfred Binet, a psychologist contemporary with James and author of *On Double Consciousness*, a work Reuel also reads, expresses his belief in an unconscious stratum of the mind: a "secondary" personality or set of personalities of which the primary self remains unaware. As in James's and, later, Freud's conceptualization of the unconscious, Binet's "hidden" self actively contributes to and informs conscious psychological experience.[7] Significantly, we see these ideas enacted in Dianthe during her illness. Speaking of herself in the third person, she tells Reuel that "in seven months the sick will be restored—*she* will awake to worldly cares once more." Then "her voice ceased; she sank upon the cot in a recumbent position. . . . She appeared to sleep. Fifteen minutes passed in death-like stillness, then she extended her arms, stretched, yawned, rubbed her eyes—awoke" with no memory of the conversation with Reuel (*OOB* 475; emphasis added). Hopkins's depiction of Dianthe's dissociated states imitates accounts of hysteria given in scientific and medical journals, as well as in James's own work.

Judith Herman notes that by the 1880s "hysteria captured the public imagination as a great venture into the unknown" (10). Charcot's Salpêtrière lectures were considered "theatrical events" (Herman 10), attended by artists, novelists, journalists, actors, and scholars. Both Freud and James studied with Charcot, though not at the same time, and James refers to the Salpêtrière lectures in "The Hidden Self" (253) as well as in his Lowell Lectures, which I will discuss later. Hysteria excited the interest of neurologists and psychologists who began listening to and recording the stories of women with an unprecedented respect.

Even after Charcot altered the perception that hysteria was evidence of demonic possession, the illness "had been considered a strange disease . . . originating in the uterus . . . with incoherent and incomprehensible symptoms" (Ellenberger 142). These symptoms, almost exclusively afflicting women, could include partial or hemi-paralysis, convulsions, anxiety or fear, helplessness, and total or partial sensory loss, including sight. Because it was a diagnostic receptacle for all of women's complaints not immediately or easily identified by physicians, one doctor describes it as "a dramatic medical metaphor for everything that men found mysterious or unmanageable in the opposite sex" (Micale qtd. in Herman 10). The term "hysteria" became a magnet for the misogyny of the almost entirely white male medical academy. Because it was often considered tantamount to malingering, some physicians actually refused to treat women complaining of its symptoms. As we know, Freud and Janet (working independently and competitively), concluded that psychosexual trauma explained hysteria's origins, and its somatic symptoms "represented disguised representations of intensely distressing events which had been banished from memory" (Herman 12). In an attempt to deal with these experiences, the victim was able to produce an altered or dissociated state of consciousness, successfully repressing the frightening events from conscious memory, but causing the symptoms. Like his predecessors, Freud called this state "double consciousness," and it is in this context—traumatic memories persistently residing in the unconscious—that he made his famous remark that "hysterics suffer mainly from reminiscences" (*Studies* 7).[8]

Announced for the first time in *The Aetiology of Hysteria* (1896), Freud revealed what was to become his most disputed finding: "I . . . put forward the thesis that at the bottom of every case of hysteria there are *one or more occurrences of premature sexual experience*" (103). (Known beyond a doubt, "premature" implied a forced or unwelcomed sexual experience.) His later renouncement, discussed in more depth in my Introduction, was particularly unfortunate because, potentially, the theory offered help to sexually abused girls and women.[9] Yet, his controversial idea that sexual trauma in childhood produces symptoms of emotional disturbances in adulthood remains a landmark theory; no longer contradicted, the causal link between childhood sexual abuse and adult psychopathology first analyzed by Freud continues to spark debate regarding the sexual and economic politics of trauma, particularly rape and incest.[10]

In view of her connection to James and his to Freud, Hopkins was almost certainly familiar with the fierce debate surrounding Freud's theory yoking childhood sexual abuse with hysteria. William James was an avid admirer of Freud's work. In fact, when the two met at Clark University in 1909, James, who was particularly interested in Freud's work on dream analysis, told him that the future of psychological thought resided with him. Earlier, in 1895, James, fluent in German, wrote a laudatory review (Richards 205) of the important new work, *Studies on Hysteria*, by Freud and Josef Breuer, in which the authors presented their theory of the etiological connection between trauma/shock and the symptoms of hysteria. A proponent of their view, James actively disseminated their ideas in the United States. Jacques Barzun notes that "in discussing hysteria, James quoted Janet, Breuer, and Freud, who were just then creating a stir throughout the learned world"; in a review for the *Psychological Review* in 1894, James "lent his authority to the Breuer-Freud position[:] . . . the hypothesis that the memory of a shock can become . . . [in the words of Breuer and Freud,] trauma(ta) wound(s)" (230, 231).

In his 1896 Lowell Lectures on Exceptional Mental States, which were open to the public and reported comprehensively in the Boston newspapers (Schrager 189), to which Hopkins of course had ready access as well as personal and journalistic interest, James cited case analyses from Freud's *Studies in Hysteria* (1895). Although Freud did not identify the nature of the violent trauma underlying hysteria's symptomatology as always sexual until 1896, the year following that text's publication (the same year as the Lowell lectures), *Studies* reported cases of sexual abuse/rape that precipitated psychological and physiological problems consistent with hysteria, and James discussed these case histories in his lectures. And, undoubtedly, he had read Freud's 1894 article, "The Neuro-Psychoses of Defense," in which the sexualized nature of hysteria was previewed. Similarly, James introduced the work of Charcot who described the majority of his patients as "young women who had found refuge in the Salpêtrière from lives of unremitting violence, exploitation, and rape" (Herman 10; see also Auerbach in Abel, Lunbeck, and Showalter, *FM*). Sympathizing with myriad problems of women suffering from hysteria, James lamented that they were "victims of sexual trouble" (Taylor 55).

While the pre-Freudian link between rape/incest and hysterical symptomatology was implicit (rape/incest was an unspoken precipitant of hysteria), the connection between female sexuality and the disease of hysteria was explicit. But, no doubt Hopkins perceived the ubiquitous, subliminal sexualized violence to which her work shows her so acutely attuned, even if the fact of sexual coercion was not overtly articulated. If contemporary critics are able to read those subtextual nuances in earlier fictionalized depictions of hysterical women, so was Hopkins. Likewise, the same is probably true for her understanding of the psychiatric case studies which were reported in the press and discussed in lectures. For example, she may very well have read Charlotte Perkins Gilman's "The Yellow Wallpaper," which appeared in *New England Magazine* in 1892. Though Gilman's narrator is white, married and upper-middle class, her story shares with *Of One Blood* the theme of sexual sadism. As Elizabeth Ammons argues, Gilman's text "offers a horrible picture of what the bourgeois white nineteenth-century ideal of femininity often really meant: bondage, masochism, madness" (*CS* 39).

In her first published short story, "The Mystery within Us," appearing in the debut issue of the *Colored American* (May, 1900), as well as in *Of One Blood*, Hopkins expresses her own special interest in maverick physicians pursuing experimental ideas about what James called "the fringe" of the human mind. It is quite plausible that Hopkins read the prolific material published at the turn of the century in medical and psychology journals on "mental healing," mesmerism, neurasthenia, hysteria, and trauma, including the new ideas of Freud and Breuer. Lunbeck points out that "one-third of the women [at Boston

Psychopathic Hospital] who manifested the symptoms of hysteria told of being subjected to unwanted male sexual aggression" (219). Widely circulated theories of psychology in the 1890s and into the first decade of the next century, which attributed the cause of hysteria to earlier sexual abuse, support my presumption that Hopkins was not only acquainted with the originating ideas of psychoanalysis but, more importantly, that they contribute directly to the narrative argument of *Of One Blood* in the character of Dianthe.

As I will discuss at length in my subsequent chapter on Margaret Atwood and Charlotte Perkins Gilman, it is well known by now that numerous physicians horrendously abused the diagnostic label of hysteria, resulting in the neglect, maltreatment, wrongful institutionalization, and even the torture and deaths of women. Many who were unjustly imprisoned in asylums wrote profound first-person narrative accounts of their experiences which examined this problem from feminist and cultural perspectives, but Victorian society's repressive and regressive structure regarding women was not overtly identified as an underlying cause of their somatic and psychological problems until much later.[11] Therefore, in the late nineteenth and early twentieth century, critical questions regarding the relationship between the diagnosis of hysteria and narrow-minded, cruelly restrictive definitions of gender remained largely unasked and have, understandably, attracted modern scholars' critical attention. Still, the fact that doctors used this diagnosis to malign women eradicates neither the existence of hysteria nor the legitimate experience of its victims. Contemporary scholars who consider hysteria an illusion or invention of the male-dominated medical establishment fabricated for the sexist purpose of keeping women as domestic slaves study only one aspect of the dilemma. In my view, critiquing and contextualizing the very serious sufferings of those with hysteria is the only way to recognize and offer respect to the women for whom this label, and of course the syndrome itself, was a tragedy. Jessica Benjamin, writing on another subject, asserts that it is always a mistake to "substitute moral outrage for analysis. Such a simplification . . . reproduces the structure of gender polarity under the guise of attacking it" (*BL* 10). The political analysis of psychiatric theory and practice is indispensable, but unless we augment it with discussion that considers internal and unconscious life, we replicate the ignorance and crudity that left women without help and hope at the turn of the century.

Dianthe's representation as an hysteric suggests that repressed sexual trauma lies in her past. In Hopkins's first novel, *Contending Forces*, Sappho Clark was a victim of rape/incest when she was fourteen, and her story, like Dianthe's, merges with mesmerism and mind study through Madame Frances, Sappho's Aunt Sally, the psychic who is raising her young son. In *Of One Blood*, when Reuel thinks about "the heartless usage to which [Dianthe] must have been exposed" (*OOB* 489), he is probably imagining sexual violation. For interwoven into her political, if not personal, history as an African American woman, Hopkins already knows what the psychologists are learning: sexual trauma is an epidemic. If the unconscious meanings of hysterical symptoms are revealed only by understanding their traumatic precipitant, then we must locate Dianthe's hysteria in slavery and rape. Additionally, memories of her racial identity, as well as those of her sexual abuse, are contained within her repressed "secondary" personality or personalities. Conceived during the rape of Mira by her master, Dianthe's childhood is steeped in mystery. Her mother was the only child of ten that her grandmother Hannah was allowed to keep; "all de res' were sold away" (*OOB* 605) and Mira's sale was arranged when, perhaps, she escaped. Though it is not clear what happened to Mira, or who raised Dianthe, we do know that the child never knew her father or her siblings. As we see in later novels by African American women—for example, Gayl Jones's *Corregidora* (1975), the white "masters'" rape is intergenerational and incestuous; like Ursa in Jones's text, Dianthe exemplifies the disastrous aftermath of slavery in the succeeding generation. Writing nearly a century before Jones, Hopkins codes and encrypts her sexual language unlike Jones, who can be explicit; for example, in *Contending Forces*, Luke Sawyer signifies his mother's rape as a "whipp[ing]" (*CF* 257), and Mrs. Montfort's rape is indicated by her "tender flesh [which] *feel[s] the lash*" (*CF* 68). Hazel Carby points to the "snaky leather thong" (the instrument used for the whipping) as Hopkins's "metaphoric replacement for the phallus" (*RW* 132).

If sexual violence resides in Dianthe's "hidden self" as it does in Sappho's secret past, so does her racial identity. She fades into a death-like trance induced by severe shock following a railway accident, but Reuel, acting as her physician, actually restores life to her.[12] (We see later in the text that in resuscitating her, he himself is reborn.) Although the other doctors consider her beyond hope, Reuel's studies in the supernatural have taught him that sometimes acutely traumatized people can appear dead but are actually in catatonic or trance states. Though revived to consciousness, Dianthe awakens with amnesia, which, according to Freud, is common in hysteria following shock (*Studies* 235). She remembers neither her name nor her magnificent singing talent, and her very light skin prevents her from identifying herself as black.

While devastating tragedies envelop this text—for example, the gruesome murders of Molly Vance and Dianthe herself—none has more horrific ramifications than the agreement made between Aubrey and Reuel to deceive Dianthe by keeping her racial identity a secret from her, confounding her "hidden self" even further.[13] In thinking about the role Reuel's deceptive silence plays in Dianthe's murder, Ammons notes that of course Aubrey is her actual killer, but "there is a level at which Reuel . . . tragically abets the white man's evil by his silence" (*CS* 82). She contends that

> perhaps the most pernicious way in which [racist] oppression works . . . is not through its blatant structure of lies, sexual assault, and murder, but through its insidious genocidal power of encouraging black people to deny and disown their racial identity, and therefore each other—the community, the group. (*CS* 82)

In fact there are at least three aspects to Dianthe's hidden self. One is the possibility that she was sexually attacked sometime in her past, but the experience is blocked from her memory. By assimilating the discoveries of prominent contributors on the subjects of trauma, hysteria, repression and mesmerism—William James and Alfred Binet directly, Janet and Freud indirectly—Hopkins invites this speculation. The second element of Dianthe's personality of which she is unaware is her consanguinity, included in which is her link with Africa; as Thomas Otten argues, the "hidden self [is] . . . that part of the personality that preserves the memory of ancient African civilization" (244). And if this second facet links her to her African history, then the third connects her to her African American history. Although she is born after emancipation, the sexual molestation, rape and miscegenation endemic to slavery are the signatures of her genealogy. When Hannah tells Dianthe that she, Reuel, and Aubrey are siblings—"all of one blood!" (*OOB* 607)—she calls attention to the incest that biologically connects these three and, thus, assigns a most concrete, specific meaning to that biblical phrase. Simultaneously, Hopkins highlights the extent to which families were shattered as a result of slavery. When we first meet Dianthe, she is described as "fair as the fairest woman in the hall" (*OOB* 453), representing immediately the embodiment, the "proof," of miscegenation through rape.[14]

Performing as a lead singer with the Fisk Jubilee Singers, Dianthe is an artist whose musical genius signifies her familial and political connections to her African American ancestry. Reminding us that she carries within herself the trauma of black U.S. history and heritage, her brilliant voice expresses the "outpoured anguish of a suffering soul."

> All the horror, the degr[a]dation from which a race had been delivered were in the pleading strains of the singer's voice. It strained the senses [of the listener] almost beyond endurance. . . . [She sang] the awfulness of the hell from which a people had been happily plucked. (*OOB* 454)

Acting as animating connective tissue between America and Africa, Dianthe's art holds the potential to unite her with her "African Personality" which would enable her, as it did Reuel, to discover her "true" racialized self, but Aubrey silences her before she can do so. In her arousing artistic performance in which her voice resonates the "anguish of a suffering soul," Dianthe sings from her "self"—her racialized identity—as a black woman. That her race, her "voice," and her art inextricably entwine explains why she stops singing after being severed from her African American heritage when she awakens from a coma with amnesia. More accurately, Reuel and Aubrey rob her of her birthright by keeping it secret.

Each of the novel's three central characters has an African "hidden self." Reuel deliberately denies his blackness by "passing"; ironically, racist Aubrey does not know that he is black because he was switched at birth with his white half-brother; likewise, Dianthe is unaware of her African identity because Reuel and Aubrey deny her that truth. Of the three, only Reuel recaptures the "undiscovered country within [himself]—the hidden self lying quiescent in every human soul" (*OOB* 448) and, not coincidentally, he is the only one still alive at the novel's close.

Exhibiting a white man's unbridled power to alienate a black woman from her husband, her brother, her art, and her community, Aubrey sadistically imprisons, rapes, and ultimately murders Dianthe. Most dramatic is the way his vicious, sexual violence reenacts and repeats her original trauma (in which her hysteria is rooted), and does so quite specifically by exploiting her helplessness. When Aubrey witnesses Dianthe, tortured and cataleptic, begging and pleading with Reuel for relief, "for the benefit of [his] powerful will" (*OOB* 475), the voyeur, Livingston, responds with strong sexual desire. Her powerlessness, especially her pain, excites him, sending him into "a trance of delight, his keen artistic sense fully aroused and appreciative . . . losing himself in it" (*OOB* 475). Describing Dianthe's inability to assert or defend herself, Hopkins tells us that "she . . . ha[s] lost her own will in another's" (*OOB* 603). That Aubrey's lust for Dianthe is undoubtedly prompted by her debilitated condition is crucial because it establishes the lethal link between erotic pleasure and sadism. In other words, her helplessness—her "invalid"ism—operates upon Aubrey as an aphrodisiac. Facilitated by Jessica Benjamin's explication on the dialectic of control, we understand that for Aubrey, Dianthe exists as a one-dimensional "other" who will restore his omnipotence. Sexually aroused by her submissiveness, he identifies, then targets her as prey. Motivated by his intrapsychic need to be recognized as an individual "self," a separate, differentiated "I," and able to achieve that only through his complete domination over another, Aubrey "takes possession" of Dianthe in an attempt to recapture the omnipotence he experienced as an infant.

The omnipotent view acknowledges no claim from or responsibility to the outside world, and experiences neither external nor internal restraint of its absolutist authority. According to Freud, omnipotence operates as a defense mechanism intended to protect one's self from the pull of the death instinct: the regressive drive toward the elimination of all tension, a primary impulse toward "nothingness." Omnipotence is projected outward and manifests as rage, aggressiveness, as "the blindest fury of destructiveness" (Freud, *Civilization* 68) and, in erotic life, as sadism. Benjamin considers omnipotence "the manifestation of Freud's death instinct. . . . Whether in the form of merging or aggression, it means the *complete assimilation of the other* and the self" (*BL* 67; emphasis added). Moreover, Freud calls attention to the "extraordinarily high degree of narcissistic enjoyment" that accompanies destructiveness, because it satisfies "old wishes for omnipotence" (*Civilization* 68).[15] Now, let us complicate our thinking on Aubrey's intrapsychic processes—the "narcissistic enjoyment" he derives from his sadistic omnipotence—by analyzing them in terms of gender and racial politics. Aubrey's political, social, and familial culture, which sanctions, even encourages violent racism, as well as the eroticization of sadism, merges smoothly with his psyche's need and wish to dominate and destroy. Inflicted by Aubrey, the fusion of this political and personal trauma is experienced by its victim, Dianthe.

Submissive behavior is an hysterical symptom often thought to be a form of sexual manipulation. But, for victims of rape like Dianthe, compliance can prove life-saving. Although it now leaves her at the mercy of powerful men, her torpidity is a post-traumatic, residual manifestation of the violent episode(s) precipitating her hysteria. For Aubrey, a predatory "master's" son, Dianthe's passivity offers him the opportunity to enact the cold-blooded drama that will "officially" initiate him into his father's powerful, white, fraternity of sadistic "property"/slave owners. Exploiting the fact that Dianthe has no memory of her past, and therefore can exert no agency on her own behalf in the present, Aubrey defines her as "slave," thus designating himself as omnipotent dominator, that is, "master." Carby implies that sexual politics reminiscent of the master-slave relationship bolster Aubrey's obsession with Dianthe; the critic notes that he "experienced an uncontrollable lust and sexual desire that was given the historical reverberations of the power dynamic between a white plantation owner and his black mistress" (*RW* 156).

If Benjamin is right that within the dominator's sadistic behavior lies his need/wish to be acknowledged as an autonomous "self," then Aubrey's rape of Dianthe—the daughter of his father and his father's slave—is not only his incestuous rape of his sister, although, of course, it is that. Aubrey immerses himself in a competitive Oedipal drama in which he "takes"/rapes his father's sexual "property," signified by Dianthe, while at the same time, he looks to that father for recognition and approval. Furthermore, by claiming his patriarchal "place" in the next generation of "masters"/dominators who subjugate Hannah's daughters, Aubrey metaphorically takes "possession" of his father's (coerced) lover, who is, indeed, his own mother, Mira. That he literally inscribes the "master" plot on/in Dianthe's body when he rapes her is his perverted attempt to reify his cultural/historical and paternal/Oedipal link with his father who signifies racism and patriarchy.[16] To *Of One Blood*'s reconfiguration of Freud's not yet developed Oedipal conundrum, Aubrey adds a uniquely sadistic twist by sacrificing the mother/lover figure when he murders Dianthe, so that the surviving "couple" remains that of son and father.[17]

According to early research on hysteria and trauma, the female body "converts" emotional pain into physical or somatic symptoms so that the body *always* "narrates" the story. Of course, the body is the site of sexual trauma; but, in addition, it operates as the site of the trauma's displacement, because it is the conduit through which the symbolic or "imagined" hysterical symptoms are expressed. In this sense, Hopkins's text, rendered by way of Dianthe's body, is an hysterical text. For example, in Toni Morrison's *Beloved*, we can read Sethe's story through the indelible mark of the chokecherry tree lashed into her back; also, in Morrison's *Song of Solomon*, Pilate, who has no navel, places in doubt the very fact of her matrilineal ancestry. Likewise, the bodily representation of Ursa's story in Jones's *Corregidora* is her hysterectomy scar. Similarly, Hopkins's novel fuses Dianthe's permanent emotional scar of neither having nor becoming a mother with trauma's inerasable bodily scars.

In *Of One Blood*, Hopkins views the politically and historically distinct trauma of white slave "master" rape upon black women and girls from the perspective of the turn-of-the century Freudian discourse on hysteria to underscore the fact that many, perhaps all, of slavery's female victims who were raped suffered from an actual, clinical *illness* during, and in the aftermath, of that trauma. Today, that syndrome would be diagnosed as post-traumatic stress disorder. Hopkins contributes to a literary tradition of black women writers who, looking at trauma through the lens of sexual abuse, document white rape and incest at a particular moment in U.S. history through a variety of genres, including fiction, autobiography, poetry, and essays. Indeed, African American women have consistently authored a tradition of historical trauma literature long before such narratives emerged in white, mainstream fiction and theory during the last quarter of the twentieth century. Examples of literature and essays published prior to *Of One Blood* aimed at exposing the trauma of white rape of black girls and women include Harriet Jacobs's autobiographical *Incidents in the Life of a Slave Girl, Written by Herself* (1861), Frances E. W. Harper's *Iola Leroy, or Shadows Uplifted* (1892), Anna Julia Cooper's *A Voice From the South* (1892), Ida B. Wells's *Southern Horrors: Lynch Law in All Its Phases* (1892), and Hopkins's own *Contending Forces* (1900).

Representing the fact that the reverberations and sequelae of white men's rape of black women during slavery and into the post-bellum era remains traumatic for African American women, even writers who are separated from slavery by many generations, such as Nella Larsen in *Quicksand* (1928), Gayl Jones in *Corregidora* (1975), Toni Morrison in *Beloved* (1987), or Octavia Butler in *Kindred* (1979), emphasize that the violent racialized and sexualized power dynamic of the white "master" who "owns" his black "mistress" continues as a literary trope because, as a *trauma*, the dynamic persists as an historical reality. The discursive pivot around which all of these texts revolve is that of sexual trauma rooted in the violent racism of American slavery. Although Dianthe expresses her victimization through the psychosomatic symptoms of hysteria, other manifestations of trauma (in other works) include mania or manic-depressive illness, "identification with the aggressor," in which the victim herself becomes the sadist, psychosis or psychotic episodes and, perhaps most frequently, suicidal depression.[18] The texts of Hopkins, Jacobs, Wells, Larsen, Morrison, and Jones, among others, cluster to form a literary tradition because they share a rhetorical strategy and a conversation—an intertextual dialogue—explicitly focused on *trauma* precipitated by racialized, sexual violence during, and as a consequence of, slavery.[19] My view is that Freud's seduction theory, which coincided in time with Hopkins's thinking on the subject of sexual trauma, formally structures *Of One Blood*, and does so by emphasizing the "hidden" political sadomasochism that victimized Dianthe, that is, the racialized, sexualized trauma of Aubrey's violence against her. Dianthe's hysterical symptomatology becomes Hopkins's entrance into her examination of the aftermath of white, "master" rape executed upon black, slave women.

Addressing the question that Jessie Redmon Fauset, Zora Neale Hurston, Gloria Naylor, Ann Petry, Alice Walker, and many other black women writers will ask decades later, Hopkins wonders how, or more accurately "if," a young black woman, such as Dianthe, can thrive as an artist when the past is dominated by violent oppression. And she answers her own question with pessimism. The readers' expectations are mistakenly hopeful when we first meet Dianthe because, unlike Sappho of *Contending Forces*, Dianthe does, indeed, actualize her artistic potential with the Fisk Jubilee Singers. But by the time of *Of One Blood*, her last novel, Hopkins has lost faith that a brilliant and beautiful African American woman artist and performer like Dianthe can survive in the racially bigoted and misogynistic United States.[20] Since Dianthe did not accompany Reuel to Ethiopia where, like him, she would have been welcomed, there is no option for her except death. But Hopkins's skepticism declares itself even in the matriarchal Telassar, the "double" to the patriarchal United States, where the kind and beautiful black Queen Candace rules. Though she is the monarch, she can claim no distinction or individuality; the city is ruled by a "Candace" for fifteen years, after which her successor, the next "Candace," takes the throne. Of course she fares far better than Dianthe, but even in the idealized Meroe, the questionably powerful queen has no "self."

That Hopkins's despair for the creative woman seeps into her utopian representation of Africa implies that, in her view, there is no emancipation anywhere for the black woman artist. *Of One Blood*, which "dramatized the violent silencing and death of the black American woman artist," was Hopkins's last major piece of fiction; shortly after its publication she "disappeared as a productive artist" (Ammons, *CS* 85).

Perhaps the commitment to internal transformation—a reconfiguration of the personality—inherent in psychology attracted Hopkins because within it she saw a useful framework for reconstructing damaging racist political perceptions. But, for Hopkins, even though the psychological paradigm invites one to wish for political as well as personal metamorphoses, the construct fails to heal. Blending a sophisticated view of the complex machinations of the mind with her knowledge of traditional African history and beliefs, Hopkins suggests radical approaches to understanding human behavior. Dianthe's demise exemplifies Freud's and Breuer's point in *Studies*—one resonating deeply within Hopkins's work—that highly intelligent and artistically gifted women, as hysterics frequently were, must be given the opportunity to work creatively at their art, if they are to avoid falling prey to severe depression. If this appears obvious to us, then we must look again at Gilman's "The Yellow Wallpaper" (1892) to remember that most women were not allowed control over their own emotional healing. Like Gilman, but more complicated, Hopkins invokes hysteria to indict both the racism and the misogyny that kill black women artists in America.

Significantly, Pauline Hopkins develops a unique racialized view of the unconscious in which she rewrites a crucial aspect of psychoanalytic theory adding precisely what Freud and his protégés omitted—specific cultural and racial analyses. Historicizing as well as racializing the meaning of hysteria, and therefore recontextualizing it, Hopkins interprets that syndrome to include the sexual, violent traumas of racist rape and incest that are the heritage of African American women. Written with acute psychological insight, *Of One Blood* works as a political indictment of the United States's racism which is responsible for Dianthe's illness. Moreover, Hopkins establishes that the view of hysteria as a disease affecting only white, middle-class women is itself racist and myopic.

Deliberately blurring distinctions between the dominant culture's so-called facts, myths, theories, and superstitions, while simultaneously defying easy categorization in established literary traditions, Hopkins manipulates narrative form to invent an unconventional framework for *Of One Blood* which leads Ammons to consider her "a radical experimenter whose work will be read in the next century as a model of early modernist innovation and revolution in the United States" (Greusser 211). Merging traditions and styles—realism, historical romance, allegory, fantasy, and mystery—into an experimental pattern that synthesizes salient intellectual, political, and spiritual ideas, *Of One Blood* stimulates and deepens insight into the unconscious.

Additionally, *Of One Blood* functions as what Elie Wiesel calls "literature of testimony" and Shoshana Felman refers to as "an art of urgency" (Felman 114). Felman explains that "the 'literature of testimony' is . . . not an art of leisure but an art of urgency. . . . [It is] a struggling act of readjustment between the integrative scope of words and the unintegrated impact of events. This ceaseless engagement between consciousness and history *obliges* artists . . . to transform words into events and to make *an act* of every publication" (114). Hopkins's "act" was to rivet her readers' attention to a sadism so profound that it can only be represented through story. She brilliantly negotiates the "integrative scope of words [with] the unintegrated impact" of traumatic experience by rendering a family so ruptured by rape, incest, and miscegenation that Dianthe unwittingly commits incest twice by marrying both of her brothers. Crucial, too, is the fact that *Of One Blood* takes place approximately two generations following emancipation, demonstrating that the sexual violence inherent in the power structure of the master/slave relationship remains an ineradicable facet of black peoples' lives.

Avowedly interested in psychic matters, Hopkins's unusual conflation and containment of diverse, even seemingly non-complementary genres mimics the way the human mind can simultaneously "hold onto" a multitude of contradictory ideas. If our conscious thoughts and behaviors sometimes appear random, fragmented, chaotic, even insane, they become coherent when contextualized within the logic of our unconscious wishes and fantasies. I believe that *Of One Blood* mirrors this mental process: Initially, it strikes us as "unrealistic" or "imaginary" that Reuel restores life to the apparently "dead" Dianthe; or, we find "unbelievable" the fact that he, Dianthe, and Aubrey are all "of one blood"; yet, within the novel's context, these are stories that belong in the tradition of realism. The mystical narratives of Reuel and Dianthe look unrealistic only until we recognize that they are motivated by powerful unconscious wishes to discover their "hidden selves." In my view, Hopkins's novel is not an hysterical text in the sense that Kahane describes a "discourse in crisis." Yet, just as the hysterical patient's story may appear "illogical," represented through disjointed, displaced, and somaticized conversion ailments, *Of One Blood*, like the hysteric's symptoms is organized by the logic of the unconscious. Thus, it can only be understood when its repressed trauma is revealed. Likewise, what appears to be *Of One Blood*'s inchoate blending of disparate literary conventions or genres is actually a sophisticated entwining of conflicting and corresponding threads, which, like the human mind, are firmly rooted in historical/cultural/psychological/spiritual realism. If no existing genre accommodates this text, perhaps it belongs to the undefinable category of "unclassified residuum," which is, according to William James, "the great field of new discoveries."

CHAPTER FIVE

Postmodern Realism, Truth, and Lies in Joyce Carol Oates's *What I Lived For*

"Honesty is an art."[1]

—Joyce Carol Oates

"If nothing else is left, one must scream. Silence is the real crime against humanity."

—Nadezhda Mandelstam

In a 1986 article for *Ms.* Magazine, titled "My Friend, Joyce Carol Oates: An Intimate Portrait," Elaine Showalter rightly points out that "despite [Oates's] position as one of the most versatile and intellectually powerful of contemporary American writers, and despite the series of important books on female experience she has written especially during this decade, Oates has never had the acknowledgment from feminist readers and critics that she deserves" (qtd. in Milazzo 128). Showalter observes that for the past twenty years, no critical discussion of Oates's work has failed to mention its "quantity" or its "violence," and she notes: "Critics have hinted [that her] fecundity is positively indecent" for a woman writer (Milazzo 129). Oates herself responds that "perhaps critics (mainly male) who charged me with writing too much are secretly afraid that someone will accuse them of having done too little with their lives" (Milazzo 129). The idea of a woman writer who is both prolific and artistically serious seems to be, for some, hard to accept. That honesty is Oates's art is certain.

Responding to the other ever present criticism of her work—its violence—Oates published an essay in *The New York Times Book Review* about twenty years ago, called "Why Is Your Writing So Violent?" in which she declared that "the question was always insulting . . . ignorant . . . always sexist. . . . War, rape, murder, and the more colorful minor crimes evidently fall within the exclusive province of the male writer, just as, generally, they fall within the exclusive province of male action" (qtd. in Milazzo 130). Revealing their sexism, these objections—too many long, "violent" novels—do not apply substantive, critical standards of literary or narrative theory to Oates's writing; instead pages are counted, months between publications are calculated, and the "appropriateness" of her subject matter is critiqued. Ironically, this sort of criticism was hurled at her *before* the publication of her twenty-eighth novel, *What I Lived For* (1994), a six-hundred page book in which she adds pornography to her large and variegated narrative repertoire, as she continues to stake out the language of explicit sex and violence for the domain of women's fiction.[2]

In the first part of this chapter, I maintain that in *What I Lived For*, Oates breaks new ground in two ways: First, she "crosses" the boundary of gender to create a culturally specific, intimately detailed, psychological and social representation of a man. It is not my contention that women have not portrayed men "realistically" in their novels before now, but rather that the depth of Oates's "firsthand" exploration of masculinity, including even the narration of sexual and orgasmic experience is, if not unprecedented, then extraordinary.[3] By adding Jerome "Corky" Corcoran, *What I Lived For*'s protagonist, to a distinguished group of fictional male characters, all of whom have been imagined by men, Oates deliberately writes herself into an exclusively masculine tradition in literary history. The male representations I am thinking of include William Dean Howells' Silas Lapham, Theodore Dreiser's Hurstwood in *Sister Carrie*, Charles Chesnutt's John Walden in *The House Behind the Cedars*, Saul Bellow's Moses Herzog, Philip Roth's Alexander Portnoy, James Weldon Johnson's narrator in *The Autobiography of an Ex-Colored Man*, Thomas Wolfe's Eugene Gant in *Look Homeward, Angel*, and Corky's probable prototype, Sinclair Lewis' George Babbitt.[4] Specifically I see Oates situating herself within the literary tradition of American realism, which of course includes women writers, but none has as thoroughly interrogated "masculinity" as she does in *What I Lived For*.

A second way in which Oates's text is innovative lies in its adroit blending of narrative approaches usually considered to be incongruous with realism. For example, although her novel is realistic, it is equally and simultaneously postmodern, offering complex social commentary from a "cross-gendered" perspective. If Silas Lapham and George Babbitt exemplify traditional realism, which Rene Wellék describes as "the objective representation of contemporary social reality" (qtd. in Habegger 103), then Corky embodies what I call "postmodern realism." By placing the title of the text in the first person and past tense—*What I Lived For*—Oates previews the ambiguity that envelopes her narrative as she invites us to begin her book with questions asked from the perspectives of existential or postmodern realism. Whose story is this? Who is the "I"/narrator? Whose "reality"/mind have we entered?

My argument in part two of this chapter, informed by psychoanalytic theory, thinks about Corky as psychologically wounded from the trauma of losing both his parents in one life-shattering moment when he is eleven years old. Shot three times by gangsters on Christmas Eve, his father's murder adumbrates his own (Corky too is shot three times), and he feels both physical and emotional pain as his father's bullets, foreshadowing his own, "tear through [him] changing [him] utterly."[5] Exacerbating Corky's loss and shock is his mother's response; finding the body only seconds before he does, she suffers an emotional "break down," for which she is immediately and permanently institutionalized. That he did and does cope with that trauma's aftermath by avoiding and denying its importance poses serious problems for him. Also, I employ Lacan's incorporation of semiotics into psychoanalysis to argue that formally structuring Oates's text, as well as determining its trajectory, is a discourse entwining power, narrative, and trauma with "desire."

Uniting these two approaches in my discussion of *What I Lived For*—one focused on literary tradition and one relying upon psychoanalytic theory—is my view of Oates as a social critic. Her contextualized rendering of a particular man—white, Irish, heterosexual, upper-middle class, whose entire life, spent in upstate New York, spanned the years 1948 to 1992—is the narrative device through which she critiques a politically corrupt culture. Her pessimistic and admonitory analysis suggests that when social and psychological forces, such as misogyny, racism, greed, shame, and loss collide, Corky, like his model George Babbitt, cannot harmoniously reconcile his need to conform, on the one hand, with his desire to tell the truth, on the other. Since his own and his culture's construction of masculinity affords him no honest way to understand his early life/trauma, his premature, violent death is inevitable.

Corky's textual existence conflates and reifies dangerous slants on masculinity only to subvert them. Constructing him in order to deconstruct his entire moral code and value system, Oates uses a radical strategy to warn us that the time to emancipate "gender" from its limited, conservative definitions and theories is now. If *Almanac of the Dead* is Leslie Marmon Silko's indictment for "five hundred years of theft, murder, pillage and rape" (Silko qtd. in Perry 327), then *What I Lived For* is Oates's condemnation of the individual, political and social tragedies that occur when sexism underlies and controls gender constructs.[6]

Perhaps informed by recent scholarship in the field of gender studies, Oates represents Corky as a three-dimensional protagonist through whom she continues, like Kate Chopin, Edith Wharton, Pauline Hopkins, and Henry James, to explore social, sexual, and gender issues.[7] Oates analyzes contemporary ideologies of masculinity to expose both subtle and blatant—frequently lethal—repercussions of sexism and misogyny. Highlighting his complexity, she depicts Corky as a composite of several perspectives on masculinity to insure that he will defy easy categorization and diagnosis. Because like any important aspect of one's self, gender identity is inseparable from one's other material or corporeal aspects, this text invites us to inquire into masculinity's complex structures and meanings.

In his study on constructs of "maleness," Peter Clatterbaugh suggests three paradigms of culturally normative masculinity, which I summarize here in order to contextualize Oates's representation of Corky within an ideological framework. Those who adhere to the first perspective, that of "moral conservatism" believe that

> men in their civilized role are . . . to be providers for families, protectors of women and children. Men compete with each other and enjoy taking risks; they are the initiators of sexual encounters; and they are socially and politically more powerful and more influential than women. Men . . . need "masculine-affirming" work in order to feel that they are contributing to society. . . . Finally, they are wary of emotional expression and tend to depend upon women for the satisfaction of their intimate emotional needs. (Clatterbaugh 17)

Clatterbaugh's second category is "profeminist" masculinity.

> For [profeminists], masculinity is created through male privilege and its corresponding oppression of women, although they allow that traditional masculinity is also harmful to men. . . . Liberal profeminism [views] both women and men . . . as subjected to a mystique (born of social stereotypes and ideals) that prevents the realization of their full humanity. (Clatterbaugh 10, 38)

The third viewpoint—"classical Marxist" or "Marxist feminists" (Clatterbaugh uses these terms interchangeably)—"locate[s] the oppression of women and the domination of men in the class structure of capitalist society" (Clatterbaugh 107). His discussion of this concept evokes the politics in Corky's office where, as the boss, "Mr. Corcoran" asserts his dominance over his female secretaries through sexist jokes: "Don't fax with me, girls!" (*WILF* 148). Angela Davis links gender bias with the obsession with private property. Clatterbaugh emphasizes that "masculinity and patriarchy are maintained by the relations of production . . . mean[ing] the relations of control over people, their labor, the products of their labor, and the productive resources" (108).

Although Corky identifies himself politically as a liberal Democrat, he fits most comfortably in Clatterbaugh's "moral conservative" group, with his "masculine-affirming" work being politics. Clatterbaugh points to the culturally accepted use of "phallic" and patronizing descriptive language about masculinity as reflecting a moral code full of expectations with which the men in this group feel they must identify and comply. Culture mandates that they "provide," "protect," "initiate," "compete" and "take risks," and their implicit reward is greater social and political power and influence than/over women. Corky mirrors this when he thinks about the upcoming 1992 presidential election, and muses: "That shit with 'Gennifer' Flowers really hurt Clinton, makes a fool of him if nothing else—a cunt's got no power except to throw shame on a man, that's *her* power" (*WILF* 463). Narcissistic white men like Corky who subscribe to Clatterbaugh's politically regressive paradigm of gender feel no responsibility for anyone else's marginalization nor do they experience any need to interrogate their own "maleness," "whiteness," or privilege. While men holding the beliefs of the "profeminists" or the Marxist feminists critique the patriarchy, the moral conservatives, representing patriarchy's most dangerous constituency, struggle for even greater power, wealth and domination, which is of course tantamount to perpetuating the oppression of others. Corky loves to hear himself referred to as part of the "'power elite'—you got to love that term, if you're in it!" (*WILF* 40). But Corky is a liberal, evidenced by his voting record. He is "on the record as a liberal Democrat solidly behind every liberal cause there is" (*WILF* 40). How are we to understand this important discrepancy between his moral and social conservatism about gender and race and his self-declared liberalism? Perhaps Corky exaggerates his sense of social responsibility when he identifies himself a "liberal" but, more likely, he accurately represents Oates's not very sanguine commentary on political liberalism. She declares that liberals *are* morally conservative, at least regarding issues of gender, race and class, despite protestations to the contrary, and *What I Lived For* clarifies and condemns this equation.

Corky relies on racism, sexism, and class privilege to express his perceived dominance, turning his narrative into a discourse on the nexus of these prejudices. For example, when Marilee Plummer, a young black woman, brings rape charges against Reverend Steadman, a black City Councilman who is Corky's political enemy, Corky feigns liberal outrage at the public sentiment that "a black man raping a black woman doesn't seem so much of a crime" (*WILF* 204). However, he later reveals his blatant and frightening racism and sexism. Inhabiting Corky's mind, the narrator tell us that "as a man, [Corky is] likely to identify with another man accused of rape, *so long as no violence is involved*; as a white man, he's likely to identify with another white man, so long as no violence, no really criminal activity, is involved" (*WILF* 205, 206;

emphasis added). That Corky can even imagine such a thing as "non-violent" rape explicitly reveals his misogyny which coexists with his supposed "broad-mindedness." He admits that "he doesn't have a fucking clue . . . about a woman's *personhood*[—]if it isn't her body what the fuck is it? *why* the fuck is it?" (*WILF* 223). And revealing his anti-Semitism, he wonders why his Jewish accountant does not immigrate to Israel to join "the Jewish people" (*WILF* 117). Defining women as "bodies," black people as "niggers," Jews as intellectually "superior," "real" men as those who go to war, Corky remains unaware of how insulting, never mind how potentially dangerous, such unconscious hate can be when it is unwittingly translated into behavior. Undercutting people's identities and individualities by applying these stereotypes dehumanizes the disempowered in the eyes of the oppressor, thus allowing those in control to rationalize their exploitation. Moreover, Corky *blindly* flexes his oppressive muscles; he genuinely believes that he is a kind, unselfish, liberal man—"a good-hearted guy, [who] inspires generosity in others" (*WILF* 268).

In a scathing commentary on liberalism's hypocrisy, Oates underlines Corky's reaction to a racially motivated murder: "Devane Johnson, 12, [black,] shot fatally in the back by the [white] UCPD Sergeant Dwayne Pickett, 34, November, 1991" (*WILF* 40). The official response to Pickett, who claims he shot the boy in self-defense, although no evidence substantiates this, will be determined by the city's political "old boy" network whose priority is exploiting the "incident's" effect for the Democratic mayor's reelection campaign. The mayor and police fear an aftermath similar to the one in Los Angeles following the Rodney King verdict if Pickett remains free; yet no one with the authority wants to bring charges against him because no one considers his a "real" crime. Revealing the depth of his ability to distort reality and deceive himself, Corky allies himself with Pickett, then tells a friend: "For sure [I] don't defend racist killer cops" (*WILF* 40). "I don't . . . think [the police are] antsy, y'know—trigger-happy. I think they have a tough job. . . . Our cops aren't racist" (*WILF* 123). Clearly his own racism obscures his vision. He prefers to slant the truth rather than reflect upon the glaring contradiction within his thoughts. Conveniently accepting Pickett's lame pretext of self-defense, Corky excuses, even supports, an obviously racist policeman's murdering an unarmed twelve-year-old boy, while he simultaneously spouts clichés to the precise contrary: "[I] don't defend racist killer cops." Upsetting the supposedly clear dualism of liberalism and conservatism, Oates's view is that the ideological differences between the two political positions are sometimes non-existent.

When Reverend Steadman, outraged that Pickett is being protected from a murder indictment, mobilizes public support and demands that he stand trial for killing Johnson, the mayor and his son, U.S. Representative Vic Slattery, Corky's childhood chum, feel their Democratic political base being threatened.

They offer Marilee Plummer fifty thousand dollars to bring spurious rape charges against Steadman to discredit him, and she agrees.[8] Subliminally and subtextually, the Slatterys's conspiracy to destroy the black politician manipulates prevalent white supremacist propaganda—the myth that the insatiable libido of black women caused black men to rape white women.[9] In a stunning example of a contemporary "master/slave" relationship, the Slattery men exploit racist stereotypes of Marilee as "temptress" and Steadman as sexual black "monster" in order to enhance their own political agenda. Reminiscent of the backlash aimed at Anita Hill for her testimony accusing Clarence Thomas of sexual harassment, a vocal faction of Union City's black community, including Marilee's family, express anger at and feel betrayed by her for bringing legal charges against a powerful black man like Steadman. (No one knows the charges are a sham, nor do they contest his guilt; they simply feel that her loyalty to a black man must take precedence over all else.) Abandoned, guilty and unable to undo her mistake, Plummer commits suicide, but her death is a murder as politically motivated as if she were assassinated. Again the ambiguity which is a trademark of this text surrounds her demise. Though I interpret it as a suicide (she is depressed and has attempted suicide before), certainly one could argue that the Slatterys kill her to keep her quiet. Yet, since they are her murderers either way, the distinction is not a crucial one. I note it to spotlight Oates's form of weaving questions, doubts, and alternative readings throughout every "realistic" portion of the text, prodding us to keep asking "what is 'really' happening?" In fact, these are questions and dynamics I return to in my chapter focused on Atwood's *Alias Grace*, a text I consider an example of "poststructural realism."

While my theoretical focus is that of psychoanalytic feminism, Oates's view complements a Marxian one when she argues that within the United States, where capitalistic conspicuous consumption forms and defines the infrastructure of every aspect of the culture, "liberalism" is extinct.[10] As we read the meticulously detailed descriptions of Corky's material possessions—his new thirty-five-thousand-dollar Cadillac and his hundred-dollar designer shirts, for instance—we see that his "things" and his power to possess them are the touchstone of his self-esteem and self-image. (The same is true for Carrie and Hurstwood.) Oates's critique of liberalism exposes a culture that propagandizes the fiction that yokes psychological well-being and money. Therefore humanity and justice can only manifest themselves when the existent hierarchical status of the dominant culture is not at risk, which means never.

Certainly Corky's self-proclaimed liberalism conflicts with the importance he attaches to a man's political power, prestige, and wealth. (To Corky, women's power is insignificant.) From the vantage point of psychoanalytic theory, the views of Robert J. Stoller offer an understanding of Corky's need for power. If Clatterbaugh's approach to constructions of masculinity is taxonomical, then

Stoller's is etiological.[11] While Clatterbaugh emphasizes political language to describe different expressions of "masculine" behavior in adult men, Stoller's psychoanalytic perspective studies the development of gender identity with a focus upon the mother/child relationship as well as the tensions and struggles that characterize the adolescent boy's entrance into manhood. Especially highlighted is the need for the boy to separate emotionally from his mother. As I contextualize Stoller's ideas within my exploration of Corky—his relationship with his mother and his acquisition of masculinity—I refer to Alfred Habegger's discussion on realism in which he, too, makes use of Stoller's theories in order to understand representations of masculinity in American realistic fiction.

In *Sex and Gender*, Stoller writes:

> There are special problems in a boy developing his masculinity. . . . In contrast to Freud's position that masculinity is the natural state and femininity at best a successful modification of it . . . I . . . feel that the infant boy's relationship to his mother makes the development of feminine qualities more likely. . . . *The boy . . . must manage to break free from the pull of his mother's femaleness and femininity,* a task that is . . . frequently uncomplete [*sic*], to judge by the amount of . . . forced hyper-masculinity one sees. (263; emphasis added)

Informed by Stoller's work, Habegger suggests that

> masculinity has an uncertain and ambiguous status. It is . . . acquired through a struggle, a painful initiation, or a long and sometimes humiliating apprenticeship. To be male is to be fundamentally unsure about one's status and hence to struggle to win the *cocky certainty known as masculinity.* When it is won, it is signified by subtle tokens of posture, dress, speech that cannot be counterfeited. (199, 200; emphasis added).

Habegger's discussion on gender and realism focuses on the works of Howells and James; still, his depiction of masculinity—the anxious and uncertain boy suffering "painful initiation" or undergoing a "humiliating apprenticeship" to emerge with "cocky certainty"—resonates with Corky's rite of passage with his peers. (Corky becomes "cocky" with one letter change.) Habegger argues that in nineteenth-century "boy's" fiction, "it was not the father that enabled the boy to escape women's sphere and define his own masculinity" (205), but rather other boys. "The biggest masculine fear of the last century [in fiction] was the fear of not . . . being able to win a place among other men and boys" (204): Habegger's point as well as Stoller's model apply to Oates's twentieth-century critique.

Corky's induction into masculinity was won in a boy's world, but the admission price was high. He sat with six other boys in the back seat of his friend's car while his drunken cohorts taunted a group of young black boys. Laughing and screaming "run niggers!" (*WILF* 563), Corky's friend Heinz blasted the horn, aimed his car at the kids and drove onto the sidewalk. Somehow, the terrified boys managed to get away unharmed. Corky remembers that episode with shame and considers his behavior "cowardly," but his all-encompassing desire for indoctrination into the fraternal order of "adult" masculinity overcame his disgust with his friends' sadistic racism.

Significant, if not surprising, Corky achieves his "manhood" through a display of vicious, macho bravado, which includes a racist attack. If Habegger and Stoller acknowledge the cruelty that can comprise the "painful initiation" into masculinity, Oates raises the stakes when she racializes that cruelty. Imprinting an adolescent experience intended to intimately bond Corky and his friends—the car ride, she irreparably contaminates those "close" male relationships. Racism becomes a permanent part of the "secret handshake" those boys/men share. Furthermore, the fact that all of this takes place as Corky strives to define his "manhood" insures an inexorable, everlasting, and dangerous link between his "male" identity and racism. One defining aspect of Corky, the man, then, is his racism. In his unconscious mind, "real" men are bonded by bigotry.

If we look at Oates's rhetorical form in her representation of the notorious car ride, we see that the loosely associated flow of the single, long, unpunctuated sentence mimics the drift of Corky's thoughts and emotions. For him, the ride is a nightmare: He is

> in the back seat staring his face locked in an idiotic grin . . . all the guys laughing like they're about to piss their pants and Corky was gripping the seat in front of him thinking he'd be sick to his stomach and at The Bull's Eye his terrible worry was there wouldn't be room enough for him in the [restaurant] booth, what if, what then, yes but there was plenty of room for Corky Corcoran that night, he was O.K. (*WILF* 563)

This sentence reveals the desperate tension and ambivalence that plague and characterize Corky's whole life following Tim's murder. Morally, he wants to do the "right thing," which is to make Heinz stop the car, but he cannot jeopardize his friends' approval. If we juxtapose the last portion of the passage from *What I Lived For* cited above—Corky's "terrible worry was there wouldn't be room enough for him in the booth"—with Habegger's observation—"one of the biggest masculine fears [expressed in novels] in the last century was the fear of not somehow being able to win a place among other . . . boys" (204)—we see Corky enacting the anxiety Habegger articulates when the insecure teenager actually, not metaphorically, searches for his place at the table. Habegger clarifies the imperative, life-and-death feeling accompanying Corky's need for acceptance; and in the context of *What I Lived For* as well as in those examined by Clatterbaugh, Stoller, and Habegger, acceptance presupposes conformity.

Corky first confronts a moral crisis pitting his need to conform against his desire to tell the truth immediately following his father's murder when he stands up to pressure from the police and his uncle by refusing to identify falsely Tim Corcoran's killers. The police know who killed him, but they need a witness in order to arrest him, and they try unsuccessfully to badger Corky into being that witness. The crux of this problem is, of course, that conformity leads to praise and love, while speaking the truth results in rejection. For illumination of this point, let us look again at the passage from *What I Lived For* excerpted earlier in which Oates describes, in one long sentence, Corky's experience of the car ride. He is

> in the back seat staring his face locked in an idiotic grin . . . all the guys laughing like they're about to piss their pants and Corky was gripping the seat in front of him thinking he'd be sick to his stomach and at The Bull's Eye his terrible worry was there wouldn't be room enough for him in the booth, what if, what then, yes but there was plenty of room for Corky Corcoran that night, he was O.K. (563)

The sentence enjambs Corky's two equally important anxieties: One concern focuses on that pivotal ride, the other on his friends not making room for him in the restaurant booth. Initially, this enjambment may appear discordant; if the first worry is one of conscience, then the second looks self-referential and narcissistic. Yet, in fact, the connection works rhetorically because it mimics how his anxieties work psychologically. Corky's mind free associates from one to the other because his fear of being snubbed underlies both. If defending the black kids, that is, behaving in a non-conformist way, means being ostracized, then the motivation to do the "right thing" evaporates—subsumed under being loved. Ironically, the fact that Corky insisted upon the truth about his father's death thirty-three years earlier and refused to conform, effectively ignoring the incessant hounding of those who wanted him to lie, causes him to feel like a coward now. Clearly, he has learned that "honesty is an art." He defines himself as a "coward" in two different contexts: the first time, it is for not lying, and the second time it is for not speaking his true feelings by asking Heinz to stop the car.

Establishing his niche within Clatterbaugh's "moral conservative" paradigm, Corky's behavior as an adolescent adumbrates his racism as an adult, most notably in his defense of Sergeant Pickett, the white policeman who killed the black boy, as well as in his support of Reverend Steadman, the black man accused of raping a black woman. Oates stamps crucial coming-of-age experiences for boys—the acquisition of a masculine gender identity and male bonding—with sadism and racism, and such an intermingling affects Corky irreparably.

Pondering men's loyalties to each other, Corky experiences "a bond of maleness that does not so much repudiate the female as transcend her: the anxious intimacy of brother-rivals who dare never accuse one another of any *manly* sin for fear of being expelled irrevocably from that intimacy" (*WILF* 327). If we amend this passage by adding "the black person" to the "female," we see again that Corky's perception of his "place" in the male world is buttressed by racialized and sexualized scapegoats. The end of the text tests precisely this bond, setting "truth" against male friendship; if Corky reveals the circumstances of Marilee Plummer's death, he dooms his friendship with the powerful Slattery family, which is tantamount to destroying his own career. Too mediocre in too many ways to achieve success without political favors, Corky could not maintain his own affluence if the Slatterys were disgraced.

The concluding drama—Corky's confrontation with Vic followed by the former's accidental murder—replays a more sophisticated, adult version of the dilemma of the adolescent car ride and, like that episode, this one is also racialized. Corky faces the same quandary as when he was sixteen: does conformity take precedence over truth or vice versa? Should he stay silent allowing the truth to be buried with Marilee, who, like the kids he taunted with his teen-age friends, is black, or should he expose the Slatterys, vindicate Plummer, and make retribution for his past "cowardly" behavior? Revealing the truth would not only ruin him and the Slatterys, but it would mean forfeiting the coveted acceptance he experiences from his wide circle of "contacts," including Oscar, his father surrogate whose support is Corky's life blood. He declares repeatedly that his loyalties are to men; although his "bond of maleness" transcends women and his pledge of allegiance "as a man" to another man, even one accused of rape, reflects his gendered narcissism, he now faces a crisis in which his entire life could be turned upside down. Perhaps his decision to tell or be silent is as crucial to Oates as is her strategy to have him murdered in a way that replicates his father's death.

Tim's complicated and politically motivated murder was also racialized. Underlying the political issues that led to his murder—labor unions, organized crime, payoffs, protection money, illegally procured government work contracts—the actual provocation was his progressive stance of hiring black workers. Refusing to conform to racist employment practices, Corky's father ignored threats, hired black workers, spurned the demand to pay off the union bosses for the "privilege" of doing so, and was murdered as a result. Infused into these three pivotal experiences for Corky—Tim's murder, the car ride, and Marilee's suicide, which indirectly leads to his own death—racism motivates the narrative development of *What I Lived For*.

If camaraderie with other boys is, according to Habegger, the ultimate need of adolescent boys for attaining the status of "masculinity," then initiating independence from their mothers must, according to Stoller, accompany, if not precede those, strong peer relationships. "Break[ing] free from the pull of his mother's femaleness" (Stoller, *S&G* 263) is, for Stoller and numerous other psychoanalytic theorists beginning with Freud, the boy's primary task in establishing his masculine gender identity, and Habegger points to Huckleberry Finn as illustrating the "basic male dream—being entirely on one's own, autonomy" (205). Mary Gordon observes that "the image of the moving boy has been central in American writing. Motion is the boy's genius" (3). But what about the boy's pull *toward* the mother or the maternal world? Even considering Stoller's point, recent psychoanalytic scholarship emphasizes that the desires of children of both genders for love, caring, safety and connectedness compel as much, if not more, than the wish for separateness.[12]

Perhaps the sometimes fractious debate within psychoanalytic circles emphasizing the importance of either the boy's separation from the mother *or* his connection to her during the transition from adolescent boy to adult man mirrors Corky's equally strong oppositional wishes to merge with his mother, on the one hand, and to separate from her, on the other. His problem lies not within his feelings themselves, but rather in the commonly held erroneous belief that conflicting emotions cannot exist simultaneously. A textual example of this psychological dynamic is expressed in his memory: He remembers "being bathed by his mother. . . . He sees only the hands gently bathing him. . . . She's leaning over him, arms around him . . . a face of such beauty, the shining eyes . . . he stares, he tries to see, with every fiber of his being he tries to see, but can't" (*WILF* 253). Directly following this, and repeated as a refrain throughout the text, Corky recites to himself: "You made me love you. Didn't want to do it. Didn't want to do it" (*WILF* 253). The enjambment of these two sentences exemplifies the depth, even in his recollections, of the tension he experiences when associating tenderness and pleasure with his mother. Clearly there is a sexualized component to these memories and I will address it later in this chapter.

As Stoller explains the male adolescent's path to autonomy, one gets the impression that the boy unambivalently wants nothing more than to escape his "devouring" mother's tentacles. (The perverse ways in which mothers are portrayed by some psychoanalytic theorists—monstrous, engulfing—are well-known, but fortunately much is being written to correct these misogynistic distortions.)[13] But for the teenager, too, emotionally separating from his mother can be experienced as sad, scary, and a loss, as well as exciting. Stoller writes that the boy must "break free from the pull of his mother's femaleness and femininity." More useful is a view in which the boy is able to negotiate powerfully complex feelings for someone of the other gender, considering sexual "sameness" and "difference" as he grows *within*, not split off from, the maternal world.

Conventional psychoanalytic theory emphasizes the need of the male child, later, the adolescent, to divorce himself from the maternal world as a prerequisite to acquiring his masculine identity. Stoller adds that the breaking away process is frequently not completed and the result is "effeminacy, passivity, or forced hypermasculinity" (*S&G* 263). But what if a desire for connection with the mother/maternal world is a natural one inherent in the human condition? If so, and if such longing provokes cultural disapproval, is even considered to be "effeminate," then boys will repress these desires, which will then surface as "forced hypermasculin[e]" behavior—Corky's muscle-flexing car ride being a case in point. While Stoller would interpret that episode as evidence that Corky's rupture with his mother's/aunt's "femaleness" is incomplete, requiring even more distance, my view is different.

The car ride reveals Corky's pressure to hide his tender feelings, which, if not inhibited, could motivate him to help the victimized black kids. I agree with Jessica Benjamin who proclaims that "these distinct psychic tendencies of our psychic organization [—to remain close to the mother while simultaneously establishing autonomy—] constitute a tension rather than, as has often been supposed, a contradiction, an 'either-or'" (*LS,LO* 85, 86). As a microcosm, then, the car ride makes apparent the intersection of the intrapsychic and the political. If Corky had felt that protecting the frightened boys expressed "manly" behavior, he would have done so, thereby preempting a racist incident. If the discourse of the patriarchal hegemony provided or promoted "masculine" status without the "necessary" prop of black (at other times, female) scapegoats, the white boys would have had no need to torment the black kids. And if psychoanalytic theory could better withstand the conflicts, ambivalences, and divided desires inherent in boys' relationships with their mothers, the boys' mandate to sever such maternal ties, so as to prevent "feminization," would most likely diminish. Adhering to rigid Manichean oppositions that allow for no intersubjectivity is a problem that, according to many Western cultural and psychological theories, is associated more often with masculinity than with femininity, and certainly applies to Corky's dissociated feelings about his mother.

Sharing a cultural and psychological construct of masculinity that emphasizes the "man's" world as viewed politically by Clatterbaugh (his moral conservative group) and psychoanalytically by Stoller are a number of writers whose works are included in the literary tradition of American realism. Examples are Dreiser, Howells, James, Lewis, Roth, Styron, Wolfe, and modernists such as Hemingway and Fitzgerald. Linking Oates's text with others fitting the criteria of realism/naturalism is, first, the "hero's" confrontation with a moral/existential crisis. Provoking the protagonist into an unprecedented introspective examination of his socially conservative, conventional life, the crisis of conscience then structures the novel's narrative in order to critique the moral decay and political corruption of society.

Also joining Oates's text with those of the early realists, particularly Howells' work (see E. Elliott 503), is *What I Lived For*'s argument against the tenets of Social Darwinism. Oates makes it clear that "survival" depends upon the confluence of psychological and cultural factors. To enforce this point, her work frequently explores the question of "what would have happened if . . .," in this case, Tim had not been murdered (see also *American Appetites*, *Because it is Bitter and Because it is my Heart*, *Black Water*, and *We Were the Mulvaneys*) to underline the complex interrelatedness of political and personal elements which contribute to the occurrence of events. For Oates, as well as for the politically progressive writers who preceded her, the reductive concept of "manifest destiny" is regressive and useless.

Deliberately writing herself into the one-hundred-year-old male dominated realist literary lineage, Joyce Carol Oates, in my view, establishes a special connection between *What I Lived For* and *Babbitt*. Both texts study the personal and political permutations of "conformity" and, in so doing, confront the high stakes of even minimal defiance of collective norms. For example, in his short-lived attempt to define him"self," Babbitt resists being coerced into joining an anti-labor vigilante group formed by his friends; however, when those "friends" "black ball" him, he loses business and money, then begs to be admitted. Acting in accordance with his conscience only until he experiences hurt or loss, Babbitt, unlike Corky, feels angry because he recognizes he is entrapped and wishes he could "break out" of society's strait jacket. He has had a taste of freedom. Corky, on the other hand, does not realize that he is imprisoned. Babbitt moves farther along, albeit temporarily, toward developing an independent "self" than does Corky. Moreover, Lewis's protagonist risks social opprobrium when, at the novel's close, he allies himself with his nonconformist son. Again invoking Habegger's relevant observation that the biggest worry of many protagonists in American realism's "boy's" fiction is being accepted by other boys, I suggest that neither Corky nor Babbitt outgrow this adolescent anxiety; rather it becomes an organizing principle of their adult lives. Conformity is the price individuals and society alike pay when the political system's power relies upon the accumulation of material wealth, thereby offering commodities as substitutes for empathy and love.

In an earlier essay, Oates writes that "nihilism is overcome by the breaking-down of the dikes between human beings, the flowing forth of passion." Perhaps *What I Lived For* represents her gloomy view of the fin de siècle if nihilism is not overcome. She predicts that the "dehumanization of power as an ideological premise," earmarked by vapid consumerism and conformity, will pervade and destroy any remnant of cultural generosity as well as intimate human relationships (qtd. in Wesley, *Refusal* 67).

Within the tradition of realism, Oates addresses several crucial questions, one of which is of particular interest to me. Concentrating on *What I Lived For* and *Babbitt* while paying special attention to Habegger's emphasis on boys' widespread anxiety regarding their masculine place in the world, I view the enactments of conformity in "boys" and "girls" fiction as different from each other. How are we to understand these gendered differences? Corky and Babbitt are willing to conform, even willing to go to extremes, for their places at the "male" table, the implications of which are demonstrated in *What I Lived For* and *Babbitt*.

Joining numerous psychoanalytic theorists, I think that within the Oedipal phase of development, boys are more preoccupied with issues of performance and competition than are girls. In the process of defining gender, boys identify with their fathers to establish their own masculine identities. At the same time, they unconsciously vie with those fathers for attention from their mothers. (Within contemporary psychoanalytic theory, it is *not* widely believed any more that the attention boys desire from their mothers is exclusively sexual. Their wishes, which can include erotic desires, are also for love and recognition. Additionally, psychoanalytic theory presumes that the young boy is heterosexual and a girl or woman, his desired love choice.) The aggression boys and adolescent males feel causes them anxiety, not only from guilt or fear of retaliation, but because, as much as they wish for "special" maternal relationships, they don't want to jeopardize loving and devoted paternal ones. Therefore, according to Freud, Stoller, and Habegger, for instance, boys ensconce themselves in same-sexed peer groups, while also needing support and encouragement from men; they are willing to sacrifice their individual values and morals to those of the group in order to win acceptance. That approval is critical because it works to reassure the boys that the aggression they direct toward their fathers will not boomerang and harm them.[14] When discussing the problem of conformity for girls, it is important to remember that psychoanalytic theory has yet to address the Oedipal phase in the context of gender development for lesbians. For heterosexual girls, the theory proclaims that their yearnings for acceptance into same-sexed peer groups are different, though not lessened, from those of boys because the identification with the mother/woman is already in place. Unlike the boy, girls do not have to "switch" or realign their parental mirroring in order to define their "femaleness."

Women in traditional American realist texts, such as Edith Wharton's Lily Bart in *The House of Mirth*, Ellen Glasgow's Dorinda Oakley in *Barren Ground*, Nella Larsen's Helga Crane in *Quicksand*, Charlotte Perkins Gilman's narrator in "The Yellow Wallpaper," or Kate Chopin's Edna Pontellier in *The Awakening* are all extremely concerned with societal acceptance. However, their anxieties are less related to finding a welcoming and approving place at the table of their peers. Their central dilemma is one of establishing an autonomous existence without transgressing society's expectations. Their needs for approbation do not, for the most part, stem from a fear of retaliation for their own aggression and competition; the female characters are preoccupied, unlike Corky/Babbitt/Hurstwood, with being "good" women/wives/mothers. They conform to the mandates of patriarchy and their guilt derives from the wish to escape that same patriarchy. In her inquiry into conformity, Oates reveals how politically dangerous it can be when it means the sacrifice of one's moral and ethical beliefs, as it does for Corky.

Corky's literal psychological trauma—his murdered father and lost mother—operates symbolically as the modern Oedipal metaphor that typifies white, Western masculinity. While I understand the contention that "perverted" behavior may be the appropriate response, even the healthy one, to a "sick" environment, I do not believe that Corky can be perceived *only* as an ordinary man in a distorted culture. Yet I do think that the social construction of masculinity, on the one hand, and his trauma and psychopathology, on the other, dovetail, or are, indeed, two sides of the same coin. Pursuing my discussion of *What I Lived For* from the perspective of psychoanalytic theory, I will think about Corky as an adult who survived a nearly devastating trauma in his childhood. He continues to experience unquenchable desire for his lost parents, evidenced in this thoughts and memories, but he refuses to acknowledge the sadness these reminiscences evoke. Still, words, phrases, and memories surface to his awareness uninvited. For example: More than once he remembers his mother, "Theresa angry, weeping over him; [he thinks] I can't! can't save you! I'm not strong enough!" (*WILF* 519). Motivating every nuance of Corky's life is his desperate need to rid himself of his painful feelings. Unaware that "desire may be insatiable," Corky is obsessed with what Mary Ann Doane calls "the constantly renewed [but futile] pursuit for a perpetually lost object" (12). While Oates advances the story forward, paradoxically, Corky travels backward toward destruction, operating as his own most formidable obstacle.

If psychoanalyst Judith Herman is right that "remembering and telling the truth about terrible events are prerequisites both for the restoration of the social order and for the healing of individual victims, . . . [and if] avoiding . . . traumatic memories leads to stagnation in the recovery process" (1, 176), then there is not even a glimmer of hope for Corky to heal. Consistent with the trope throughout this book that ignoring one's personal and political histories potentially precipitates violence, his evasion of his defining trauma—the sudden, permanent and simultaneous loss of both of his parents—may precipitate his own death sentence. Additionally, his steadfast refusal to allow unconscious desire to surface, his stubborn need to keep his feeling of "wanting" severed from its source, leads unreflective Corky on a doomed quest like the one described by Doane.

Continuing my exploration of the relationship between "desire" and trauma, I want to recall Peter Brooks's observation that "it is important to pursue the notion of desire as that which is initiatory of narrative, motivates and energizes its reading, and animates the combinatory play of sense-making." According to Brooks, "we need . . . to talk about desire not only as the motor force of plot but as the very motive of narrative" (*RP* 48). Early trauma influences the complex and variegated permutations of desire which "motor" Oates's plot; Corky's desire actually organizes Oates's narrative, or in Brooks's words, desire is "the very motive of narrative." Approaching the subject of desire from a different perspective, Lacan complements Brooks's point that the feeling of desiring *itself* propels the behavior of the subject or the action of the text. As a major contributor to an extensive conversation focused on desire, Lacan restructures Saussure's linguistic of the sign in two ways that are relevant to my reading of *What I Lived For*: First, he reconfigures Saussure's symmetrical relationship between the signifier and the signified, designated as s/s, by transposing a capital S for the signifier to indicate its greater power, represented as S/s. Second, he poses a metaphoric relationship between insatiable desire and the object of that desire, which then replaces his symbol S/s with the designation Desire/object. Lacan privileges the experience of "wishing" over what-is-wished-for evidenced by the capital S, and thus intersects with Brooks's paradigm. Viewed in this way, the desire and its longed-for object are forever separated by the same figurative slash that keeps apart the signifier and the signified, but in Lacan's version, the slash is renamed the "bar of repression," indicating the repression or inaccessibility of the actual desire. In his construction, desire is only and always Oedipal/sexual, therefore unconscious and taboo.

The feeling of longing, the emotional experience of desire, though disconnected from its source, is quite conscious in Lacanian theory. Likewise, in Oates's novel, desire is conscious, especially when it works as the determining force for Corky Corcoran. However, my reading of *What I Lived For* expands Lacan's limiting application of desire to encompass more than incestuous and sexual yearnings; for example, Corky's "real" desire is to reunite with Tim, his murdered father, and his institutionalized mother. At the same time, I agree with Lacan that this wish is unconscious. Brooks concludes that "unconscious desire becomes, in the later life of the subject, a motor of actions whose significance is blocked from consciousness, since interpretation of its scenarios of fulfillment is not directly accessible to consciousness" (*RP* 55). Moreover, Corky's impulsive mania is the "language" through which his repressed memories and semiconscious fantasies are expressed; in addition, he employs his "lunacy" to avoid precisely those traumatic memories. Unaware and disinterested in what motivates his behavior, Corky is controlled like a puppet by his unconscious desires.

I locate Corky "within" Lacan's bar of repression, stuck in the black hole between his experience of desire and the object of that desire. Six hundred pages long, *What I Lived For* is divided into two distinct sections: a thirty-four-page prologue comprising the murder/trauma, taking place over four days including Christmas, 1959, and the body of the text, also taking place over four days and including a holiday—this time Memorial Day, 1992. Textually separated by blank pages and thirty-three years, this division rhetorically mimics the schism within Corky's psyche. In other words, Saussure's slash, Lacan's repression bar, and Oates's blank pages indicate the psychological inaccessibility of this earlier time to Corky. Still, fueled by the urgency of desire while remaining ignorant of its origin, his frenetic, "notched-up" behavior, represented by *very* long, unpunctuated, fast-moving, action-building sentences, thrusts him into "a motor of [floundering] actions," and these actions become and comprise his narrative. Corky desires to undo the prologue, reverse the murder, love and be loved by his parents, but he is unconscious of this, realizing only an insatiable and nagging "wanting of something," which he sublimates into money and sex, looking to material commodities and sexual encounters for his misplaced gratification.

Freud defines sublimation as "the power to replace [an instinct's] immediate aim by other aims" ("Leonardo da Vinci" 452). While he is talking about sublimating sexual urges into, say, work, I reverse his structure to suggest that, in Oates's text, Corky's wish for his parents is sublimated into sexual activity. Corky feels urgently "propelled like a shot off a shovel" (*WILF* 199) into action if he senses his emotional pain threatening to emerge, but his responses bear no resemblance to the feelings precipitating them. He satisfies his sexual desires, but since they are not the "real" source of his yearning, he "end[s] up cruising the city, his nightspots, even the Irish Bar down by the docks, restless and pugnacious and close to getting into one or two fights" (*WILF* 207), which indeed almost invariably characterizes his moods. Another time, feeling hurt, after Thalia deserts him, "like he's been hit over the head . . . *and* kicked in the balls" (*WILF* 306), he goes out to get drunk and "on a crazy impulse" (*WILF* 478), buys the bar—"brandishing his check-book like it's his cock in his hand" (*WILF* 309). (This language as well as the represented behavior exemplifies Corky's "hypermasculinity" as I described it earlier in this chapter.) With the inner voice of his accountant, Corky questions what he is doing "buying a heavily mortgaged jazz nightclub in downtown Union City, not even checking out the books, the insurance, the actual condition of the premises, what madness in the midst of [his] own financial problems and in the depths of the recession!" (*WILF* 309). But since he represses the particular desire underlying his excited mania, that desire manifests itself in an activity that he doesn't understand; he describes his behavior as "beyond a mistake[;] [it is] a mystification." And later he wonders, "why does [he] do the wild impulsive things he does, it's as if another man makes these decisions" (*WILF* 329), and Corky is stuck carrying them out. Looking at Oates's construction of Corky, we find a consistently believable, psychologically accurate, realistic first-person narrative representation, which serves to remind us once more of this protagonist's position in the literary tradition of American realism. Still, paradoxical pressures situate him in an almost surreal disharmony with his social environment. His psychological "being," as it were, is anathema to the cultural construct of "masculinity" that he embodies. Recovering from a trauma demands "tell[ing] the story of the trauma. [Doing so] . . . actually transforms the traumatic memory, so that it can be integrated into the survivor's life story" (Herman 175). But such a process is one that Corky will not undertake under any circumstances. We know he wants to avoid emotional pain, but even more importantly, shedding his veneer to confide his innermost feelings is antithetical to the construct of "masculinity" that he represents.

Emphasizing *What I Lived For*'s postmodernity, Corky is the "I"/narrator of the title. Structured as his "autobiography," the text reflects his life's purpose—what he lived for—which is to illustrate the explosive consequences of political power when used as a weapon for personal gain. Yet, to read with, and not against, the moving current of Oates's postmodern representation, which evokes more than it resolves, we must accept uncertainty, instability, and ask what, if anything, including human personality, is secure or reliable. Constructing her protagonist in order to deconstruct him, Oates subverts sexist and racist representations within a strata of American culture by satirizing the extreme of a Social Darwinian ethic in which only the most unscrupulous, money- and power-hungry men are fit to survive. Marilyn Wesley, writing before the publication of *What I Lived For*, rightly points out that Oates's wealthier characters frequently earn and maintain their fortunes by "operat[ing] as agents of the inhumane power deployed by the institutions they serve . . . [for instance,] law, medicine and politics" (*Refusal* 69). Additionally, Oates juxtaposes Corky's emotional needs against society's imposed demand for conformity, and the conflict, for him, proves disastrous. (Lewis sets up the same binary for Babbitt.)

Patriarchy's inscriptions, now consolidated *within* Corky, are locked in irreconcilable and lethal opposition to his psychological need to talk about and understand his past. Corky "never talks about his family [*sic*] never even his mother[;] . . . it's like he's forgotten his background" (*WILF* 312). In fact, one way of thinking about his ambiguous death is that this profound, unendurable opposition is its cause. (Although one could argue that Corky does not die and is actually talking at the novel's close, such a view explains neither the physical impossibility of his speaking while on a respirator, nor why his friends come to pay off their gambling losses for the baseball pennant race four months before the playoffs.) Trapped within a rigid definition of gender, Corky believes that expressing his emotions will sabotage his power and dominance, and as he says repeatedly, having no "male" power is tantamount to death. The weight of his trauma caves in on him because his cultural environment (or his interpretation of it) prevents him from rehabilitating and (re)claiming his past. This then is what his unexamined quest for power tells us—living for prestige and acceptance with no moral center is a doomed existence. Such is the case in most texts in realism's lineage. Reminiscent of the ghost-child in Toni Morrison's *Beloved*, Corky comes back from death to tell his story, evidenced in the past tense—"liv*ed*" of the title. Still, it is too late.

One critic asserts that when "negotiating the representation of violence, the reader finds him- or herself more vigorously placed and more intensively manipulated than in most texts" (Tanner, 13). Certainly this manipulation of the reader operates forcefully in *What I Lived For* as it does in most, if not all, of the books I discuss. Not until Budd Yeager visits the protagonist does the reader surface from inside Corky's deteriorating mind. Yeager offers an "outside" view on the past two days and four hundred pages; he tells Corky: "Some friends are a little worried about you lately . . . they think you've been acting strange, the last couple of days" (*WILF* 466). Tanner explains that "the seductive power of [violent narrative] representation lies, at least in part, in its ability to naturalize its own conclusions, to obscure its manipulation of the experiential dynamics of violence by veiling the ideological assumptions inherent in its linguistic maneuvers" (10). Oates's strategy is not to obscure violence, but rather to reveal it as insidious. By locking our perspective inside Corky's mind, she seduces us into his story, then introduces Yeager, who, simply by carrying that "extra-textual" message, reminds us that reading *What I Lived For* demands alert, critical analyses of the patriarchal, capitalistic, racist political systems that determine the rise and fall of Corky Corcoran. Insisting that reading is an action, Tanner writes that "the experience of reading may become an opportunity for interrogating the mechanisms of representation and the conventions of reading through which the material dynamics of violence are depicted" (10). If we do not politically contextualize this narrative, we commit Corky's error of obstinately denying responsibility for his impulsive and dangerous behavior.

Literary Trauma analyzes how textual violence imagined by women undermines dominant discourse. In Oates's narrative, as well as in those by Silko, Allison, Jones, Hopkins, Atwood, and Gilman, violence defines both personal and historical pasts. Close to the heart of each of these books is the idea that until/unless the brutal past is understood and accepted, it will be destructively repeated. To some extent, Corky does finally grieve for his parents when he weeps uncontrollably at their grave sites after learning the true circumstances surrounding his father's death. Ideally, then, he would rescue his past and emancipate himself from the confining construct of masculinity that bears his signature. Perhaps it is too late. Enigmatically, he replicates his father's death; he is even hit by the same number of bullets. Earlier in the text, Corky holds his unloaded gun to his head in a mock macho pose and wonders what he would do if he was ever "in a position where he could save somebody else's life but he'd be paralyzed, or run like hell saving his own [*sic*]. The shame of it afterward, he'd never outlive" (*WILF* 210). Though he does not outlive what is perceived to be his heroism for (in my view) unintentionally "saving" Vic's life, I am interested in Oates's foreshadowing of that event.

In one sense, Oates brings us to Corky's death through a narratively conventional, linear path consistent with the novel's formal day-by-day chronological structure, and thus adheres to the tradition of realism. At the same time, the text is cyclical, moving in time from Corky's childhood to beyond his death, deconstructing itself at every "realistic" turn, thereby fusing realism with postmodernism. Corky is shot almost immediately after his (potentially) life-changing conversation with his uncle in which he "learns what he seems not to have known nor even guessed: [His father] brought his own death upon himself, yet not intentionally, seeming not to know he would die, even as he seems to have willed his death. [Like his own,] *an inevitable death. Yet in its way accidental*" (*WILF* 573; emphasis added). But Corky dies before he can make use of his new knowledge. His death appears to be unalterably fixed since the novel's inception. In his review for *The New York Times* (October 19, 1994), James Carroll writes that for this protagonist "character is destiny. . . . This blind, drunken, skittish human pinball game has in fact been an arrow-straight moral odyssey, aimed at the truth." Corky's fate, sealed the day Tim is shot, runs as straight as "the trajectory of a bullet" (*WILF* 16) to the same end.

On a more hopeful note, Corky's evolution has a purpose that transcends his corporeal existence—that of communicating his story, the objective of which is to alert and forewarn. Metaphorically portraying his death, Oates describes "the death of a large star [as] a sudden and violent event" (*WILF* 187).

> The star evolves . . . but when it runs out of . . . fuel, it collapses under its own weight in less than a second. It might seem that this implosion would be a chaotic process, but in fact it is quite orderly. Indeed, the entire evolution of the star is toward a condition of greater order, or lower entropy. (*WILF* 187)

If, what Corky lived for is not precisely "a condition of greater order or lower entropy," it does mandate (re)shaping and renovating stereotypic definitions of gender. Additionally, narrating the story in Corky's voice even through the epilogue helps to redeem him. Telling his "life" is Corky's first generous act serving to mitigate somewhat the text's pessimism.

Oates, whose novelistic signature is the representation of emotionally intense and complicated family relationships, emphasizes Corky's memories of his mother. A central concern in *What I Lived For* is his conflated and confused longings for sexual, romantic, and maternal love with sex/pain/violence. Corky's trauma, including his convoluted relationship with his mother, causes these yearnings to converge. For example, as he makes love with Christina, he fantasizes about Theresa: "His blood courses hotly into [Christina]. They shared the same heartbeat. As with Theresa, long ago. Before he was born. Snug and secret upside down breathing not air but blood, fueled in blood, Corky has never been so happy" (*WILF* 76). And four hundred pages later in a chapter entitled "The Kiss," Corky remembers an encounter with Theresa when she escaped from the hospital. He was twelve years old; it was the first and only time he was to see her after Tim's death.

> Theresa moaned and rocked from side to side holding [Corky] in her thin, strong arms, and kissed him wetly, hotly, with a terrible hunger, on the mouth, and he began to fight her *as always he did at such times* but then abruptly ceased, it was to be the last kiss between them and thus the last struggle and she wept over him . . . and *a single heart beat between them.* (*WILF* 474; emphasis added)

In the single heart beat he shares first with his mother, then with Christina, the romantic language of sex meets the symbiotic language of maternity. With his mother, in particular, the image of a wet, hot, hungry kiss from which he struggles to escape is more erotic than maternal. The meaning of this kiss to Theresa is inexplicit because her son becomes confused with her husband in her delusional mind, but since Corky "*always*" struggles against his mother's embraces, perhaps this kiss is incestuously tinged.[15] While this reading may be overdetermined, I point out that Corky clearly experiences anxiety or discomfort from Theresa's touches and kisses; this is a crucial dynamic for any incest argument, in addition to precisely how physically intimate the behavior is. (It is also true that twelve-year-old boys struggle against their mother's embraces, but this passage is blatantly encoded in sexual language.)

Later, while having sex with Charlotte, his ex-wife, Corky again links his sexual experience with maternity. He feels "a little scared . . . the way the woman is clutching, caressing him, hands moving up and down his body, reclaiming it, *like she's given birth to him*" (*WILF* 448; emphasis added). Still another time, he is driving his car thinking about Charlotte, when suddenly he remembers: "Theresa hugging him so tight against her the breath went out of him like a blow, his ribs cracked open. . . . Kissing him hot and wet and so hungry on the mouth like nobody's ever kissed him since. Nor ever will. And nobody so beautiful" (*WILF* 476). Enjambing sex, pain, and Theresa, Oates represents, even mimics, Corky's aversion to and voracious desire for sex.

Corky's thoughts during sex yoke Theresa with images of power, pain and violence, and a case in point is when he makes love with Charlotte and muses: "Every fuck a rape. But not every rape a fuck, they say it's not sex but the desire to hurt, to humiliate, to kill. But why isn't *that* sex too?" (*WILF* 446). And during that same sexual encounter, he recalls his college roommate asking him if he "ever want[ed] to fuck [his] own mother" (*WILF* 446). These simultaneous thoughts reveal his con-fusion regarding Theresa, sex and "the desire to hurt, to humiliate, to kill." British psychoanalyst Stephen Frosh thinks about why men sexually abuse women and children. He discusses "the nexus . . . of hostility/rage/sexuality centring on that splitting-off of sex from intimacy which is a crucial element in masculine sexual socialisation" (113). He explains that

> the extent to which . . . specific experiences [such as the quality of early childhood relationships and the advent of trauma] enable a man to deal with the potential splitting of intimacy and dependence from sexuality, and hence the degree to which he can come to a more integrated absorption of maternal and paternal images, that is the primary determinant of his capacity to overcome sexual rage and use sex for contact rather than control. (114)

Perhaps Corky's sexual desire to hurt expresses his wish to declare himself an autonomous being separate from his mother. Brooks notes that a universal aspect of the human condition "is in essence the desire to be heard, recognized, understood, which, never wholly satisfied or indeed satisfiable, continues to generate the desire to tell, the effort to enunciate a significant version of the life story in order to captivate a possible listener" (*RP* 54). When Corky characterizes his life as "*a fight between an 'It' and an 'I'*" (*WILF* 304), maybe he addresses Theresa who he thinks "quit being a mother to him as if incapable of recognizing him except to know his name . . . but incapable of feeling it" (*WILF* 91). He recites that "all a man wants, no matter what it costs him [is] to be the real thing" (*WILF* 556). Juxtaposing Brooks's theory that the desire to be "known" forms narrative with Jessica Benjamin's that authentic recognition from an important "other" forms subjectivity, we see that provoking Corky's narrative of desire is, in part, his attempt to construct an identity.

What Oates accomplishes in *What I Lived For* is multifaceted, far-reaching and visionary. Perhaps she even comes close to her "laughingly Balzacian" desire "to put the whole world into a book" (qtd. in Bender vii). Alerting us to the violent and sometimes fatal ramifications of Western white, masculine, heterosexual politics, Oates warns that these social and cultural constructs stymie human intimacy and personal growth, which inevitably thwarts political action.

CHAPTER SIX

Intertextuality and Poststructural Realism in Margaret Atwood's *Alias Grace* and Charlotte Perkins Gilman's "The Yellow Wallpaper"

"Tell all the Truth but tell it slant—"

—Emily Dickinson[1]

"The truth may well turn out to be stranger than we think."

—Simon Jordan in *Alias Grace*

In her ninth novel, *Alias Grace* (1996), Margaret Atwood examines, for the second time, the story(ies) of Grace Marks, a sixteen-year-old domestic servant, accused in 1843 of conspiring to murder her employer, Thomas Kinnear, and his housekeeper/mistress, Nancy Montgomery, in Kingston, Ontario.[2] Along with James McDermott, a third Kinnear employee who was, according to some, Marks's co-conspirator and lover, while others, including Grace herself, say he was her intimidating persecutor, she was found guilty and sentenced to death. Pleading that she was still a child as well as supposedly witless, Grace's lawyer won a stay of execution for his client commuting her sentence to life imprisonment; McDermott, who confessed to carrying out the killings, shooting Kinnear, and hacking Montgomery with an ax, then strangling her, was hanged. Ambiguity still shadows Grace's role in these crimes: Was she the instigator and/or mastermind behind them? Did she assist McDermott in the strangling, tightening her own handkerchief around Nancy's neck, as he claims? Or, at the very least, did she fail to warn Nancy that her life was in danger? And, if she was involved, what was motivating her? Still, critical as these questions are, they remain inadequate for Atwood who wonders about the entirety of Grace's life:

what was she like, what did she think/feel/fantasize/experience, even read and wear? Atwood researches old trial reports, and relies upon her imagination to endow Grace with such a humanely, individualized personality that both the reader and the character move beyond the relentless question of did she or did she not do it. Without diminishing the tragedy of two deaths, Atwood enables us to care about more than Grace's guilt or innocence.

Emphasizing that Marks's narrative is enigmatic and protean, Atwood chooses a patchwork quilt as a metaphor or emblem for her newest novel. Grace is an expert quilter and each of the novel's sections is named for a quilt pattern. In keeping with Atwood's symbol, I have divided this chapter into four sections, although the divisions are not cut with a scalpel; they frequently overlap, and are "pieced" together like patchwork. My first segment continues my exploration into how, for specific protagonists, personal/psychological sadomasochism converges with and is contextualized by political/cultural sadomasochism and, the result, inevitably, is trauma. In *Alias Grace*, a complex novel of nineteenth-century scientific, social, psychological, and political ideas touching on provocative subjects such as U. S. slavery, abortion, and sexual liaisons between "masters" and servants, the axis around which Grace's traumas spin and intersect is the "Irish Question," which involved severe anti-Irish prejudices.

In the second section, I discuss *Alias Grace*'s intertextual relationships: by this I mean the novel's references to two other texts, which contain different versions of Grace Marks's story—Susanna Moodie's *Life in the Clearings* (1853) and Atwood's *The Servant Girl*, a television drama written in 1974, produced by the Canadian Broadcasting Corporation.[3] Atwood provides the unusual opportunity to juxtapose three perspectives or interpretations of one historical episode, written over a period of about one-hundred-forty years. From these three works, intertextual relationships blossom into a remarkable assembly of dialogues among almost fifty texts. Additionally, in this section, I discuss how Grace insistently "undoes" or deconstructs aspects of her story almost as soon as she presents them to psychiatrist Simon Jordan, her interlocutor, leaving the reader, as well as Simon, on constantly shifting, unstable, un"fixed" ground.

My third section will show that Atwood has extensively researched the theories of selected nineteenth-century scientists, psychologists, and medical practitioners whose work was devoted to the study of the human mind. She renders an intricate, scholarly history of specific ideas which influenced how certain mental disorders were treated—from bleedings to the modern "talking cure," with much, such as phrenology and hypnosis, in between. Atwood's aim is to contribute to the evolving, organic discourse on psychological phenomena, central to cultural and literary studies, that has been ongoing for two hundred years; she does so by bringing to light several early and now forgotten pioneers in the "discovery" and study of consciousness. Pivotal to the formal structure of

Alias Grace, as well as to my argument, is that Grace's first-person narrative voice emerges for the first time to tell *her* story within the context of a psychotherapeutic relationship. Through such a construct, Atwood declares that the popular and frequently contentious nineteenth- century discourse provoked by the heretofore unprecedented study of the mind, specifically "alternate" or "secondary" states of consciousness, such as multiple personalities and somnambulism, frames her novel. On the subjects of dissociation, amnesia, repressed memories, and hypnosis, this section bears obvious connections to my earlier chapter on Pauline Hopkins's *Of One Blood*.

Charlotte Perkins Gilman's "The Yellow Wallpaper" (1892) is the primary focus of my fourth section, especially Gilman's aim of exposing the patriarchal "mental health" system, which institutionalizes, sanctions, and sometimes even promotes, the captivity of women. While the lunatic asylums were abominable, the systematic processes of infantilizing, humiliating, and devaluing women before they even set foot inside those places are an emphasis of "The Yellow Wallpaper."[4] Gilman's text examines how patriarchy can drive women crazy, and the particular signatures emblematizing that "craziness"; I will look closely at how psychological and cultural sadism(s) produce trauma for the story's unnamed narrator.

For Grace Marks and the thousands of Irish immigrants forced to leave their country because of religious persecution and the poverty resulting from, among other causes, the potato famine of the 1840s, the horrendous, frequently fatal, six- to eight-week journey across the Atlantic was certainly traumatic.[5] Grace describes the experience to Simon, beginning with the sleeping arrangements. The "beds" were

> hard rough wooden slabs . . . poorly nailed together and six feet long and six feet wide, with two persons to each, and three or four if children; and two layers of them, one on top of the other. . . . In case of breach of discipline [of the captain's rules] we would have to be locked up in a cubbyhole. . . . The doctor was not to be pestered with trifles. . . . All the passengers were stuffed in together, with no walls between, and most as sick as dogs; . . . not only could you hear the retchings and groanings of your neighbors . . . but hardly any air got in, and so the hold became fouler and fouler and the stench was enough to turn your stomach inside out. . . . [She apologizes to Simon for her "indelicacy" when she tells him] there were no proper ways to relieve yourself. . . . With the . . . noise and the stink, and the rats running to and fro . . . it was like being a suffering soul in Hell. I thought of Jonah in the belly of the whale, but . . . he only had to stay three days, and we had eight weeks . . . and [Jonah] did not have to listen to the moaning and vomiting of others.[6]

Underlying the appalling conditions aboard these ships, politically sanctioned ethnic prejudice allowed immigrants to be conveyed in subhuman conditions; many, like Grace's mother, died along the way, and those who survived the journey were disillusioned and met with hostility in Canada. Although the boats usually docked in Quebec first, many people, including Grace's family, continued on to Toronto "which was where they said the free land could be obtained" (*AG* 124).

In a more individualized and psychological sense, Grace's poverty, which forced the immigration, is inseparable from her personal trauma—the death of her mother. Weakened over the years by her husband's abuse, Grace's mother, who raised nine children and suffered an additional four pregnancies—three babies died and she had one miscarriage—did not live to reach Canada. Grace never knows with certainty the cause of her death, but the doctor thinks "it was most likely a tumour, or a cyst, or else a burst appendix" (*AG* 119). Wrapped in a sheet, her dead mother is cast overboard—"buried at sea"—as the twelve-year-old Grace, her drunken father, and her siblings watch. Devastated by the loss, Grace explains to Simon

> I did not cry. I felt as if it was me and not my mother that had died; and I sat as if paralyzed, and did not know what to do next. . . . As soon as the sheet was over her face I had the notion that it was not really my mother under there. . . . It must have been the shock of it that put such things into my head. . . . And then all was over, so quickly, and the next day went on as before, only without my mother. (*AG* 120, 121)

Of course Grace's reaction of shock and denial to her mother's death is completely expected and normative, particularly for a child; what is noteworthy, certainly less ordinary and leads to trauma, is her last sentence—"all was over, so quickly, and the next day went on as before, only without my mother."

That the circumstances of Grace's life afford her neither the time nor the privacy or the adult help to mourn her loss does not diminish the necessity of her doing so. As with Corky Corcoran (also Irish) in Joyce Carol Oates's *What I Lived For*, who was eleven years old when he watched his father die, and about whom I discussed this same phenomenon, Grace will become "stuck" in this trauma if she does not acknowledge and experience her pain. Also like Corky, who loses his mother when his father dies, Grace is virtually orphaned; and for her, it happens in a foreign country. Her father, cruel, usually drunk, mercenary, and an arsonist, forces her, as the oldest child, to assume the care of her eight younger siblings. Eventually, when the rent is due, he sells her into domestic service, leaving her nine-year-old sister to raise the other children. With the exception of the few times he came to her place of employment or sent his younger daughter for the purpose of coercing money from Grace, she never sees her father or any of her family again, including at her trial.

Separated from everyone she loves—her siblings and her mother's sister who stayed in Ireland—Grace eventually makes a good friend at her first job, Mary Whitney. But Mary dies shortly thereafter, when she is fifteen or sixteen years old, bleeding to death from a botched abortion, as she sleeps in bed next to Grace. Mary's death represents a cruel second merging of personal and political trauma for Grace, as well as for Mary. Her death, attributed to misogynistic indifference and self-righteous contempt for women's medical needs, is complicated by the fact that her pregnancy results from a sexual liaison with the "master's" son. Punctuating the penalty of "class-crossing," the young man's mother, who suspects the truth about her servant's sexual encounter with her son and the resultant cause of her death, accurately senses that Grace too knows the truth. Afraid that Grace may gossip, she dismisses her from her position, causing her to lose her best friend, her job, and what had become her home all on the same day.

Before she turns thirteen, then, Grace's life has been defined as that of a penniless, orphaned, Irish immigrant, whose future is limited to domestic servitude. Significantly, anti-Irish sentiment impacts directly and negatively upon her trial three years later, at least in part because of the Mackenzie Rebellion. Popular, Irish radical, William Lyon Mackenzie, involved with the movement for political reform first as a journalist and then as a member of the provincial Parliament, later served as mayor of Toronto from 1834–1836. In 1837, he led a short, unsuccessful rebellion with the aim of setting up a democratic government in Toronto. As Mary Whitney explains to Grace, the rebellion "was against the gentry, who ran everything, and kept all the money and land for themselves" (*AG* 148); describing Mackenzie's dramatic escape following the failed rebellion, Mary uses words nearly identical to those of Atwood who sketched the same story in her 1996 interview with David Brown. Mary's historically accurate account, relayed to and received by Grace with awe, is that "Mackenzie escaped through ice and snow in women's clothing, and over the Lake to the States, and he could have been betrayed many times over but was not, because he was a fine man who always stood up for the ordinary farmers" (*AG* 149). Adding two interesting facts to Mary's account, Atwood notes that, against all odds, Mackenzie's group nearly won the rebellion, and second, after spending some time in the United States, he changed his mind regarding the virtues of its government; he requested and, surprisingly, was granted the right to return to Canada (Atwood to Brown).

Specifically relevant and quite damaging to Grace is the fact that the Mackenzie Rebellion was still being written about in the same newspapers that were covering her trial: there were "editorials either denouncing . . . or praising him, depending [on] which political faction owned that particular newspaper" (Atwood qtd. in Brown). The Tories dominated Toronto by 1843, the year of Grace's trial, because radicals and most anti-Tories who were not hanged, imprisoned, or impoverished by having their land confiscated after their rebellion failed, escaped to the States. Grace was Protestant, not Catholic, but that was outweighed entirely by majority public sentiment against the Irish. The case's "evidence" was evaluated from the vantage point of ethnic bias. Reverend Verringer explains to Simon that "the Tories appear to have confused Grace with the Irish Question, although she is a Protestant; and to consider the murder of a single Tory gentleman—however worthy the gentleman, and however regrettable the murder—to be the same thing as the insurrection of an entire race" (*AG* 80). Adding one more ironic twist to Grace's trial was the fact that her lawyer, Kenneth *MacKenzie,* no relation to the Rebellion's leader William Lyon *Mackenzie*, was, nonetheless, occasionally confused with him.

In her Afterword to *Alias Grace*, Atwood writes that "the combination of sex, violence, and the deplorable insubordination of the lower classes was most attractive to the journalists of the day" (461). Grace became a phenomenon, a "celebrated murderess" (*AG* 22), "a folk hero . . . [though not] a canonical murderer" (Auerbach Rev. 3); she generated an enormous amount of written commentary that is inseparable from the "private" person of Grace Marks. In Atwood's view, Grace was constructed, projected upon, and shaped by the texts of strangers, whose words formed her far more than Grace informed what was written about her. Stylistically constructed in what I call "poststructural realism," *Alias Grace* is Atwood's return, not only to the story of Grace Marks, but to her own earlier work, *The Servant Girl*, produced by Canadian Public Television in 1974. Intricate, overlapping textual relationships operate within *Alias Grace* that blur, even dissemble, boundaries between fiction, "fact," and story. Atwood's interweaving of fictional or literary characters with historical or "real" figures, including her own play, mimics what actually occurs in the aftermath of the murders, especially during McDermott's and Marks's trial.[7] Atwood believes that "people were just making the story up from the moment it happened. They were all fictionalizing; . . . projecting their own views onto these various people" (qtd. in Miller 2). That the 1853 journalistic account of Grace's story, upon which Atwood relied for *The Servant Girl*, was itself based on McDermott's confession as (re)told by his lawyer, Mr. MacKenzie, is only one example of the Gordian knot in which drama and fiction were (mis)taken for "fact" and "evidence." Remaining intimately involved with Grace's life while simultaneously transcending her individual dilemma, *Alias Grace* probes how a version of "reality" is constructed;

this text examines what molds perceptions of "truth," and how sexual, cultural, even textual politics influence the processes wherein a specific account of a violent episode develops into an established consensus. Crucially, this debate takes place within a highly sensationalized double murder trial—in a court room, not a class room—emphasizing that even if "what really happened" the day of the murders remains a mystery, it is profoundly important how the versions of the story are told and heard, because they will/do determine whether McDermott and Marks live or die.

The Servant Girl reflects Atwood's certainty, in 1974, of Grace's guilt. The play also indicates the author's overall trust in a "monologic" (Todorov 63) interpretation of concepts such as truth and knowledge.[8] With her interest in Grace's story initially sparked by a kind of anthropologic-tour guide book entitled *Life in the Clearings* by journalist Susanna Moodie, Atwood wrote her first version of the murders predicated on the assumption that "non-fiction meant true" (Atwood qtd. in Miller), and relied on Moodie's book for her source material. Moodie's earlier book, *Roughing it in the Bush* (1852), is her unhappy account of the first seven years of her experiences and those of her family as immigrants to the Canadian colonies from England. Although that book was intended to dissuade other British "gentlefolk" from making the same rough journey—Moodie's family spent those seven years living in the woods—she wrote *Life in the Clearings* only one year later in part to compensate for the relentless gloom with which she had rendered Canadian life in the earlier text. The later book focuses on city life, especially in Toronto, where she discovered fascinating tourist sights, among them the new penitentiary and lunatic asylum. In those days, one could visit either institution, and request a "viewing" of a particular prisoner or inmate, as though s/he were an exotic zoo animal, or a horse on the auction block. Escorted by a guard, the prisoner would be displayed for the sightseer.

When Moodie accompanied her husband to the Provincial Penitentiary in Kingston, making precisely this request—to "look at the celebrated murderess" (Moodie, *LC* 157), Grace Marks, the prison's most notorious inmate, had been incarcerated for nine years, and was twenty-five years old. Moodie saw Grace a second time in the Lunatic Asylum in Toronto, where the "murderess" had been transferred temporarily for "hysteria," and recorded her observations in two chapters of *Life in the Clearings* (1853). Written ten years after Grace's conviction, Moodie's text endorses the widely-accepted view of the crime: sixteen-year-old Grace, in love with Kinnear, the gentleman master, manipulates the weak-willed McDermott into killing her perceived rival Nancy, by promising him sexual favors. Her jealousy of the many, material gifts Kinnear bestows upon Nancy also fuels her rage. But when Grace protests McDermott's wish to kill Kinnear, he realizes her true motive for wanting Nancy dead; he demands his "reward," kills Kinnear anyway, and threatens to kill Grace too if she tries to escape. Although Atwood now refers to Moodie's narrative as an interesting "little Victorian play," it was the only version she "knew for quite a long time" (qtd. in Wiley), and accepted it as "truth."

Life in the Clearings poses serious problems for contemporary readers, including Atwood. Most significant is the fact that, in its entirety, Moodie's version is based on McDermott's confession to his lawyer the night before his execution. Presumed to be candid because he knows he is about to die, the confession appeared in the Toronto *Star and Transcript* in 1843. This account, which would become an authoritative source on Grace, as well as the foundation for subsequent narratives including Atwood's play, is based upon Moodie's questionable ability to remember the ten-year-old report from the *Star* in which McDermott's "honest" confession, as told to Kenneth MacKenzie, was published. Moodie presents the following as facts: the accuracy of her memory (which she later admits is wanting), the veracity of McDermott's confession (because he dies at sunrise), MacKenzie's verbatim conveyance of the confession to the press, and the newspaper's capacity to publish it with no subjective interpretation. Although she is "not very certain as to dates . . . and the name of the township, and the county in which [Kinnear's farm] was situated, have [been] forgotten," she reassures us that her memory problem applies only to what is "of little consequence to [her] narrative" (*LC* 158). Still, it is surprising that she errs on both of the victims' names. She refers to Nancy as Hannah Montgomery and Mr. Kinnear as Captain Kinnaird, although he never held such a title. Additionally, only in Moodie's version does McDermott confess to "cut[ting] [Nancy's] body in four pieces, and turn[ing] a large washtub over them" (*LC* 164). Considering how the newspapers sensationalized this event, it seems certain that an item such as a dismembered female body would not have been overlooked. But, even if one were to agree that the forgotten details do not matter, or, more importantly, that the confession honestly represents McDermott's involvement with the murders, it is untenable to grant him, as Moodie does, the authority to tell Grace's story.

The dialogue among *Life in the Clearings*, *The Servant Girl*, and *Alias Grace* expands to include Dickens's *Oliver Twist*. Both Moodie's text and Atwood's novel report that when Grace's lawyer visited her in prison after she had been confined for several years, she confided in him that she "was haunted by Nancy's bloodshot eyes" (*AG* 375). *Alias Grace*'s Reverend Verringer and Simon Jordan are familiar with and discuss the Moodie account; Verringer tells Simon that "Mrs. Moodie . . . has stated publicly that she is very fond of Charles Dickens, and in especial of *Oliver Twist*. I seem to recall a similar pair of eyes in that work, also belonging to a dead female called Nancy" (*AG* 190). In Dickens' novel, Bill Sykes, paralyzed with fear and guilt after he murders

Nancy, is haunted by "widely staring eyes . . . that were everywhere" (353). And in a letter, Moodie refers to *Oliver Twist* as a novel "that has done much good in the world, and every benevolent mind must feel grateful to the author" (Moodie, *Lifetime* 161). When Simon asks Grace about being haunted by Nancy's eyes, she tells him that she did not say eyes followed her, she said peonies. Parenthetically, the reader never understands the urgency of the peonies, but we know they are quite meaningful to Grace. The image of red or white peonies repeatedly occurs to her in connection with the day of the murders, and she makes a point of burying peonies with Mary Whitney. While Simon is obsessed with the concept of free association as the way to unlock Grace's memory, he does not yet realize that "free" refers to Grace's actual associations, which he must pursue wherever they lead, rather than trying to extract specific ones from her. Still, regarding Moodie's report of "haunting bloodshot eyes," Grace tells Simon, "I have read what Mrs. Moodie wrote about that . . . [and] I don't like to call anyone a liar. . . . I suppose it's more the usual thing, to have eyes [rather than peonies] following you around. It is more what is required, under the circumstances, if you follow me. . . . They [Mackenzie and Moodie] wanted to have things done properly" (*AG* 359).

What Grace means is that the lawyer and the writer wanted to cast a perception of truth, design a consensus of reality, and create a text about "her" that, in fact, need not even resemble her, as long as it satisfies public expectations of a "celebrated murderess." Perhaps Atwood is trying to articulate the verbal equivalent of a patchwork quilt. While she is comfortable with the fact that the seams between fiction and non-fiction can be both apparent and invisible, and she pokes fun at her self of twenty years ago who believed that "non-fiction meant truth," she is clearly not at ease with Moodie's unconscious or unacknowledged blending of journalism, observation, and fiction. That Atwood continues to remind us that this discourse is embedded in a murder trial is critical, because it implies that a nuance of (mis)understanding can determine Grace's entire future; the stakes could not be higher, and as Simon later says "the small details of life often hide a great significance" (*AG* 162). In other words, in postmodernism, "'truth' is a process, in the patterning rather than the 'patterns'" (Greene 203); but of what use is such a postmodernist stance if Grace's judge hates the Irish?

Successfully deconstructing the Moodie account by revealing its biases and actual errors, Atwood, of course, challenges *The Servant Girl*; in a postscript to *Alias Grace*, she writes that since her earlier play "relied exclusively on the Moodie version, [it] cannot now be taken as definitive" (467). Yet her novel is not intended to replace the 1974 play. Doing so would imply that a unitary or unified "Grace Marks story" exists, thereby replicating the binary view that Atwood critiques, and ultimately finds unworkable. She accentuates that "the *fullness* of

Grace is the point" of her new novel (qtd. in Wiley; emphasis added). She may view her two accounts as companion pieces, with the novel offering Grace a voice that is quite different from the myriad stories projected upon her. Comparing the two texts is invaluable: it allows us to see Atwood's incorporation of feminist literary theory into her more recent rendering of Grace. She (re)locates her protagonist *outside* of the either/or patriarchal dualism of Guilt verses Innocence that categorizes the earlier accounts.[9] Refusing to accept Simon's notion that Grace's story has ended—"the main story, that is, the thing that has defined her" (*AG* 91), Atwood elaborates "the fullness of Grace" because she steadfastly believes that there is more to say about any individual personality than maybe she did, or maybe she did not, commit murder, as important to one's life as that question is.

While most of Grace's contemporaries concur with Simon that the "episode" of the Kinnear-Montgomery murders indelibly defines her, few agree as to what that definition entails. Reminiscent of Hester Prynne's scarlet "A," Grace's symbolic "M" for murderess operates as a Rorschach inkblot; she exists only as the passive recipient of whatever views are projected upon her. Descriptions of Grace by people who knew her, some of whom served as witnesses at her trial, include "evil," "very nice," "conniving," "weak-willed," and "quite amiable" (Atwood qtd. in Miller 2). Significantly, Grace's objectification takes place in print, and she reads it all. If she is a "subject" for others' unauthorized "Grace Marks" texts, then she is merely an "object" of her own. Or, more to the point, she authors no story of her own. Surrounded by a plethora of narratives constructed by strangers devoted to capturing some new exciting angle on her, Grace's capacity to realize/invent/develop an autonomous autobiography is stolen from her. Scrutinizing the textual material in which her name appears, she hopes to discover a version of her persona that feels familiar. When teenagers seek out role models in their families, teachers, friends, and celebrities, they are not only looking for someone to emulate; they want to encounter a reflection of themselves. In a sense, it is a recreation of Lacan's mirror stage, when the baby discovers an image that reflects back her/him "self." No person in Grace's life does or did that for her, with the possible exception of her mother; the closest thing she has are the disconnected written words of outsiders, to which she clings despite the fact that they actively thwart her potential to be anything but an "alias."

Complicating the process of establishing an identity for herself is the problem that much of what Grace reads makes no sense to her. For example, she notes with disappointment that what really seems to interest the lawyers, judges, reporters, doctors, "the gentlemen and the ladies both" is whether or not James McDermott was her "paramour." "They don't care if I killed anyone, I could have cut dozens of throats, it's only what they admire in a soldier, they'd scarcely blink. No: was I really a paramour, is their chief concern, and they don't even know themselves whether they want the answer to be no or yes" (*AG* 27). When she looks in the mirror, Grace muses that what has been written about her includes "that I am an inhuman female demon, that I am an innocent victim . . . that I have blue eyes, that I have green eyes, that I have auburn and also brown hair, that I am tall and also not above the average height . . . that I am of a sullen disposition with a quarrelsome temper that I am a good girl with a pliable nature. . . . And I wonder, how can I be all of these different things at once?" (*AG* 23). Though Atwood attributes to Grace an ironic, wry, quite enjoyable sense of humor, I think that her question—"how can I be all of these different things at once?"—is also serious. If we remember that she has been in prison since she was sixteen, without a mother for four years prior to that, witnesses her only friend die a horrifying death, was perhaps raped at the asylum, and surely was not loved or cared for by her father, it is no wonder that her identity has been formed through what others write about her.[10] Searching for her own narrative, Grace obsessively pores through the books, papers, poems, articles, even a scrapbook on famous criminals that the Governor's wife keeps, wishing to find out who she is. That it may do nothing to clarify the events of the murder or help her be released from prison is not the point. Without a story and identity, she has no "self."

Intertextual dialogue contributes to the novel's structure with the extensive interweaving of excerpts of poetry and fiction by Emily Bronte, Elizabeth Barrett and Robert Browning, Charles Dickens, Emily Dickinson, Nathaniel Hawthorne, Henry Wadsworth Longfellow, William Morris, Coventry Patmore, Edgar Allen Poe, Christina Rosetti, Wallace Stevens, and Alfred Lord Tennyson, which blend together with excerpts from the *Kingston Penitentiary Punishment Book*, the Toronto *Star and Transcript*'s published "confessions" of Marks and McDermott, quotations from the Medical Superintendent of The Provincial Lunatic Asylum, and statements from the daily journal of the Warden of the Provincial Penitentiary, both of whom were actually in those positions during Grace's respective incarcerations. In addition, Atwood incorporates excerpts from Susanna Moodie's *Life in the Clearings* as well as selections from Moodie's letters and poems. Also quoted are small portions of William Harrison's "Recollections of the Kinnear Tragedy," written for *The Newmarket Era* (1908); excerpts regarding the murders from the *History of Toronto and the County of York* (1885) (author unknown); and newspaper coverage of the murders and trial from *The Examiner*, the *Toronto Mirror*, and the Kingston *Chronicle and Gazette* (1843). An excerpt from Isabella Beeton's *Book of Household Management* (1859–1861) on "hysterics" is offered; and then Beeton's book is referred to twice more: once because original police reports from the murders state that a bloodied copy of the book was found in Nancy's bed, and again when Grace reads a few pages before using it for toilet paper.[11]

Since almost all, if not all, of the cited excerpts are epigraphs, we immediately confront an enjambment of fiction and non-fiction; in fact, we encounter a rich assortment of literary traditions before we even get to the first page of narrative. Like other texts in this study, *Alias Grace* operates as a metanarrative, critiquing itself in a relentless challenge to think about the existence of "truth," and the possibility of "knowing." Juxtaposing a varied assembly of writings—for instance, two "real-life" murder confessions, Tennyson's poetry, and Beeton's *Household Management*—as, in a sense, "pre-text," introduces a central dilemma both for the text and for Grace: how does our critical perspective change, and I think that it does, when we read not only different genres and styles, but intertextually. Never alleviating the tension between which documents and characters she imagines and which she unearths by her extensive research into these murders, Atwood highlights a crucial aspect of her text—the merging of historical and reconstructed "fact" with fiction or story.[12] I suggest that the "pre-texts" adumbrate the novel's postmodern synthesis of intertextual dialogue; put another way, the unusual blending of epigraphs preludes the way that writing "speaks" to other writing in *Alias Grace*. Still, Atwood writes flawlessly from the tradition of realism, evidenced in Grace's remarkably detailed descriptions of her everyday life. Feeling like a work in progress in its dynamism and vibrancy, *Alias Grace* configures and (re)structures as we read it.

When Grace tells Simon to speak with the lawyers, judges, and newspaper men if he wants to learn about her "because they seem to know my story better than I do myself" (*AG* 41), she means that when it came time to testify at her trial, MacKenzie "said that the right thing was *not* to tell the story as I truly remembered it, which nobody could be expected to make any sense of; but to tell a story that . . . had some chance of being believed" (*AG* 357; emphasis added), again confusing and conflating Grace's "truth," story, and memory. Clearly the professional men constituted themselves her "author"ities.

The fact that Grace's voice had little influence on the trial proceedings may be tragic, but it is not surprising; the combination of the misogyny in the legal system in 1843, her young age, class prejudice, and her status as an Irish immigrant, albeit Protestant, could certainly operate to convict her without just cause. What initially appears striking is that when she first researched this story, a reader/writer/critic as brilliant and astute as Margaret Atwood did not recognize that all of her source material was, in fact, propaganda for McDermott's representation of Grace. Several accounts were published at the time of the murders, in addition to Moodie's, and almost all view Grace from the same vantage point—that of the jealous, enraged, narcissistic, seductress-whore-girl-woman, cold enough to plot the murder of her rival. *Alias Grace* represents a change over the past twenty years in literary and cultural, particularly feminist, discourse that continues to move away from "phallocentric" or "monologic"

(Todorov 63) interpretations and readings in which only men have power. And for Atwood personally, Grace's story lingered in her mind

> beneath the threshold of consciousness [until its] reappearance. . . . I started going back to the newspaper accounts of the time, once I had figured out where [the murders] had taken place, because Susanna Moodie didn't tell us. . . . Then it became a much more ambiguous story. . . . [The decision to write a new version] was based on the discrepancies among the different accounts. . . . They didn't agree with one another. (qtd. in Miller 1)

Feminist studies mandate that scholars pay long overdue attention to women's neglected experiences and, with that in mind, Atwood imbues Grace with her own first-person narrative voice.

Likewise, motivated by psychoanalytic feminism, there is a similar process taking place in the field of psychiatry, stressing the personal and political relevance of the study of women's intrapsychic experiences. Interestingly, by evoking the possibility that Grace suffers from trauma and/or multiple personality disorder, Atwood opens an unusually thorough if not unique exploration within a novel into the evolution of psychological thought.

Psychoanalytic theory paid little attention to women's trauma since Freud moved away from the seduction theory shortly after publishing it in 1896 but, as I discuss in my Introduction and in previous chapters, that is fortunately changing. Within the past ten or fifteen years, trauma resulting from domestic abuse has emerged as a serious topic in public discourse; it is a subject of interdisciplinary academic conferences and scholarly publications, as well as a recurrent theme in essays, newspaper and magazine editorials, memoirs, and novels. Returning with a renewed commitment to understanding domestic and child abuse after initially discovering and abandoning it, some psychiatrists are reviewing old professional literature, such as the case of Mary Reynolds, the first documented instance of multiple personalities in 1816, to whom the fictional Dr. DuPont refers in reference to Grace (*AG* 405).[13] Just as Atwood revisits *The Servant Girl*, psychiatry, too, wants to (re)place trauma accurately within its social/historical/medical context.

Much textual evidence exists to suggest that Atwood deliberately participates in or replicates psychiatry's clinical return to trauma with her own narrative return to Grace. For example, Dora, Mrs. Humphrey's servant, with whom Simon has a hostile relationship, certainly evokes Freud's well-known hysteric, "Dora" (Ida Bauer), the most famous casualty of his abandonment of the seduction theory.[14] In several versions of this analytic relationship, "Dora" was angry at Freud because he refused to empathize with her experience as a victim of sexual abuse by her father's lover's husband, Herr K., beginning in her adolescence. As a result, "Dora" left her analysis with Freud. In *Alias Grace*, when Dora, the housekeeper, gossips with Grace about the sexual escapades in the Humphrey home, Grace can hardly believe these licentious stories "of two such outwardly respectable people" (*AG* 427), a comment that Atwood directs toward the Freud-"Dora" and Herr K.-"Dora" relationships as well as to the one between Simon and Rachel Humphrey. This is, of course, the essence of the disturbing, and never resolved relationship between Freud and "Dora": the analyst could hardly believe his patient's complaints "of two such outwardly respectable people," meaning "Dora's" father and Herr K.[15] And today, some admirers of Freud still want to blame "Dora" for her analyst's insensitivity, believing such an explanation to be more plausible than the fact that underlying Freud's disrespect toward "Dora" was gender-based bias. Like the actual Freud, Atwood's fictional Simon is "outwardly respectable," so virtuous, in fact, that the Governor's wife wants him to marry her daughter, Lydia.[16] Then, imitative of Freud's sadism toward "Dora," Simon sleeps with Rachel Humphrey, his married landlady, toward whom he directs his sadistic sexual fantasies; finally, like Freud again, Simon abandons both Rachel and his patient, Grace. And, during all his time, Simon and Dora continue to quarrel. If Freud deserted "Dora" by giving up the seduction/trauma theory, then Simon flees Rachel, leaving Grace in the dust, in a parody of the actual analyst's behavior. All three—Freud, Simon, and "Dora's" father—seduce and abandon and, perhaps, Atwood thinks of herself in that role regarding her first narrative treatment of Grace.

As I have discussed, Freud's seduction/trauma theory exemplifies a phenomenon in psychiatry in which a theory or treatment technique evokes interest and research for a time, then is given up as a result of conservative political backlash, followed by a renewed (re)discovery of its value much later.[17] A corresponding process is taking place regarding the use of hypnosis, first called mesmerism, named for F. A. Mesmer's much debated theory on animal magnetism. A German psychiatrist noted in 1989 that "the shifting perception of mesmerism according to different paradigms illustrates the problem of every innovative psychological theory" (Hoff). In the early part of the nineteenth century, hypnosis was used successfully to treat a broad range of somatic complaints, including phantom limb pain and symptoms of hysteria. But its use declined with the advent of psychoanalysis, because the newer treatment of neuroses encounters the patient's unconscious through his/her slips of tongue, free associations, defense mechanisms, and "resistance." Requiring the patient to be alert and verbal, psychoanalysis was thought to be at cross purposes with the induced state of suggestibility necessary for hypnosis. However, after a long hiatus, hypnosis, like trauma theory, makes a comeback. Recognized anew as a beneficial treatment technique, it appears successful in helping people with multiple personality disorders to uncover repressed memories of sexual trauma. Significantly, Atwood proposes that it may be relevant to understand Grace Marks as a multiple personality, because of the "alternate" personality of Mary Whitney who emerges during her hypnosis with Dr. DuPont. If Grace is experiencing "the bizarre alternations" (*AG* 405) in personality that afflicted Mary Reynolds, who was diagnosed with "multiple personality disorder" in 1816 (and many similar cases were reported between then and 1853), perhaps she, too, suffers from that same illness. Furthermore, a multiple personality disorder could explain Grace's participation in the Kinnear-Montgomery murders without her remembering doing so.[18]

Atwood returns to Grace Marks after twenty years, during which time a postmodern sensibility has permeated cultural and literary studies. I suggest that the cycle of rethinking, revisiting, remembering, and reworking one's earlier ideas, theories, and stories operates as an organizing trope within *Alias Grace*. That Simon's abandonment of Grace mimics Freud's of Dora is *not* a coincidence. Moreover, the psychiatry profession's return to clinical as well as theoretical work regarding treatment techniques for trauma and amnesia, including hypnosis, coincides with Atwood's resurrecting Grace. Put another way, in fiction's world, where we imagine/"make-up" and transcend "real" time and place, Atwood revives Grace so a contemporary "Dr. Simon Jordan" will treat her accurately and kindly for her amnesia; symbolically, Grace as "Dora" is also resuscitated, and treated for her sexual trauma by someone who genuinely believes in her story. Hence, Atwood makes reparation to both women for their abandonments by their psychiatrists.

Articulating an intriguing, credible, psychologically consistent, and sympathetic interpretation of Grace as a victim of trauma and multiple personalities, Atwood allows us to believe in the protagonist's sincerity, humor, and humanity; we root for her, and hope that Verringer's group will finally win her a legal pardon. We consider that she may have been hoodwinked or intimidated by McDermott into becoming involved in the murders. We know that trauma uncannily repeats itself, and we can perhaps understand how a terrified Grace stayed with her persecutor in the same way abuse victims frequently cannot escape their dominators. But, Atwood's unique, postmodern twist is that she is *not* arguing for this version of Grace's story. Fascinating and plausible as it is, she deconstructs it immediately. That no monologic, patriarchal interpretation can explain complex people, emotions, and motivations is Atwood's point; and that transcends Grace's narrative. What she scrutinizes, challenges, and pulls apart is not any particular version of a story or an event, but the idea of any one explanation—"certainty" itself. She questions the usefulness of concepts such as "truth," "knowledge," "fact," and "story" and wonders if they are workable. But again, despite the fact that she blends and conflates them, she openly struggles against an entirely subjective approach, such as Moodie's, that appears to have no guidelines and make no distinctions. Atwood may not believe that nonfiction means truth, but she knows it contains differences, however subtle, from the meanings of "fiction" and "imagination." Offering no resolution—to do so would be antithetical to her text—she evokes important discursive issues through Grace's deconstruction or "undoing" of her narrative.

In her review of *Alias Grace*, Hilary Mantel thinks of "Grace [as] a deceiver. She is never simply what she seems" (4). Certainly, Atwood neither simplifies nor reduces her to an "essence." We can never say "she is *really* like this," or "*actually* feels/thinks that." I suggest this is because Grace herself consistently dismantles her own story from a nineteenth-century "dear reader" stance; we watch her do it but, consistent with her character, she does not explain or critique her behavior. Existential doubt permeates this novel, while at the same time, it could not be more steeped in realism, exemplified by the minute, obsessive detail with which Grace's daily chores are described. Like Oates's *What I Lived For* and Hopkins's *Of One Blood,* this text also raises postmodern questions about "self," "identity," and "truth" as it *simultaneously* adheres to the tradition of realism. A provocative Grace challenges us to acknowledge the self-imposed contradictions of her realities. For example, in her initial conversation with Simon when he explains that their talking together may help to restore her memories of the murders, Grace responds: "perhaps I will tell you lies, I say. He says, perhaps you will. Perhaps you will tell lies without meaning to, and perhaps you will also tell them deliberately. Perhaps you are a liar. I look at him. There are those who have said I am one, I say. We will just have to take that chance, he says" (*AG* 41). Immediately, she calls attention to the veracity and accuracy of her story. Does she lie, and if so, when? She could not possibly have "made-up" the poignant story of the ship's journey from Ireland, and her mother's death, or could she? And the relentless question of why—what motivates her—haunts us.

Seducing the reader with beautiful imagery, of which there is a dearth in this "prison novel" (Auerbach Rev. 1), Atwood opens the segment named for the quilt pattern "Fox and Geese" in Grace's voice:

> Today when I woke up there was a beautiful pink sunrise, with the mist lying over the fields like a white soft cloud of muslin, and the sun shining through the layers of it all blurred and rosy like a peach gently on fire.
>
> In fact I have no idea of what kind of a sunrise there was. . . . The windows [are so] high up . . . you cannot see out of them. . . . They do not want you looking out, they do not want you thinking the word *out*. . . . And so this morning I saw only . . . a swathe of daylight the same all the way through, like lard. (*AG* 237)

Like *Beloved*'s Baby Suggs, who spends the last years of her life pondering colors because there were none during slavery, or Amy Denver who intends to walk from Kentucky to Boston to *feel* carmine velvet, Grace lures us into this section with relaxing, sensual images of pink, white, rosy and peach. But after one paragraph, the tone of the writing snaps from seductive to sarcastic, suddenly shattering our security and reminding us that this is not a text into which we should relax. It requires diligence. Clearly, Grace's fantasy is understandable when we remember that the only sunrises she will ever see are those that she imagines, but the juxtaposition of beauty and serenity with prison/gray/steel/lard underscores the enigma and complexities of Grace, as well as those of "truth" itself. The questions of "what is 'really' happening" and "can I 'know' this character at all" pervade our thoughts, just as they do in Oates's text.

Grace admits that she knows several ways of acting to satisfy others' expectations of her: "I had now been a servant for three years, and could act the part well enough" (*AG* 224); "I have a good stupid look which I have practised" (*AG* 38); "I've learnt how to keep my face still" (*AG* 26), so as to appear repentant. Importantly, Grace's inscrutability opens the book. Walking around the prison yard, she has a fantasy, possibly it is a delusion or an hallucination, about saving Nancy: "This time I will run to help, I will lift her up and wipe away the blood." Almost immediately following, in her sotto voce to "dear reader," she remarks that "this is what I told Dr. Jordan, when we came to that part of the story" (*AG* 6). Easily overlooked because it appears so early in the book, this ambiguous, short statement, set slightly apart on its page, conveys content, but no meaning. Grace is *not* necessarily telling us that she wishes she had saved Nancy or, if given another chance, that she would save her; she expresses no feelings and, indeed, she is not even confiding that she actually had the fantasy. Simply and directly, her words inform us *only* that "this is what [she] told Dr. Jordan." With this remark, Atwood introduces us to Grace's enigmatic style of revealing and concealing herself simultaneously; in addition, Atwood underscores how language colludes with Grace's ability to remain mysterious. Beginning with its title, *Alias Grace* raises philosophical, political, as well as semiotic issues regarding the relationship(s) between words and their "real" meaning(s), and does so by asking the reader to ponder the process by which s/he reads Grace's ambiguity. For example, do we unwittingly attribute "meaning" to statements that are designed to remain cryptic? Do we gloss over what is encoded, so that we unconsciously read Grace's statement—"this is what I told"—as "this is what happened"? If so, how does that differ from the "fictionalizing" (Atwood qtd. by Miller 2) and projections that constructed the sensationalized and contradictory "Grace Marks" stories? Viewing Grace as a victim of personal and cultural sadomasochism and trauma, I suggest that the story's logic is psychological, a perspective that deliberately does not address her role in the Kinnear-Montgomery murders. At the same time, I see Atwood offering her character's most impenetrable moments as a parody of poststructuralism in that, at these times, Grace's words are not rooted within any particular hermeneutic system.

In fact, Grace makes no disclosure more remarkable or disquieting than the one that unfolds following Mary Whitney's death. She awakens to discover that Mary has bled to death during the night following her abortion; she summons help from the other servants, who keep her busy washing sheets, washing Mary, burning the mattress, changing Mary's nightdress, and combing her hair. Eventually, all is in order and the presence of the mistress is requested. The servant, Agnes, explains to Mrs. Alderman Parkinson that Mary has died suddenly of a fever, concealing the abortion, and Grace thinks that "for a woman as pious as [Agnes] was, she lied very well; and I stood by Mary's feet, keeping silent. And one said, Poor Grace, to wake up . . . and find her cold and stark in the bed beside you." Instantly, Grace discloses that "*then it was as if that had really happened;* I could picture it, the waking up with Mary in the bed right beside me, and touching her, and finding she would not speak to me, and the horror and distress I *would* feel; and at that moment I fell to the floor in a dead faint" (*AG* 179; emphasis added). What could Grace possibly mean by "*as if* that had really happened"? Did it perhaps not happen? Is she imagining the "horror and distress" she would feel, *if* she had cause to? Or is my reading overdetermined? Perhaps I should remember that she is a thirteen-year-old girl, alone in the world, who recently watched her mother die and now finds her best (and only) friend's bloodied, dead body lying next to her in bed. That she experiences shock and faints is no doubt expected and appropriate.

But, why does the persona of Mary Whitney emerge from Grace's hypnotism at the end of the text? (Certainly I will discuss the problems inherent in that hypnosis; but its legitimacy is very possible, despite those problems.) Does Mary exist only as Grace's alias, her other "personality"? Mary Whitney is the name Grace assumed when she escaped with or was kidnapped by McDermott; did she take the name of her young dead friend, or had "Mary" been a dissociated other "self" all along? Who is the alias of the novel's title? Atwood resolves nothing and, in her review of *Alias Grace*, Nina Auerbach refers to Grace's story as one that "denies more than it reveals, though she tells most of it herself" (1). If one looks for clues, one discovers only more ambiguity. When Simon tells Grace that "the small details of life often hide a great significance," she responds by teaching him how to look at quilt patterns—"you can see them two different ways, by looking at the dark pieces, or else the light" (*AG* 162), suggesting that those significant small details are simply a matter of subjective perspective.

If Leslie Marmon Silko's *Almanac of the Dead* operates as an historical text from which we can learn about the political policies determining U.S.

expansionism, imperialism, and genocide toward American Indians, and if Toni Morrison's *Beloved* asks us to (un)/(re)cover stories from slavery's Middle Passage, then from *Alias Grace* we learn aspects of the history of Western ideas that influence, even form, our thinking about the human mind. Beginning in the early nineteenth century, with a primary focus upon ideas relevant to Grace's mysterious memory lapse, Atwood traces medical, scientific and psychological thought from its belief in "bad blood" to an early link between dissociative disorders and exposure to toxic substances—a theory which contributed to the much later use of sophisticated medicines for mental illness. She brings us into the twentieth century with Simon Jordan's use of the "talking cure" "to wake the part of [Grace's] mind that lies dormant—to probe down below the threshold of her consciousness . . . to discover the memories [of the murders] that must perforce lie buried there" (*AG* 132). Grace's confiding in Simon enacts the modern doctor-patient relationship, which then defines the background for Atwood's study of the history of psychological thought.

Indeed, as the topics of hysteria, double consciousness, amnesia, memory, and hypnosis are heatedly debated among Drs. Jordan, DuPont, and Reverend Verringer, Grace and Simon actuate the much discussed relationship between psychiatrist and patient. Simon, who is working on the nascent concept of "free association," which will become a mainstay of contemporary psychoanalysis, tries a number of techniques during their daily sessions to jar Grace's memory and kindle images of the murders. For example, he brings her fruits and vegetables with the idea that their aliveness may elicit feelings of remorse for those she helped to kill. When that fails, he switches to vegetables and roots that grow underground in the hope that her associations will run along the lines of grave-corpse-murder. Rendering these scenes with considerable humor, Atwood has given several reviewers of *Alias Grace* a chance to poke fun at psychiatry, but these representations of Simon also poignantly reflect a pioneering, pre-William Jamesian, pre-Freudian "scientific investigator" (*AG* 83), continuing to develop new strategies as he struggles to "re-establish [Grace's] chain of thought, which was broken, perhaps, by the shock of the violent events in which she was involved" (*AG* 85).[19] If Hopkins's *Of One Blood* acknowledges the fascination that "the new psychology" held for professional and lay people, alike, Atwood's scholarly research credits forgotten or neglected physicians—"alienists," as psychiatrists were then called—for their insistence upon a view of the human mind as a complex, multi-layered organism, even capable of bearing multiple personalities.

Simon is hired as an authority in "cerebral diseases and nervous afflictions" (*AG* 78) by a group of anti-Tory, progressive thinkers who, believing in Grace's innocence, hope he will assist them in their mission of procuring her a pardon from the judge by providing medical documentation stating she suffered "latent insanity at the time of the murders" (*AG* 80). Potentially, such a diagnosis could commute her sentence. Opening the trope of psychiatric illness and treatment early in the novel, Simon engages in conversation with Dr. Jerome DuPont, "a trained Neuro-hypnotist, [*sic*] of the school of James Braid" (*AG* 83). Instantly disparaging Braid, Simon acknowledges that he has heard of him as "a noted authority on clubfoot and strabismus . . . but surely professional medicine does not recognize these other claims of his. Is not this Neuro-hypnotism simply the reanimated corpse of Mesmer's discredited Animal Magnetism?" Patiently, DuPont explains that "Mesmer posited a magnetic fluid encircling the body, which was certainly erroneous . . . [but] Braid's procedures involve the nervous system alone. I might add that those who dispute his methods have not tried them. They are more accepted in France, where the doctors are less prone to craven orthodoxies" (*AG* 83). Aligning DuPont with the theories of James Braid, whose ideas are entirely anathema to Simon, Atwood evokes a central and continuing debate in psychiatry regarding the uses of psychoanalytic and/or neurophysiological treatment approaches, of which hypnosis is an example. Despite the fact that Simon refers to him as that "Scottish crackpot" (*AG* 133), one psychiatrist writes in the *American Journal of Psychiatry* today that

> Braid is both a neglected and integral figure in the history of dynamic psychiatry . . . who established hypnotic phenomenon [*sic*] as data suitable for scientific inquiry. . . . He elaborated a sophisticated psychophysiology with an emphasis on the psychology of suggestion and the phenomenon of double consciousness. His espousal of hypnosis as a tool of scientific investigation and his innovative use of hypnosis to cure hysterical paralysis profoundly influenced the debates of the 1880s and 1890s concerning suggestive therapeutics and the nature of hypnosis. (Kravis)

Laying "the foundation of medical hypnotism" (Tinterow), rather than promulgating the ideas of animal magnetism, as Simon claims, Braid's theory in the early 1840s brought "the age of mesmerism or animal magnetism . . . to a close"; in fact he was the first to replace the word "mesmerism" with "hypnotism" (Tinterow).

Regarding this debate between DuPont and Jordan, two points are especially noteworthy. One is that the fictional Simon, like the historic Freud, Pierre Janet, and William James, studied with Jean-Martin Charcot at the Salpêtrière Clinic in Paris. Simon's first impression of Grace, when they met in her cell at the penitentiary, was that "he'd seen many hysterics at the Salpêtrière in Paris who'd looked very much like this . . . [and] all was as it should be" (*AG* 59). Since Charcot's most notable contribution to the study of human behavior is his discovery that hysteria is a psychological, not a neurological, disorder—

a discovery he came upon through his work with hypnosis, a treatment method for hysteria for which the Salpêtrière was famous—why was Simon aghast at DuPont's association with Braid? First, Simon is unaware of Braid's sophisticated elaboration on the concept of "suggestibility" and his coining of the term "hypnosis"; then, he seems to be under the erroneous assumption that the hypnosis he studied with Charcot in Paris is of a different, maybe "purer," sort than what DuPont/Braid practice. Simon's elemental confusion regarding salient ideas within his field of "expertise" is unquestionably a deliberate communication to us from Atwood—a clue—to pay close attention to his inner contradictions, which, as we later learn, run quite deep.[20]

Although Dr. Jerome DuPont astutely represents the legitimate medical findings of Braid, a neglected brilliant-surgeon-researcher-healer, he, Jerome DuPont, is alias Jeremiah the Pedlar; though he, too, may be brilliant and conversant in sophisticated theories of the mind, he lies when he introduces himself as "a trained Neuro-hypnotist, of the school of James Braid." His persona is a sham—he learned hypnotism at the fairs, where he had an act as "a medical clairvoyant" and "traded in Mesmerism and Magnetism" (*AG* 267). But like every revelation in *Alias Grace*, this evokes more questions than it resolves. Does Atwood represent Braid through Jeremiah to discredit the physician and hypnosis? Is she foreshadowing the hypnosis which Dr. DuPont/Jeremiah performs near the end of the book that will represent Grace as a "multiple personality" with Mary Whitney as her "alternate self"?[21] Or is that hypnosis a ruse designed to secure a favorable letter from Simon to the judge? As Jeremiah tells Grace in an earlier context, feigning the hypnotic trance is "wellnigh foolproof" (*AG* 267). On the other hand, the fact that Jeremiah lies to the Governor's wife, Mrs. Quennel, Reverend Verringer, and Simon does not, by itself, inauthenticate his hypnosis of Grace. It would not be surprising for Jeremiah to (mis)represent himself as the distinguished Dr. DuPont in order to help his old friend; yet, again, this reveals nothing about the validity of the hypnosis. However, a topic that does emerge clearly from this uncertainty is that of recovered and false memories, a contentious contemporary debate, at the center of which lies a very fundamental question: when it comes to recalling previously repressed events, how does one know how, who, or what to believe? While psychiatrists and scholars in many fields are strongly opinionated on this issue (see my Introduction), Atwood raises the dilemma not to settle or even to discuss it, but to root the contemporary debate on the human mind within nineteenth-century discourse, where it rightfully belongs.

Without resolution on these issues, Atwood's inquiry into the study of the mind expands to include other theorists. If Drs. Jordan and DuPont discuss James Braid in a quasi-contentious manner, other names—J. F. Herbart

(1776–1841), Moreau de Tours (1804–1885), French philosopher and scientist Maine de Biran (1766–1824), the Marquis de Puysegeur, a student of Mesmer's, and Thomas Laycock (1812–1877) whose research on epilepsy proved critical, elicit respect as Simon thinks about studying their important works in the hope of learning something about Grace.[22] "He must reread Herbart's theory of the threshold of consciousness—the line that divides those ideas that are apprehended in full daylight from those others that lurk forgotten in the shadows below" (*AG* 140); Simon is referring to the German philosopher whose ideas about drives and the unconscious were an historical antecedent to Freud's early theories, which reflected the psychoanalyst's earlier interests in biology and neurology. Believing that repressed memories in the unconscious lead to increased tension, Herbart does "much to bridge the gap between psychological and neurophysiological aspects of Freud's ideas about . . . psychic determinism" (Kanzer). Participating in another intertextual dialogue with an historical figure, Simon's thoughts flow from Herbart to Moreau de Tours who "considers the dream to be the key to the knowledge of mental illness" (*AG* 140). A Rumanian physician, de Tours (1804–1885) believed that dissociative states or trances were not symptoms of a "mental disease," but rather a reaction to "toxic causes." Emphasizing toxicity and antidotes, de Tours contributed enormously to the effort to pharmacologically treat mental illnesses. Indeed, in one particular article he is referred to as the "father of psychopharmacology" (Nica-Udangiu).

Atwood's choices of theorists are interesting. The only obvious aspect of her method of selection is that she deliberately chooses forgotten or neglected men, a few of whom had rather arcane interests, which are not always accurately represented by Simon.[23] It is unclear how well-known these men were in Toronto at the time that Simon was "investigating" Grace, but we do know that the excitement surrounding the "new psychology" generated numerous publications—articles, papers, books, even heated written debates—in the middle of the nineteenth century. Although the fascination with the subject of mental illness peaked in the last two decades of that century, Atwood had many options in selecting the physicians, and since nothing about *Alias Grace* is arbitrary, I suspect that the specific names and ideas were carefully chosen. Juxtaposed with Herbart and de Tours is Maine de Biran (1766–1824); interestingly, some of the novel's most beautiful and poetic language appears in Simon's musings about him. He "believed there was an inner New World to be discovered, for which one must 'plunge into the subterranean cavern of the soul'" (*AG* 300).

> Maine de Biran held that conscious life was only a sort of island, floating upon a much vaster subconscious, and drawing thoughts up from it like fish. What is perceived as being known is only a small part of what may be stored in this dark repository. Lost memories lie down there like sunken

> treasure, to be retrieved piecemeal, if at all; and amnesia itself may be in effect a sort of dreaming in reverse; a drowning of recollection, a plunging under. (*AG* 140, 141)

If the intertextual relationships in *Alias Grace* start with dialogues among that novel, *Life in the Clearings*, and the drama, *The Servant Girl*, they elaborate to include Simon's "conversations" with the texts of scientists and philosophers to whom he now looks for guidance with Grace. By combining and conflating "real" and fictional psychologists, doctors, even penitentiary wardens and asylum directors, Atwood creates an obstacle course into which Simon blindly marches to fulfill his mission of uncovering Grace's repressed memories. Of course, in this text, such a quest for "truth" is a fool's errand. However, were he willing to learn, Grace could have taught him what the "free" in free association means; or, how to "really" look at patchwork; or, to notice that "there is a good deal that can be seen *slant*wise" (*AG* 229), referring specifically to Dickinson's line "Tell all the Truth but tell it slant—"; in other words, she could teach him what is valuable about postmodernism; but, Simon skips town before such an exchange can take place. Inverting the typical reading of "Dora's" abandonment by Freud and, metaphorically, Grace's by Simon, which focuses solely on the patient's loss, Atwood reveals that the doctors also lose—they miss the opportunity to learn from the women about the protean, multi-dimensional qualities of "truth" and human experience.

In *Alias Grace*, Atwood studies the sexual politics of two political institutions in which women continue to be held captive: the legal system and the mental health system. In so doing, she links *Alias Grace* with still another literary work—Charlotte Perkins Gilman's "The Yellow Wallpaper" (1892). Intersecting and diverging on many points, each of these "Victorian" texts looks closely at an ongoing dialogue between a male physician (who is also the husband in Gilman's story), and a female patient/prisoner in order to critique the larger convergence of patriarchy and the mental health system.

In "The Yellow Wallpaper," Gilman explores and indicts the etiological connections among privileged, white, Victorian women's depression, their patronized and subhuman care by their husbands, and the extension of that deplorable treatment into the public world where they are rendered silent and invisible. Scrutinizing the sexual politics of the daily domestic life of her nameless narrator—an upper-middle-class, white writer, married to a physician with whom she has a new baby—Gilman exposes how madness results when a woman is denied the right to tell/write her story. If the primary intersection of "The Yellow Wallpaper" and *Alias Grace* is the psychological wish or need of each protagonist to define for herself a unique, individual persona, then the most obvious point of divergence is the fact that Gilman ignores the politics of class hierarchy, while Atwood scrupulously analyzes them. Additionally, in this section, I examine the intertextual relationships among the three "Victorian" texts included in this book—Hopkins's *Of One Blood; Or, the Hidden Self* (1902–1903), Gilman's "The Yellow Wallpaper" (1892), and Atwood's *Alias Grace* (1996)—all of which convene at the nexus of sexual trauma, sexual sadomasochism, racism, misogyny, depression and hysteria. (Obviously, Atwood's text is not authentically Victorian, but since it is so in content, style, and cultural/political/intellectual contexts, and focuses on an historical Victorian figure whose life spanned 1827–1873, I feel it is appropriate to include it here.)

First, however, I want to address the very important issue of the invasion and pervasion of Gilman's racism into "The Yellow Wallpaper." Despite the fact that I discuss neither the wallpaper, per se, nor Gilman's use of the color "yellow," I believe that our readings of this story have been permanently altered since the appearance of Susan S. Lanser's enlightening and now well-known 1989 essay on the manifestation of racism within "The Yellow Wallpaper."

In her essay, "Feminist Criticism, 'The Yellow Wallpaper,' and the Politics of Color in America," Lanser points out that "if we locate Gilman's story within the 'psychic geography' of Anglo-America at the turn of the century, we locate it in a culture obsessively preoccupied with race as the foundation of character, a culture desperate to maintain Aryan superiority in the face of massive immigrations . . . openly anti-Semitic, anti-Asian, anti-Catholic" (425). Lanser confronts Gilman's choice of the color "yellow" for the wallpaper and explains that it was anything but arbitrary. "Yellow" was a racist reference to minority immigrants, primarily though not exclusively Asian, whose "invasion," called the "Yellow Peril," generated such psychotic anxiety in California, where Gilman wrote "The Yellow Wallpaper," that the Chinese Exclusion Act was legislated in 1882. Lanser notes that "'yellow' readily connoted inferiority, strangeness, cowardice, ugliness, and backwardness" (427). Her meticulous research reveals that Gilman's later work is replete with evidence of her membership and active participation in racist organizations that "upheld Protestant supremacy. [She] belonged for a time to eugenics and nationalist organizations; opposed open immigration; and inscribed racism, nationalism, and classism into her proposal for social change" (429). Strikingly, Gilman is not disturbed by the irreconcilability of her narrow minded racism with her progressive feminism.

If we look at the yellow wallpaper itself as the text onto which Gilman projects and documents her racism—as Ammons puts it "Gilman's own racism [is] . . . unconsciously encoded in the wallpaper" (*CS* 39)—then the narrator's emancipation of the woman held captive behind it is a liberation from a perceived horrible, inescapable entanglement with the feared, dreaded immigrant "other." In this reading, the protagonist's decline into psychosis can be interpreted as an escape to a utopian reality where there is no yellow paper that "stained everything it touched" ("YW" 27), or a smell "that creeps all over the house . . . a peculiar . . . most enduring odor. . . . A yellow smell" ("YW" 29). Gilman was an out-spoken feminist, but clearly her progressive politics were directed toward and intended solely for white women. Ammons points out that along with Gilman's racism that is "encoded in the wallpaper" so are the "limits of this story's 'universality'" (*CS* 39). That only white women concern her is so ingrained in her mind that she never thinks to mention it.

What Gilman's narrator does mention, however, albeit only to herself, is an emphatic and urgent wish: "if I were only well enough to write a little it would relieve the press of ideas and rest me. . . . It's so discouraging not to have any advice and companionship about my work."[24] For this story's protagonist, the ability, read "permission," to write her story becomes an issue, quite literally, of life and death. Before she becomes entirely absorbed by the wallpaper, she plots ways of writing in secret when her husband and his sister Jennie are gone. She confides: "I know John would think [my need to write] absurd. But I *must* say what I feel and think in some way—it is such a relief!" ("YW" 21). For Gilman as well as for her protagonist, there is a straightforward, logical link between story and sanity. If the fictional narrator expects John to consider her "absurd," she is surprised that Jennie, "a perfect and enthusiastic housekeeper . . . thinks it is the writing which made [her] sick!" ("YW" 17). Maybe she anticipates empathy from a woman. Because writing is her work, she is denied not only the ability to express herself, but also the pleasure, routine, and identity associated with work itself.

Like Grace Marks, Gilman's narrator needs a story of her own. But, she is thwarted in her every attempt to write one and, thus will never be "whole." If she acts upon what she instinctively knows—that to write her story asserts her independent self—she will not only incur the wrath of her husband, she will violate the normative view of Victorian womanhood, "femininity," and motherhood. Authorizing her own text eradicates John's because the rigidity with which her culture defines gender allows for only one story—the seminal master('s) plot. Still, she asks to be taken seriously within John's terms and "text" when she suggests to him that perhaps she has an actual psychological problem, rather than the "temporary nervous depression—a slight hysterical tendency" ("YW" 10), for which she is being treated. Above all, her wish to be self-reliant and well is incomprehensible to John, so she translates it into the patriarchal language that this marriage acknowledges. But, the language of patriarchy is foreign to her; her feelings do not translate properly and she ends up asking for exactly what she wants least—illness. Verbally metamorphosized, her desire for self-sufficiency becomes a plea that John consider her "really" sick as opposed to "nervous," "depressed," or "hysterical"; the problem is that she does not want to be ill, she wants to be listened to and heard, experiences which would, in all likelihood, lead toward health.

Acknowledging her inescapable double-bind situation, the narrator of "Wallpaper" writes, on the one hand, "I am glad my case is not serious!" according to John; yet he "does not know how much I really suffer. He knows there is no *reason* to suffer, and that satisfies him. . . . He never was nervous in his life" ("YW" 14). She fears that because "John is a physician . . . I do not get well faster. . . . He does not believe I am sick!" (9). If Gilman's heroine establishes herself as clinically or "really" sick, she enjoys the pyrrhic victory of being believed, and therefore loved, by her husband. Or, she could autonomously declare herself sane though unhappy, and leave him as Gilman actually found the strength to do in her own life. But defying and denying every cultural, social, maternal, and "feminine" obligation and responsibility expected of her require more strength, more independence, and more self-confidence—in other words, less depression—than this heroine can muster. Notably, neither choice addresses the pain of "these nervous troubles [that] are terribly depressing" ("YW" 14) because John, representing the medical profession, which stands in for power, interprets her "self" and story. As an omniscient man and "physician of high standing" ("YW" 10), he exploits his wife's helplessness, prescribes that she be silent and still and, needless to say, under the guise of love, brings along his sister to stand guard over her and enforce his edict. Psychosis, which offers a compromise, allows her to "escape" John, establish her own reality, and liberate her "alternate" self from inside the wallpaper without exposing herself to his misogynistic rage.[25]

When Gilman's unnamed narrator asks her husband to consider the possibility that she has a "serious" problem, he responds by declaring: "you will never for one instant let that idea enter your mind! There is nothing so dangerous, so fascinating, to a temperament like yours" ("YW" 24). Not content merely to monitor everything she *does*, he now mandates what she thinks; but, in fact, he must because they are engaged in an undeclared war, and at stake is whose version of reality will be accepted. Also, his meta-message is "don't think about yourself, think about me!" Compounding her depression is the fact that, like all victims of domestic abuse, she internalizes her persecutor's projections, so that, although she has a whispering voice inside telling her otherwise, she believes that John as man, husband and physician "knows" what is right, and she really would be crazy to disobey him. Ultimately, what drives her mad is her recognition that to live "sanely" in John's text as a "perfect and enthusiastic housekeeper" like Jennie is suicide. She grasps for the life-saving alternative of psychosis. However, unlike Atwood's Grace, who never loses control of her text, Gilman's protagonist is defeated. Certainly, one could argue to the contrary that she, like

Grace, remains in charge of her story by "choosing" psychosis; in the context of "The Yellow Wallpaper," I refer to her emotional breakdown, not only as a choice, but as one with its own logic. But, I simultaneously believe that she is traumatized, beaten down, and "driven crazy"; her relentless suffering and gradual decline inform us that she does not freely or consciously elect to be psychotic. Though she selects the only alternative in which physical survival is possible, John as patriarchy wins; she is "knocked off her feet," reduced to crawling on the floor like the infant she is treated, and does not enact what would have been her "true" choice—that of feeling and being treated as a competent, adult woman.

Despite Simon's protestations to the contrary, he, like John, needs Grace to tell "her" story his way. Consciously, he is sincere when he explains to her that he wants to hear *anything and everything* she thinks and feels, but she does not quite believe him and, perceptively, she is right. Underlying his toting fruit and vegetable props back and forth is his wish to direct her "free" associations, and she often senses that she disappoints him by not saying what he hopes she will. He worries that his career is at stake; Grace is potentially Simon's big break. He hopes to make his reputation by cracking the Grace Marks case, magically turning his prestige into money, and then opening his own asylum modeled upon the newest and most humane scientific theories and treatments. One senses the ambivalence in his wish; surely he wants fame and money, but, at the same time, he is genuinely committed and works hard to help those who suffer from mental illness. Still, he unwittingly tries to dominate or direct Grace's thoughts, but a pan-optic Grace remains in charge.

Ironically, Grace's authority over her story evolved from her status as an icon, making her a source of unremitting gossip, newspaper reports, and contradicting projections. In contrast to Gilman's character, Grace has a plethora of "identities" from which to choose; or maybe, in the face of such an abundance of written material about "herself," she vows never to divulge any facet of her authentic self/story again. Quite literally, she has nothing else to keep privately unto herself—not even her nightdress. The "nightdress you wear one week, next to your skin while you sleep, may two weeks previous have been lying close to the heart of your worst enemy, and washed and mended by others who do not wish you well. . . . We own nothing here and share all in common, like the early Christians" (*AG* 27). As Grace senses Simon working hard to "approach her mind as if it is a locked box, to which [he] must find the right key" (*AG* 132), she may confabulate new twists and turns in her story to insure that she unveils nothing. Yet she must continue to cultivate his trust so he will write to the judge on her behalf. Could it be that what is expected of an imprisoned "celebrated murderess" affords more flexibility than is allotted to Grace's Victorian counterpart, Gilman's married, straight-laced, hard-working, rich, "free," terribly depressed narrator?

Excerpts from Gilman's portrait of her emotional breakdown, written in 1887, appear in *Women of the Asylum: Voices from Behind the Walls* (Geller and Harris 1994), a collection of twenty-six first-person narrative accounts by women involuntarily incarcerated in asylums in the United States between 1840 and 1945. Gilman describes how she eventually recognized that her "mental illness" was actually a serious depression attributable to her "mistaken marriage," after which she was able to procure an amiable divorce.[26] But before that, she sought the "rest cure" treatment prescribed by S. Weir Mitchell, "the greatest nerve specialist in the country" (Gilman qtd. in Geller 166), and his methods almost killed her.[27] The sadistic treatment is an enactment of what many American, middle- and upper-class white, professional men thought about women. Not only does the "rest cure" fail to treat an illness, it does not put up much of a facade of attempting to do so. Its goal was straightforward: simply put, women were not allowed to do anything except lie quietly on their beds and "rest" for weeks at a time. They could not read, write, converse, or even feed or bathe themselves. They were regressed to infancy, humiliated, and expected to be grateful for it. Interestingly, the fact that men colluded, perhaps consciously, perhaps unwittingly, to assist each other eliminate the "nuisance" of their wives, is reminiscent of Freud's "Dora." Husbands, fathers, brothers, and sons "handed over" protesting women to Mitchell with the request that he return them quiet and subdued.[28] "Dora's" father delivered her to Freud asking him to cure her of her bizarre idea that he was having an affair with a married woman and, in order to keep the woman's husband from interfering, he *gave* "Dora" to the husband.

Addressing the violent, sexual exploitation of women across borders of race, ethnicity, social class, and psychological make-up, I focus on the three "turn-of-the-century" works in my study: "The Yellow Wallpaper," *Of One Blood* and *Alias Grace*. These texts "speak to each other"; they engage in intertextual dialogue around a specific configuration of sexual sadism that results in trauma. In each text, a white, male protagonist—a physician in every case, acts as a foot soldier enforcing the supremacy of patriarchy by silencing women.[29] To differing degrees, John, Aubrey, and Simon manipulate and exploit women's psychological and culturally induced passivity and subservience because they find it sexually gratifying. Inextricably entwined with, if not precipitated by racism and issues of class privilege, the women's subordination by a privileged, white man twice leads to death: Dianthe is a victim, murdered by Aubrey, and Grace is an agent of death. Of course, each coerced female character has a unique personal drama and political-historical context within which her trauma is enacted.

From a psychoanalytic perspective, I will discuss the eroticization of sadism across race and class boundaries. That this is equally useful in understanding the traumas of Gilman's heroine, a writer, wife, and mother, whose privileged New England literary family could have been the "masters" or employers of the other two; Dianthe, a Fisk Jubilee Singer, whose maternal ancestors were slaves; and Grace, a prisoner serving a life sentence for murder, whose impoverished Irish immigrant family bordered on starvation, is what allows these three texts to engage in intertextual dialogue.

Defeated by a formidable, white, patriarchal doctor who is also her husband, "The Yellow Wallpaper's" narrator is held captive in a room intended as a nursery. She writes that the bed is nailed to the floor, "the windows are barred for little children, and there are rings and things in the walls" ("YW" 12). Surely the room could have been a nursery, but her description of a nailed-down bed, barred windows, and "rings and things in the walls" could just as easily portray a torture chamber. Instead of an actual slave-master, this character's keeper is her "loving" and prestigious husband—"a physician of high standing"—("YW 10"). Like Dianthe, Gilman's protagonist is denied autonomy by her husband; she is alienated from her work, her art, her friends, family, and her new baby. Though she may not lose her life, she certainly loses her mind. Or, more to the point, it is stolen from her. That this entire story takes place in a bedroom leaves no doubt that the nature of John's sadism is sexual.

In *Of One Blood*, the critical moment occurs when Aubrey decides he must "have" Dianthe sexually. She is still in the hospital when he observes her in a dissociated, trance-state begging Reuel for help. Importantly, her dependence and pain excite him into "a trance of delight, his keen artistic sense fully aroused and appreciative . . . losing himself in it" (*OOB* 475). In Hopkins's description of Aubrey's intense lust for Dianthe, unquestionably induced by her helplessness, we see the sadistic link between his erotic pleasure and her suffering; eventually, he recreates the master-slave relationship through his rape, captivity, and domination over her. Vulnerable, powerless, and trapped, Dianthe is ultimately murdered by her husband-brother, the son of her mother's and grandmother's "master."

In *Alias Grace*, Simon's sadism is, for the most part, restricted to his fantasies; of the three male characters, he is the most complex, three-dimensional and likable, rendering his sadistic thoughts and wishes all the more interesting. In the context of sadomasochism, however, Simon's relationship with Grace is less relevant than his with Rachel Humphrey, which is an explicitly sexual one. While Rachel initiates the sadomasochistic dynamic into their love-making, Simon is perfectly content to participate. He describes her "act" as a prostitute's in reverse: "a whore must feign desire and then pleasure, whether she feels them or not" (*AG* 365), but Rachel Humphrey does the opposite. Keep in mind that the sexual dynamics between Simon and Mrs. Humphrey are one issue about which this text is *not* ambiguous. Unquestionably, he does not coerce her into sleeping with him; she initiates their erotic encounters by awaiting him in his bed every night.

> [Rachel's] pretence is a pretence of aversion—it's her part to display resistance, his to overcome it. She wishes to be seduced, overwhelmed, taken against her will. . . . She presses close . . . then she draws back, aghast at herself . . . and bends away from him in an attitude of flight. . . . At the moment of her climax—which she attempts to disguise as pain—she always says *no*. . . . The [erotic] encounter begins with tears, quivering, and reluctance: she sobs, she reproaches herself, she pictures herself as ruined, wallowing in shame, a soul condemned. . . . She has never stooped so low, indulged in such abasement. . . . She writhes with humiliation. . . . Her other game is that she is trapped, at the mercy of his will, as in the obscene novels obtainable at the seedier bookstalls of Paris, with their moustache-twirling Sultans and cowering slave-girls [who have] . . . chained ankles. . . . [Simon] would like to make an incision in her—just a small one—so he can taste her blood, which in the shadowy darkness of the bedroom seems to him like a normal wish to have. (*AG* 364-366)

Simon's relationship with Rachel Humphrey could be a clinical vignette describing sadomasochism. If during sex "he's driven by what feels like uncontrollable desire" (*AG* 366), out of bed he feels nothing but disdain and hatred toward her. But it is exquisitely intense hatred: "Tonight he'll hit her, as she's begged him to; he's never done that before. . . . He wants to punish her for his own addiction to her. He wants to make her cry. . . . He has an urge to beat her away, as if she's a spiderweb across his face, or a skein of entangling jelly. Instead he kisses her" (*AG* 408). Concentrating on the artistic, supposedly romantic imagery of the weak woman and the powerful man, Atwood observes that Simon's interest in the vulnerable, unprotected woman reflects nineteenth-century art, especially paintings. She tells Laura Miller that the helpless woman was "eroticized in the art of the period, in the painting, in the operas, in the poetry. It was really a very attractive thing to the male artist of the period, rescuing the . . . crazy fainting woman" (qtd. by Miller 5). In other words, the art of the period to which Atwood refers, incorporates this sadomasochistic dynamic. In fact, the novels take it one step further; if John, Aubrey, and Simon want to rescue the supplicating woman, they want to first inflict the pain that weakens her.

As I discussed earlier, Simon's need to control his conversations with Grace interferes with his ability to learn more from and about her. While that is problematic, it is not sadistic. No evidence suggests that he derives pleasure of any sort from her captivity. Once, when she circumvents his questions regarding her participation in the murders, he feels unusually enraged, and is suspicious of his reaction. He thinks that "he'll pry [the answer] out of her yet. He's got the hook in her mouth. . . . He wonders why he's thinking in such drastic terms. He means her well, he tells himself. He thinks of it as a rescue, surely he does" (*AG* 322). Simon does want to rescue Grace, but this passage implies that ambivalence may underlie his conscious and stated wish to help her more than is evident. That he thoughtlessly and suddenly deserted her is probably more indicative of his narcissistic, immature need to "escape" from Rachel Humphrey than to hurt Grace. Still, his train "was halfway to Cornwall" (*AG* 413) before she even passes through his mind.[30]

Perhaps the literary style of poststructural realism characterizing *Alias Grace* reflects the fact that, in most cases, nothing based upon "reality" determined the treatment of women within the mental health and/or legal systems. In other words, women's actual psychological conditions or the crimes for which they stood accused were frequently secondary, if not incidental, to the culturally sanctioned sexual and cultural politics—misogyny and class privilege—embedded within these two institutional systems. Enforcing this point, Atwood found as she researched *Alias Grace* that

> some . . . women [on trial for murder] killed people and got off because we didn't like the people they killed; [they] were not approved of. It is also pretty obvious that some of [the women on trial] didn't kill anybody, but got convicted because they were doing other things that were not approved of, usually having an affair. . . . If a woman was involved in a case, and . . . adulterers' love letters [were produced], her chances for beating the rap went plummeting downward. (Atwood qtd. by Miller 3)

Paying scrupulous attention to every known scintilla of evidence related to the murders of Thomas Kinnear and Nancy Montgomery, Atwood critiques Grace, in part, as a victim of the patriarchal cultural phenomenon that defined her as a "celebrated murderess" and from that moment on, quite literally, became the "author"ity on/of her identity. That Grace Marks may have been guilty and received a "just" verdict is irrelevant to my argument: the verdict against her seems not to have been based upon the merits or lack thereof of her case. As Grace reminds Simon when he confronts her with the "fact" of her confession published in the newspaper: "Just because a thing has been written down, Sir, does not mean it is God's truth, I say" (*AG* 257).

CHAPTER SEVEN

CONCLUSION

WORDS FINALLY SPOKEN

> "The goal of reflection is emancipation from self-incurred bondage."
>
> —Seyla Benhabib

My exploration of literary representations of sexual sadomasochism reveals, unsurprisingly, that when the dominant culture is patriarchal and racist, the psychodynamic of sadism is most often enacted with white men in the role of the oppressor and women of color as well as white women (in Allison's novel, a young girl) in the role of victim. Simon Jordan, Atwood's protagonist in *Alias Grace*, is a sympathetic fellow rendered with complexity, fullness, depth and, therefore, may appear to be an exception to my depiction of sadomasochistic male characters. His fantasies of helpless, tormented women evoke his sexual excitement and, conversely, that sexual excitement evokes his wish to disempower the "other." He participates in the dynamic of sexual sadism, but does so psychologically, without inflicting physical pain on either Grace or Rachel Humphrey. But since "the term *trauma* is understood as a wound inflicted not upon the body but upon the mind" and "is not, like the wound of the body, a simple and healable event" (Caruth, *UE* 3), Simon causes both women to experience trauma when he cavalierly abandons them. The sadism in his desertion of Grace cannot be overdetermined because he represents her very last hope for freedom.

Like all interpersonal dynamics, sadomasochism is not static. It encompasses a wide range of behaviors, including very blatant as well as more subtle expressions of eroticized cruelty. In these texts, each act of sexual violence is uniquely contextualized by sociopolitical issues of race, social class, historical time and place. Thus, no two victims—not Atwood's Grace, Oates's Corky, Jones's Ursa, Silko's Lecha, Gilman's never-named narrator, Allison's Bone, or Hopkins's Dianthe—experience their traumas identically, although, of course, they share certain responses to events.

With caution, I venture a generalization regarding the alignment of gender and sadomasochism. That women *feel*, but do not *act*, aggressively or violently toward men is not surprising. (Although a considerable factor, disparities in physical strength between men and women do not alone account for this phenomenon.) Obviously, men perform violence upon women, but the reverse is much less frequent. My attention is directed to the fact that in the fiction I studied, the women are *not* sadistic. Deservedly furious, enraged women imagine their revenge against the men who oppress, imprison, beat, rape, humiliate, and abandon them, but they do not act upon it. Put another way, and this is my point, no female character *traumatizes* a male character.[1] Within the women's psyches, the forces of political or cultural sadomasochism do *not* converge with the dynamics of personal or psychological sadomasochism to the extent that they inflict trauma. Crucially, the women's anger directly targets the specific abusive men who, as agents of patriarchy, are responsible for their subjugation. For example, Allison's Ruth Anne wishes Glen dead; Ursa stops herself from castrating Mutt at the last possible second, in part, because she recognizes that Corregidora is more an enemy than her former husband; Silko's revolutionary commander, Angelita, is ready to kill, but she is a trained soldier, and Zeta kills Greenlee for rendering her invisible with one too many racist jokes. Other angry female characters who wish revenge on their white, male dominators include Silko's Lecha, Atwood's Mary Whitney, Gilman's narrator, Allison's Shannon Pearl, and Oates's Thalia.[2] Thus, the gendered difference is related neither to the intensity of the women's anger nor the violence of their fantasies. In these texts, the women feel and express rage, the men, sadism, and the difference lies in the link, for the men, between inflicting pain and sexual gratification.

As I have argued in the preceding chapters, female characters, such as *Bastard*'s Ruth Anne and *Grace*'s Rachel Humphrey yoke sex and suffering in their "masochistic" fantasies of humiliation and physical pain. For each, that connection remains imagined, and neither text indicates that it slides into actual sadism. In other words, we have *no* female character that correlates with, or even closely resembles male protagonists, such as Serlo, Glen, or Corregidora.[3] Can we hypothesize as to why this is so? Are we, as feminist literary critics and scholars, unconsciously shying away from women's expressions of sadism in fear that if we discover it in ourselves, we will relinquish a moral high ground? If so, the fact of such a denial would reify Western patriarchal proscriptions of "womanhood." But, arguing against this is the fact that in several disciplines, scholars are beginning to discuss "how domination is anchored in the hearts of the dominated" and to "conceive [of] domination as a two-way process, a system involving the participation of those who submit to power as well as those who exercise it" (Benjamin, *BL* 5). Furthermore, novels that re/deconstruct the expected alignment of gender roles in the psycho-political dynamic of sadomasochism are beginning to appear.

An example of one such novel, Sally Patterson Tubach's *Memoirs of a Terrorist* (1996), represents the excruciatingly intricate and, to a large extent, indecipherable experience of sexual trauma through the story of Megan Lloyd, a political revolutionary, who was raped by her father when she was fifteen years old. Having repressed the memory of incest from her conscious awareness, Megan engages in political terrorism and, in the process, merges her unconscious wish for violent revenge against her father with her confused political vision. Significantly, Tubach demonstrates that the personal is political by imagining a world in which global violence stems from the consequences of incest, particularly from Megan's repression of her memories of that rape. Tubach creates a context wherein the sexually victimized woman develops into the sadistic victimizer; Megan eroticizes her pain, projects it outward, and murders her lover during an encounter of sadomasochistic sex, inverting her usual role in this relationship as the masochist.[4]

In addition, two novels reflecting Susan Lanser's observation that "it is impossible to separate the text of a culture from the text of an individual" are Alice Walker's *The Third Life of Grange Copeland* (1970), and Gloria Naylor's *Linden Hills* (1985). Each book examines intergenerational abuse in which a violently exploited and abandoned young boy grows up to brutalize his own young son in a perverse attempt to compensate in adulthood for his earlier impotence. The prevalence of this theme in several novels by twentieth-century American women writers underscores the importance of an ongoing, public debate on violence against women.[5] Importantly, such a conversation continues the work begun by the first wave of the women's movement, which called for a reevaluation of gender relations more than a century ago. Likewise, from the perspective of many contemporary victims of rape and incest, the continuation of an open dialogue on trauma and sadomasochism is necessary; without it, as we have seen, it becomes easy to "forget," that is, repress, the excruciating narratives of women and children that underlie and define patriarchy.

Although investigating the politics and psychodynamics of submission is fraught with potential minefields, making work on the subject difficult, such a query is essential.[6] Further literary analyses on the nexus of trauma, memory, sadomasochism, gender, race, and psychoanalysis is certainly timely, and could include a study examining these issues in fiction by nineteenth- and twentieth-century American male writers. Such a project is likely to yield insight into the enactment of these narrative tropes and cultural realities in American fiction. Among the many male writers to include in such a study, Ralph Ellison,

William Faulkner, Nathaniel Hawthorne, Henry James, Charles Johnson, N. Scott Momaday, John Okada, Philip Roth, William Styron, John Edgar Wideman, and Richard Wright come to mind.

The collaborative relationships between political activists and scholars enables further investigation into psychic trauma. As I hope my study illustrates, power lies in the capacity to find or *create* individual, personal meaning from a traumatized and tortured past. If traumatic events are not repressed, they can be *used*: victims remember and imagine stories to be repeated and passed on. That is, when the stories of the past are consciously recognized, the cycle of violence can end, because the *narratives*, not the sadomasochism or the trauma, are repeated and passed on.

Notes

Chapter One

1. The Modern Library's 1998 publication of the "Top 100" novels of all time, which includes nine novels by eight women writers (two by Edith Wharton are listed), none of which is in the top ten, does not reflect the serious, persistent efforts of feminist critics. This is worth noting since it is likely that more people will read and be influenced by the Random House list than by any of the excellent lists of women writers offered by feminist publications in response. (See the *Women's Review of Books* August, 1998; also, the on-line magazine, *feminista* vol 2, no. 3/4.)

2. Beginning in the early 1920s, Freud's disciples, including Karen Horney, Melanie Klein, Joan Riviere, and Jeanne Lampl de Groot, were the first psychoanalysts to diverge from his Oedipal theory to construct different paradigms of female sexuality, which were also rooted in psychoanalysis.

3. As I will discuss in this Introduction, such theorists include Mae G. Henderson, Toni Morrison, Hortense Spillers, Claudia Tate, and Michele Wallace.

4. In her essay "The Occult of True Black Womanhood" (*Signs* 1994), Ann duCille confronts insidious racist remarks expressed by white feminists, Jane Gallop and Adrienne Rich, whose comments reflect the academy's current obsession with, perhaps fetishization of, black women writers, currently viewed, according to duCille, as a "kind of sacred text" (21). duCille considers Gallop's statement in which she admitted that black feminist critics now inhabit the place in her psyche previously reserved for her revered Lacan; in other words, for Gallop, black critics now represent The Law of the Father. Turning to Adrienne Rich's description of the black woman who helped to raise her, "my Black mother," as Rich calls her, duCille points to Rich's inability to view her "Black mother" as anything but her possession. Both Rich and Gallop fail to recognize that they are talking about *other women*—"another woman [in Rich's case] who is not her black mother but a laborer whose role as mammy is also socially, politically, and economically constructed" (52).

On the other hand, superb scholarship by white literary critics cognizant of race issues does exist. For example, du Cille observes: Elizabeth Ammons' *Conflicting Stories: American Women Writers at the Turn into the Twentieth Century* (1991) "represents a positive turn in literary studies . . . [as well as] a model we all would do well to follow" (duCille, "Occult" 31). Also, in my view, *Speaking the Other Self: American Women Writers* (1997), edited by Jeanne Campbell Reesman, is an excellent and very diverse multicultural collection of essays which grew out of the 1993 San Antonio American Women Writers Conference.

5. Smith cites several critical anthologies as well as a number of critical works by individual women writers of color. Included are: *This Bridge Called my Back: Writings by Radical Women of Color* (1981), eds. Cherríe Moraga and Gloria Anzaldúa; *All the Women Are White, All the Blacks are Men, But Some of Us Are Brave: Black Women's Studies* (1982), eds. Gloria T. Hull, Patricia Bell Scott, and Barbara Smith; *A Gathering of Spirit: North American Indian Women's Issue* (1983), ed. Beth Brant; *Cuentos: Stories by Latinas* (1983), eds. Alma Gomez and Cherríe Moraga; *Home Girls: A Black Feminist Anthology* (1983), ed. Barbara Smith; *Gathering Ground: New Writing and Art by Northwest Women of Color* (1984), eds. Jo Cochran, J. T.Stewart and Tsutakawa Mayami; Claudia Tates's *Black Women Writers at Work* (1983); Cherríe Moraga's, *Loving in the War Years: Lo Que Nunsa Paso Por Sus Labios* (1983); Paula Giddings *When and Where I Enter: The Impact of Black Women on Race and Sex in America* (1984); Barbara Christian's *Black Feminist Criticism: Perspectives on Black Women Writers* (1985).

6. In Goldberg's collection, *Multiculturalism*, essays that were especially helpful to me include those by Ramon A. Gutierrez, Peter McLaren, and Judith Stiehm. Also useful, though not included in that collection, are articles by Bonnie TuSmith, Frances R. Aparicio, and Wahneema Lubiano.

7. Also, in the United States, see the work of Jean Baker Miller, Judith Jordan, and all Works in Progress papers from the Stone Center for Developmental Services and Studies at Wellesley College. British psychoanalytic feminists, Juliet Mitchell and Jacquelyn Rose, and French psychoanalytic feminists, Luce Irigaray, Julia Kristeva, and Hélène Cixous, have all made seminal contributions to the project of joining feminism(s) and psychoanalysis.

8. An example of this very problematic critical approach, which Peter Brooks calls "something of an embarrassment" (*Storytelling* 20), is Dr. William Snyder's biography of Thomas Wolfe, *Ulysses and Narcissus* (1971). In it, Snyder analyzes Wolfe's novels to illuminate the writer's life, and concludes that "Wolfe is . . . a deeply neurotic man who suffered from insufficient gratification of his strong life urges for love and fame. . . . He certainly can be classified as a psychoneurotic" (219). In my view, this kind of specious work did as much to deter serious scholars from reconsidering the use of psychoanalysis for literary criticism as did Freud's gender biases or his neglect of cultural analysis.

9. Despite the fact that I am critical of Felman's work on trauma later in this Introduction, I believe, also, that her work toward establishing the concept of psychoanalytic literary criticism is indispensable.

10. In *Leadership, Love, and Aggression* (1983), black sociologist Allison Davis employs psychoanalytic theory to study the lives of Frederick Douglass, W. E. B. Du

Bois, Richard Wright, and Martin Luther King, Jr. In his essay, "Psychology and Afro-American Biography," Arnold Rampersad wrote that an African American biographer "explains very little . . . if [s/he] does not attempt to explain the mind" (18). He considers Davis's book "required reading" and, because it is "the first [work] to attempt a psychoanalytic reading of black leaders," Rampersad refers to it "an act of courage" (9).

Selwyn R. Cudjoe has a different view. In his essay on Maya Angelou, he writes: In African American biographies "one's personal experiences are presumed to be an authentic expression of the society. . . . The Afro-American autobiograph[y] . . . tends to be bereft of any *excessive subjectivism* and *mindless* egotism. Instead, it presents the Afro-American as reflecting a much more *im-personal* condition, the autobiographical subject emerging as an almost random member of the group. . . . *Me-ism* gives way to *our-ism* and superficial concerns about *individual subjec*t usually give way to the *collective subjection* of the group" (9, 10).

11. It appears that in his Preface to *The Words to Say It*, Bruno Bettleheim, not Marie Cardinal, first described her text as an "autobiographical novel." In her Introduction to *In Other Words* (1977), Cardinal's first book following the publication of *The Words to Say It*, Carolyn A. Durham acknowledges Morrison's tribute to Cardinal. In addition, Durham contextualizes the 1977 text within contemporary discourse on French and American feminist literary theory.

12. Spillers considers the "lack" to be that of psychoanalytic theory missing from African American literary scholarship. She maintains: "I think it is safe to say . . . that the psychoanalytic object, subject, and subjectivity constitute the missing layer of hermeneutic and interpretive projects of an entire generation of black intellectuals now at work. The absence is not only glaring but also perhaps most curious in its persistence" (136).

13. For personal narratives on childhood sexual abuse and incest, see the collection, *Interpreting Women's Lives: Feminist Theory and Personal Narratives,* eds. The Personal Narratives Group.

14. Of course, women attacked or raped by strangers experience trauma; however, my definition of personal trauma presumes a prior relationship that makes this *particular* woman the target.

15. As Charles Richet, Charcot's student, noted in 1880: "Among the patients locked away in the Salpêtrière are many who would have been burned in former times, whose illness would have been taken for a crime." Likewise, in the United States, William James pointed out that "the gradual rehabilitation and rescue [of those with hysteria] will count among the philanthropic conquests of our generation" (Herman 16). That Charcot saved many lives by diagnosing and hospitalizing depressed and hysterical women who would otherwise have been burned for practicing witchcraft is indisputable. True, too, is the fact that it never occurred to him that women were individuals whose personal stories might lie outside his "grand narrative," in which hysteria was attributed to dysfunction in a woman's uterus and brain. Patriarchy's influence on the study of hysteria often had no regard for the political or social status of women, much as the abolitionist movement worked, with honorable intentions, toward the cessation of slavery, but frequently did not consider African Americans citizens deserving of the vote.

16. In the chapters which focus on the texts by Allison, Atwood, Gilman, and Hopkins, I will deepen my discussion on the subject of the professional institution of medicine as an extension and agent of patriarchy.

17. Essays from several perspectives on this subject can be found in the collection, *In Dora's Case: Freud—Hysteria—Feminism*, eds. Charles Bernheimer and Claire Kahane. Most of the essays in this volume approach Freud's case study as a literary text.

18. For example, a recent *New Yorker* article, "The Politics of Hysteria" (April 6, 1998) by Joan Acocella (the magazine's dance editor), argues that Multiple Personality Disorder (MPD) "and its underpinning, recovered memory, have been caustically criticized by a number of feminist writers, among them Janice Haaken, Ruth Leys, Debbie Nathan, Wendy Kaminer, Carol Tavris, Louise Armstrong, and Elaine Showalter." With accuracy, Acocella could say that each has written *about* MPD. While Haaken and Armstrong agree that there may be instances of abuse in the psychotherapy relationship (as there are in other professional relationships), they oppose the idea of "false memory." They do not "caustically criticize" the syndrome of MPD, the concept of recovered memory, or the individuals who complain of those experiences. Haaken's essay in *Signs* is developed in her book, *Pillars of Salt: Gender, Memory, and the Perils of Looking Back* (Rutgers UP, 1998). Louise Armstrong's *Kiss Daddy Goodnight* (1978) is the first collection of incest narratives to be mass marketed in the United States (Tal 155). I agree with Acocella regarding Kaminer and Showalter. Focused on recovered memories of satanic ritual abuse, Lawrence Wright's *Remembering Satan* (1994), which first appeared as a three part *New Yorker* series, is often cited as the first publication to expose "false" memories. For an excellent bibliography on the subject of memory and childhood trauma, which includes publications intended for clinicians, scholars, and general readers, see Susan Riviere.

19. Among the feminist theorists in agreement with the FMSF's ideology, Elaine Showalter explains her views in *Hystories: Hysterical Epidemics and Modern Media* (1997); she states that the phenomenon of recovered memory is so pervasive it *must* be imagined. When asked why psychotherapists and patients would insist upon the credibility of "fantasized" memories of childhood sexual abuse, Showalter continues her tautological logic: "Some of [the reasons] come from the availability of this explanation for a variety of anxieties and discontents in women's lives" (147). Identifying herself as one who believes in psychoanalysis, but allies herself with the side of Freud who disavowed his own seduction theory, Showalter endorses the analyst's explanation of his relationship with the famous "Dora" (Ida Bauer), who confided in Freud a history of sexual molestation since childhood. Freud believed that Dora was abused, but insisted that she enjoyed, fantasized, and perhaps even initiated the sexual advances of her father's lover's husband. Oddly, Showalter has co-opted psychoanalytic theory for the very group she disdainfully refers to as "anti-Freudian zealots" (*Hystories* 12). Persuaded by the arguments of Frederick Crews, whose own prolific writings on his split with Freudian theory center on his contempt for the recovered memory movement, Showalter writes: "I am convinced that [Freud] did force such reminiscences [of sexual abuse] on his patients, eliciting confabulations rather than actual memories" (42).

20. Significantly, in *Female Malady* (1985), Showalter expresses a view on Freud's relationship with Dora that is quite different from the one she indicates in *Hystories*. In

the earlier text, she writes: "Freud failed Dora because he was too quick to impose his own language on her mute communication. . . . Like the Victorian nerve-doctors who saw themselves locked in combat with their hysterical patients in a contest for mastery, Freud wanted to demolish Dora's intellectual defenses" (160). Of course, views change over time, but perhaps *Hystories* would be better understood if Showalter explained her radical shift.

The problem with Frederick Crews's work is not his disdain of "countless untrained operators who use the yellow pages and flea market ads to solicit 'incest work,'" if, in fact, his accusation is true. (He offers no evidence that it is.) But, rather than expose the alleged charlatans who, according to Crews, have made an industry out of other people's pain, he blames psychotherapy patients, the process of psychoanalysis, feminism, psychotherapists with an "explicit feminist agenda [such as] Herman," and, most of all, Freud. See Crews's two-part article, "The Revenge of the Repressed," in *The New York Review of Books* (Nov. 17 and Dec. 1, 1994); *The Review* printed ten pages of letters to the editor, "'Victims of Memory': An Exchange" (Jan. 12, 1995), written in opposed, angry response to Crews. See his article in the same publication, "The Mindsnatchers," June 25, 1998. In a dismissive summary, he equates the belief in repression with the belief in god. "The idea may be true, but it is content with too many eventualities to be falsifiable—that is, amenable to scientific assessment."

21. "Anna O" (Bertha Pappenheim), an early hysterical patient of Josef Breuer, coined the phrase "talking cure."

22. I would like to thank one of my anonymous readers at SUNY Press for bringing this important point to my attention.

23. See Kalí Tal's analysis on the appropriation of "Other People's Trauma" (OPT) in *Worlds of Hurt: Reading the Literatures of Trauma* (1996).

24. See reviews on *Alias Grace* by Laura Miller, Francine Prose, and Nina Auerbach.

CHAPTER TWO

1. Obviously there are numerous Native American cultures and tribes. I write collectively of Native American cultures only when research reveals that the particular tradition I am discussing inheres in nearly all, if not all, tribes. For example, while particular ceremonies vary from tribe to tribe, the tradition of ceremony and of ceremonial ritual is inherent to all the Native American cultures that I researched.

2. For a very interesting analysis of *Almanac*, see Elizabeth Cook-Lynn's chapter, "The American Indian Fiction Writers: Cosmopolitanism, Nationalism, the Third World, and First Nation Sovereignty" in *Why I Can't Read Wallace Stegner and Other Essays* (1996). Cook-Lynn praises Silko's novel, noting that it "seems to stand alone in creating a fictionalized pantribal nationalism. . . . It is the foremost Indian novel in which we see the clear and unmistakable attempt to describe Indian nationalism in what [Silko] sees as modern terms" (90). But, according to Cook-Lynn, the

novel "fails in this nationalistic approach, since it does not take into account the specific kind of tribal/nation status of the original occupants of this continent" (93). In her interview with Ellen Arnold (*SAIL* vol. 10 #3 1998; 1-33), Silko responds to Cook-Lynn's criticisms: "The old folks would say, just like in *Almanac*, all of those who love the earth and want to do this are welcome. That's the old, old, way. That attitude about nationalism comes in much later, that's much more a European way of looking at things. . . . A lot of times when my work is attacked, it's attacked by people who aren't aware of how much they've internalized these European attitudes" (10, 11). Also, see Yvonne Reineke's essay, "Overturning the (New World) Order: Of Space, Time, Writing, and Prophecy in Leslie Marmon Silko's *Almanac of the Dead*" in the same issue of *SAIL* as Arnold's interview. Reineke considers the novel from the perspectives of postcolonial theory and the Fourth World. For an interesting analysis of American Indian literary theory from a feminist perspective, though it does not include *Almanac*, see Paula Gunn Allen's *The Sacred Hoop* (1992), which does discuss *Ceremony* and Silko's earlier work. See also Amy S. Gottfried's chapter on *Almanac* in her book, *Historical Nightmares and Imaginative Violence in American Women's Writings* (Greenwood 1998), in which she discusses representations of art and violence in several contemporary texts.

3. Leslie Marmon Silko, *Almanac of the Dead* (New York: Penguin, 1991) 174; all further citations are to this edition and abbreviated as *A* in the text. Additionally, it is worth mentioning that when Silko felt stuck during the writing of *Almanac*, she read all eighteen volumes of Freud—"Whoosh, right through" (Silko qtd. in Arnold 31), the influence of which is woven through the novel's entire tapestry. While Silko considers *Almanac* her tribute to Marx, she refers to her newest novel, *Gardens in the Dunes* (1999), as her tribute to Freud.

4. Another example of the "clinical detachment" and objectification of art, which Gloria Anzaldúa refers to in the epigraph which opens this chapter, is the story of the Laguna's stone figures, known as the "little grandparents." They were made by kachina spirits and stolen from the Lagunas by anthropologists, only to show up later in a museum behind glass.

5. Certainly the rehabilitation of white people is not a priority for Silko. But Seese's important role in the novel is consistent with the author's devotion to the ways of the old people: "I refuse to forget how generous, how expansive, how inclusive [was their] way . . . of seeing the world and of seeing beings" (Arnold 11).

6. For Silko's comments on cultural repression, see her interview with Donna Perry in *BackTalk* (1993). She states that white peoples' capacity to "forget"/repress the era of United States history that resulted in the Indians' genocide is "one of the tragedies of the United States." It is "a sort of collective amnesia about the past, sort of like the Germans during the Jewish Holocaust" (321).

7. The best-known version of the remaining almanacs is the Popul Vuh (Council Book) of the Quiché Maya of Guatemala. *Popul Vuh: The Mayan Book of the Dawn of Life*, translated by Dennis Tedlock, 1985.

Additionally, in the novel, the original almanacs are written on parchment made from horse gut, while Seese is transcribing the current copy onto computer disks. Reminding us that what is of real value will endure, Silko, at the same time, undermines the stereotype of the passive, slow Indian by linking the ancient with the technologically modern.

8. In her interview with Thomas Irmer in Germany, Silko tells him that stories about serial killers, including Jeffrey Dahmer's cannibalism, kept appearing in the news as she was working on *Almanac*. As we know from the novel, and as she repeats in the interview, she blames capitalism for his sort of sexual perversion, because that economic system sanctions the notion that parts can be severed from their whole, even when the parts are human limbs.

9. Severance from the earth is demonstrated in its extreme through Serlo's psychotic scheme to construct Alternative Earth modules designed to orbit around the earth during the war to protect those of "superior lineage." They are "self-sufficient, closed systems, capable of remaining cut off from earth for years if necessary" (*A* 543).

10. Certainly, this rhetorical switch is intentional and meaningful; it is not an example of what Alice Jardine calls a "tear in the fabric," "slippage" in the narrative (25, 26), or a moment in which the author has lost control of her text.

11. Authors who discuss the sexualized demand for power include Robert Stoller, Jessica Benjamin, Sigmund Freud, Judith Herman, and Elizabeth Waites.

12. I want to thank Judith Sanders for bringing this very important point to my attention.

13. *Lonely Planet Guide to Mexico* 1989, qtd. in Judith Sanders "Response to *Almanac of the Dead*" unp. 1994.

14. Menardo's death, attributable to his betrayal of his history and his ancestors' spirits foreshadows the assassination of Bartolomeo later in the novel. He too abandons his history, denying that anything of importance took place in Cuba prior to Castro, and in the only incidence of organized violence on the part of the native people, Bartolomeo is hanged in front of the people he betrayed.

15. In describing a similar phenomenon in *The Mill on The Floss*, George Eliot describes Maggie Tulliver's ability to "decode" Latin and make it her own.

16. See Bernard Hirsch who refers to Silko's narrative strategy as "accretion" (154). Interesting and descriptive, his theory complements Allen's theory of "accretive ritual structure" explained in *The Sacred Hoop*. Feminist theorists, such as Luce Irigaray, Hélène Cixous, or Alice Jardine, might interpret Silko's writing as "from the female body": circular, cyclical, non-linear. But Silko chooses to unite her storytelling with the spiraling red-tailed hawk, a coded, visual, and personal description. In its accommodation of all kinds of disparate concepts, *Almanac* is an excellent example of Bakhtin's idea of the novel as a "baggy Monster" (*Dialogism* xviii) having room for everything.

17. In her collection of essays, *Yellow Woman and A Beauty of the Spirit: Essays on Native American Life Today* (1996), Silko addresses "An Expression of Profound Gratitude to the Maya Zapatistas, January 1, 1994." She writes that the rebel fighters in Chiapas are participating in the "same [500-year] war of resistance that the indigenous people of the Americas have never ceased to fight" (153).

18. In their shared view of stories as generative—"the driving force of the revolution"—Silko instinctively links Angelita and Marx with EZLN leader, Subcomandante Marcos. (Ejército Zapatista de Liberación Nacional/The Zapatista National Liberation Army, EZLN, is the actual revolting army in Chiapas.) Silko's words alone

appear on the back cover of Marcos' book, *Shadows of Tender Fury* (1995), in which she points out that he "uses stories—ancient as well as recent—to reveal the origins of the 1994 Zapatista uprising." While Angelita, Marx, and Marcos are scholars of revolutionary ideology, they wait for messages from the dead ancestors and the "earth's natural forces" (*A* 518) to determine the time for rebellion. I use the word "instinctively" because *Almanac* was published three years before the EZLN uprising. But of course it is possible that Silko *was* aware of the impending insurrection in Chiapas and quite deliberately incorporated a disguised Marcos into her text.

CHAPTER THREE

1. Of course all domestic abuse is rooted in sociopolitical issues. The distinction I emphasize is one between impersonal sadism established within and carried out by institutional/governmental power structures—Nazi concentration camps, for example—and sadism inflicted upon a specific individual known to the assailant, such as incest. Where these two intersect is an important aspect of this chapter.

2. My thinking regarding this paradigm is based on several years of professional practice as a psychiatric social worker.

3. Different theorists attribute different ages and time spans to this developmental phase. Recent research in psychology and pediatrics places a recognition of gender difference at around age two. Like all markers of childhood growth and development, these ages are approximations and generalizations. Also, this paradigm applies to boys as well as girls, but since the protagonists of the two texts examined here are female, my discussion focuses on female development.

4. Adam Phillips writes: "In what could, broadly speaking, be called object-relations theory, we have potentially guaranteed subjects or selves in relation to potentially knowable and facilitating objects in search of personal development through intimacy. A modernized Freudian, on the other hand, can easily see the self as merely a function of representation—where else is it except in its descriptions?—in a world of comparably oblique objects" (57). Phillips is describing the unavoidable "lack" at the center of Freudian drive theory since the self is defined in terms of its desires, and no object can appease such desire; object-relations theorists interpret desires as wishes for "objects"—that is, relationships—and recognize the "non-perverted," non-pathological desire for intimacy. Object-relations theorists include Michael Balint, Jessica Benjamin, Christopher Bollas, John Bowlby, Nancy Chodorow, Carol Gilligan, Otto Kernberg, Margaret Mahler, and D. W. Winnicott.

5. Examples of theorists who do not perceive that pleasure is derived from intellectual curiosity include Peter Brooks, particularly *Reading for the Plot* and *Body Work*, Julia Kristeva, and Toril Moi, articulated especially in "Patriarchal Thought and the Drive for Knowledge." In addition: I make the point that further work is required to engage psychoanalysis with theories that are not formed by gender bias regarding

women's intellectual awakening. But, this is not intended to imply that theorists who are engaged with other aspects of Freudian theory support or endorse his unenlightened view on this issue. Certainly, the whole subject of curiosity in psychoanalysis demands deeper scrutiny.

6. Dorothy Allison, *Bastard out of Carolina* (New York: Plume, 1992) 112, 113; all further reference will be to this edition and abbreviated as *B* in the text.

7. My use of the term "masochism" should not be misconstrued to mean enjoyment of or pleasure in pain. Quite specifically, I describe a dynamic wherein Ruth Anne and Ursa experience acute self-hatred, shame, and humiliation because they blame themselves for their victimization. Their feelings of self-loathing become deeply entangled with sexual feelings for complicated sociopolitical and psychological reasons. Though Ruth Anne derives erotic pleasure by masturbating while *fantasizing* violent, sadomasochistic scenes, she is alone and safe at those times; no sexual fantasies accompany the actual beatings.

8. Gayl Jones, *Corregidora* (Boston: Beacon Press, 1975) 3; all further reference will be to this edition, and abbreviated as *C* in the text.

9. Incorporating Sophocles' text into my discussion on Allison and Jones may appear as a device intended to "authenticate" the contemporary novels by invoking a Greek "classic." In fact, my view is that Sophocles' work, like Freud's (and that of a number of other thinkers), is extremely relevant to my work.

10. Desire is inherent in questions. Shoshana Felman argues that:

> A question, Freud . . . implies, is always a question of desire; it springs out of a desire which is also the desire for a question. Women, however, are considered merely as the *objects* of desire, and as the *objects* of the question. To the extent that women, 'are the question,' they cannot *enunciate* the question; they cannot be the speaking *subjects* of the knowledge or the science which the question seeks. (Felman, de Lauretis, *Alice Doesn't* 111, 201 n.13)

Freud's question is "what does a woman want"?; de Lauretis wants to know "how a (female) child with a bisexual disposition become[s] a little girl and then a woman"? (*Alice Doesn't* 112). Ursa answers her question of "what is it a woman can do to a man" by confronting the urge within herself to inflict pain. Oedipus' journey is marked by questions; the sphinx's riddle—his rite of passage—is "what walks on four legs in the morning, two at noon, and three in the evening" (de Lauretis, *Alice* 157, 211 n.77). His answer of "me/Man" gains him access to his father's "place" as king and husband to his mother. The question that leads to his demise is who killed Laius, the answer to which is also "me." Irigaray observes that the question of our time is that of "sexual difference." Important issues are raised in *Corregidora* through questions, all of which can be discussed in a dialectic of "desire."

11. In a perverted mockery of slavery's commodification of women, Mutt threatens to "auction" Ursa to the highest bidder. He shouts loudly and repeatedly: "Piece a ass for sale, anybody wont to bid on it?" (*C* 159).

12. Because Allison writes that her protagonist represents her (see "A Question of Class" in *Skin*), and because Ruth Anne is identifying with Raylene, I refer, in this instance, to Bone as lesbian even though she has not identified herself as such. An additional point: Within the context of the novel, we can only speculate as to whether or not Bone discovers the story of an untortured identity within herself. After all, she is only twelve years old when *Bastard* ends. However, since Allison allows us to identify Bone with her, we know for certain that Ruth Anne uses narrative to heal.

13. Other twentieth-century fiction and poetry whose characters' "wear" the unauthorized masters' texts on their bodies include: Margaret Atwood's *The Handmaid's Tale* (1986); Willa Cather's *Sapphira and the Slave Girl*; Pauline Hopkins's *Contending Forces;* Maxine Hong Kingston's *The Woman Warrior* (1975); María Christina Mena's "The Vine-Leaf"; Janice Mirikitani's "The Spoils of War"; Toni Morrison's *Beloved* (1987); Alice Walker's *The Third Life of Grange Copeland* (1970) and *The Color Purple* (1982); and Edith Wharton's *Ethan Frome* (1911).

14. See note 13; all of these works represent domestic war novels.

15. A sense of "miracle" surrounds this birth which immediately follows a near fatal car accident. For different reasons, Anney, like Ursa's mother, is emotionally detached from the actual birth of her daughter. In both cases, only their bodies give birth.

16. In her collection of essays, *Skin: Talking about Sex, Class and Literature* (1994), Allison discusses her commitment to making literature out of her "true" story, writing that being afraid and ashamed of her past nearly killed her. I suggest that, if Allison is registering any disapproval of Anney's behavior, it is that she lived too long in denial.

17. Another aspect of the novel's ending adumbrated by its opening is that Anney, "strictly speaking" not at Bone's birth, is not with her at the end either, having chosen to live with Glen instead.

18. Jones argues in the last part of this statement that women abuse or oppress men as well as the other way around. An additional point is that Ursa's blurring of boundaries between time and people parallels that of Sophocles' Oedipus. In part, it is this confusion in Oedipus that "fates" him to kill his father and marry his mother.

19. Patricia Hill Collins writes "that women repeatedly use the metaphor of voice to depict their intellectual and ethical development." She quotes Belenky et. al, *Women's Ways of Knowing* (New York: Basic Books, 1986):

> The tendency for women to ground their epistemological premises in metaphors suggesting speaking and listening is at odds with the visualmetaphors (such as equating knowledge with illumination, knowing with seeing, and truth with light) that scientists and philosophers most often use to express their sense of mind. (16)

Again in Collins's words: "This emphasis on voice in women's culture parallels the importance of oral communication in African American culture" (Collins 113 n.2).

CHAPTER FOUR

1. In addition to her long novel, *Contending Forces*, and three serialized novels, Hopkins published short stories as well as numerous political/social editorials and commentaries in the *Colored American Magazine*, including a series on "Famous Women of the Negro Race" in which she applauded the work of Harriet Tubman, Sojourner Truth and Frances Harper, among others. She also worked on that publication as an editor and although her exact position remains vague—it is not stated in the magazine—it is clear that she had substantial editorial influence until the publication was bought by Booker T. Washington with whom she had strong ideological differences.

2. I agree with Benjamin's convincing argument that the master's sadistic/sexual pleasure derives from the "*knowledge of his power*" over his slave/ victim; however, her assertion that this occurs *in place of*, rather than in conjunction with, the master's direct sadistic enjoyment of inflicting or observing her *actual* physical pain is problematic. Because sadism is such a complex, multi-dimensional phenomenon, "either/or" analyses are unnecessary, which Benjamin herself states elsewhere. (See Scarry 1985).

3. Pauline E. Hopkins, *Of One Blood; Or, the Hidden Self* 1902; rpt. in *The Magazine Novels of Pauline Hopkins*, ed. Hazel V. Carby. The Schomburg Library of Nineteenth-Century Black Women Writers (New York: Oxford University Press 1988) 506. All further references are to this edition and cited as *OOB* in the text.

4. Boston Psychopathic Hospital is now the Massachusetts Mental Health Center in Boston.

5. Although this chapter was completed before the publication of Cynthia D. Schrager's excellent article, "Pauline Hopkins and William James: The New Psychology and the Politics of Race" in *The Unruly Voice*, ed. John Greusser (1996), we both discuss *Of One Blood* in the context of discourses on psychology and mysticism, predominantly as they are espoused by William James. My focus differs considerably from hers, however, in its emphasis on hysteria, sexual trauma, psychoanalytic theory, and James's relationship with Freud.

6. It is interesting to note that both Dianthe and Reuel do communicate telepathically with the "other world." For example, Reuel's introduction to Dianthe occurs in a prophetic vision. Also each communicates with Mira, and Reuel "heard" Molly Vance cry for help as she was drowning.

7. Alfred Binet is now remembered for his contribution to the development of the I.Q. test for children, known as the Stanford-Binet.

8. In another essay, I deal in depth with the impact of W. E. B. Du Bois's concept of "double consciousness" on *Of One Blood*. That piece thinks about Du Bois's relationship with William James and discusses their intermingling concepts of "double consciousness" and the "hidden self," respectively. Serving as the primary prototype for Reuel as well as for Will Smith, the protagonist of *Contending Forces*, Du Bois is important in Hopkins's work. His theory on the "black soul" and Edward Blyden's on the "African Personality" underpin Reuel's recovery of his racialized "hidden self" for which he returns to Africa as King Ergamenes. Additionally, the frequently contentious discourse on Pan-Africanism is a primary focus of my other essay on *Of One Blood*.

9. See Judith Herman, *Trauma and Recovery*, ch.1; and Jeffrey Moussaieff Masson, *The Assault on Truth: Freud's Suppression of the Seduction Theory*.

10. Several feminist scholars have written about the politics of rape. Especially useful are the works of Susan Estrich and Susan Brownmiller.

11. Charlotte Perkins Gilman's "The Yellow Wallpaper," published in 1892, clearly places the blame for the mental "health" system within the patriarchal culture. Written from a white, feminist perspective, it condemns the medical profession's infantilizing and sadistic treatment of women diagnosed with hysteria. Instances of these destructive methods are described in "The Yellow Wallpaper" and also in the biographies of Edith Wharton by R.W.B. Lewis, Cynthia Griffin Wolff, and Judith Fryer. Wharton and Gilman were under the care of the same physician—neurologist, S. Weir Mitchell. See also Elaine Showalter, *Female Malady* (1985), chapter 6; Ammons, *Conflicting Stories*, chapter 3; and Ehrenreich and English. For a collection of writings by women committed to asylums against their wills, which includes an entry by Gilman in which she describes her experience with Mitchell, see Geller and Harris.

12. In *Studies on Hysteria*, Freud notes that railway accidents were considered a primary cause of trauma precipitating hysteria in men (321), for whom, as Showalter informs us, Charcot had a special wing at the Salpêtrière (*FM* 148). Shell-shock, the trauma associated with male hysteria, was not necessarily associated with sexuality.

13. I agree with James's view that the "hidden self" is *not* by definition a pathological condition. In fact, it is a defense mechanism, which is tantamount to a survival technique. However, I think about it as a problematic and confounding state because, as I argue throughout this book, the issues at stake in recognizing one's personal/psychological and political past can be ones of life and death.

14. Hopkins has been criticized for making her female protagonists light-skinned. In my view, she does so to accentuate her very important point regarding the sexual violence of slavery—white rape and the resulting miscegenation. The light-skin is also interesting in the context of Professor Stone, the British "authority" in archaeology who leads Reuel's Ethiopian expedition. Perhaps Professor Stone for Reuel echoes Professor James for Du Bois, a white academic with views that could enhance rather than undermine black self-definition.

15. For Freud's most complete discussions on the "death instinct," see: *Civilization and Its Discontents* (1930); *The Ego and the Id* (1923); and *Beyond the Pleasure Principle* (1920).

16. In her section on "The Sexual Politics of Black Womanhood" in *Black Feminist Thought: Knowledge, Consciousness, and the Politics of Empowerment*, Patricia Hill Collins writes: "Contemporary portrayals of Black women in pornography represent the continuation of the historical treatment of their actual bodies. African American women are usually depicted in a situation of bondage and slavery, typically in a submissive posture, and often with two white men. As [Laurie] Bell observes, 'this setting reminds us of all the trappings of slavery: chains, whips, neck braces, wrist clasps'" (169). While Collins and Bell are commenting upon contemporary pornographic images of enslaved women, Aubrey imposed an identification on Dianthe almost one hundred years ago that is undoubtedly consistent with current depictions. Sadly, racialized renderings of victimized women—racist sadomasochism—continue to imbue the specific cruelty and violent domination of slavery with sexual excitement.

17. Since Aubrey's reenactment of Sophocles' story is taking place unconsciously, and the unconscious is unaffected by Western notions of "time" and "place," the strength of the psychodynamic is not diminished by the fact that the consanguineous relationships are unknown to everyone except Hannah, or by the fact that Aubrey's father is already dead.

18. Many twentieth-century novels by black women, such as Zora Neale Hurston's *Their Eyes Were Watching God*, Toni Morrison's *The Bluest Eye*, Gloria Naylor's *The Women of Brewster Place*, Alice Walker's *The Third Life of Grange Copeland* and *The Color Purple*, reflect a different version of gendered, racialized sexual sadism. In these texts, black men, not white "masters," perpetrate and perpetuate violent emotional and physical sadism, including rape and incest, upon women and young girls. At work here is the psychodynamic in which the black men have "identified with the aggressor" as a defense against their own literal, threatened, or metaphoric castration; they become the sadists as their only perceived means of obtaining power or authority and, unwittingly, enact the sexualized master/slave dynamic.

19. Of course, slavery need not be the literal historical site of the sexual violence in these texts which have been written over the course of more than a century. But the rape and incest in these novels, stories, and essays historically and psychologically reverberates with the master/slave power dynamic.

20. For an excellent discussion of Dianthe and Sappho as black women artists, see Elizabeth Ammons (*CS* ch.5).

Chapter Five

1. "Honesty is an art" is Oates's epigraph for her review of two collections of Raymond Chandler's fiction in *The New York Review of Books*, December 21, 1995. Chandler's work is republished by Library of America.

2. Four of the twenty-eight novels are published under Oates's acknowledged pseudonym, Rosamond Smith. Subsequent to the completion of this chapter, her published work includes collections of short stories, plays, poems, a children's book, and several novels.

In addition, Showalter advances this argument in *Sister's Choice: Tradition and Change in American Women's Writing* (1991), which she dedicates to Oates, but this also predates *What I Lived For*.

3. For a recent attempt to produce an anthology comprising empathic constructions of male characters in short stories written by American women writers, see: Patricia Ellen Martin Daly, ed. *Envisioning the New Adam: Empathic Portraits of Men by American Women Writers*. In my view, the problem with this collection is that the stereotypic representation of women as "victim" is simply reversed and it is the men who are helpless. The "new Adams" are not three-dimensional, fully developed representations.

4. I want to thank Elizabeth Ammons for bringing this very important point to my attention. Specific connections (perhaps overdetermined) between *What I Lived For* and *Babbitt* include similar descriptions of the Union City and Zenith Athletic Clubs,

respectively. Also Seneca Doane is Babbitt's Socialist friend; Seneca is both a street and a bar in Oates's text.

5. Joyce Carol Oates, *What I Lived For* (New York: Dutton, 1994) 6; all further references to this work are to this edition and cited as *WILF* in the text.

6. Clearly, Corky perpetuates racist and classist stereotypes as well as sexist ones, and I will consider these. Still, my discussion focuses on gender issues because I am thinking about Oates's postmodern-realistic representation of a man.

7. For gender research focused on constructs of "masculinity," see the work of James Doyle, Stephen Frosh, David Gilmore, Michael Kimmel, J.H. Pleck, Lillian Rubin, David Savran, and Robert J. Stoller.

8. Though I did not closely examine the character of Marilee Plummer in my chapter, I want to point out that Oates represents her as a deeply conflicted young woman, whose problems the Slatterys exploit.

9. I also discuss this dynamic in my chapter on Pauline Hopkins's *Of One Blood*. For other in-depth explorations of this racialized and racist phenomenon, see Carby's *Reconstructing Womanhood* and Ammons' *Conflicting Stories*, chapter 2. Ammons discusses this subject in the context of Frances Ellen Harper's *Iola Leroy*.

10. Of course I take this phrase from Thorstein Veblen.

11. Stoller also postulates a paradigm for female gender development; but since I am focusing on Corky, my attention is primarily on constructs of masculinity.

12. See the work of Jessica Benjamin, Nancy Chodorow, Carol Gilligan, Jean Baker Miller, and D.W. Winnicott.

13. As I discussed in chapter 1, feminism's influence on psychoanalysis is responsible for the latter's recent sophisticated, complex, and three-dimensional reconfigurations of gender identity. Misogynistic representations of the intrusive, engulfing mother are less believable and have almost disappeared. That more fathers actively co-parent also helps to change demeaning stereotypes of mothers.

14. I join others (see note 12) who believe that boys do not have to "break away" from their mothers in order to form a masculine gender identity. Identification with the same-sexed parent can occur within a closely attached relationship with the other parent. Also, I am focusing on nuclear heterosexual families because that is the familial configuration Oates represents in *What I Lived For*.

15. In her 1992 essay on incest in the novels of Joyce Carol Oates, Marilyn Wesley notes that of her then twenty-two novels, eight are "concerned with relations incestuous in tone, if not in fact" (251).

CHAPTER SIX

1. Poem 1129. c.1868.

2. An autopsy revealed that Nancy Montgomery was pregnant at the time of her death; she had previously given birth to an illegitimate child.

3. Atwood originally named her television drama *Grace Marks*; the CBC changed the title to *The Servant Girl*. I have not viewed the play. All my information

comes either from what Atwood has written about it in her Afterword to *Alias Grace* or discussed in interviews.

4. "Lunatic asylum" was the term of the day. In fact, one of Susanna Moodie's two chapters on Grace Marks is entitled "The Lunatic Asylum."

5. Although Atwood never specifically mentions the potato famine, the family left Ireland in poverty, and the famine coincides in time with their departure.

6. Margaret Atwood, *Alias Grace* (New York: Doubleday, 1996) 115, 116; all further references to this text are to this edition and will be cited in the text as *AG*.

7. Grace Marks and James McDermott were tried together in one trial and shared the same lawyer, Kenneth MacKenzie. They were only tried for Kinnear's murder; after they were found guilty and sentenced to death, there was no cause for the second trial.

8. I am referring to Bakhtin in my use of the concept "monologic," and intend it as an opposing term to his idea of the dialogic. However, Bakhtin does not altogether believe in the existence of the "monologic," because he views even a monologue as an intertextual dialogue (Todorov 63).

9. Clearly, Atwood was thinking about the "prison" of a patriarchal, binary world-view when her unnamed narrator in *The Handmaid's Tale* (1986) describes her sadistic guard, Aunt Lydia, as "in love with either/or" (8).

10. In her Afterword to *Alias Grace*, Atwood notes that penitentiary records show that when Grace returned there from the asylum, there was concern that she was pregnant. She was not, but Atwood points out that the wards of the asylum were segregated by gender, and not easily accessible to each other; the doctors were the men with the easiest access to the patients. Within the fictional text, Reverend Verringer tells Simon that Grace was suspected of "being in a delicate condition" upon her return from the asylum.

11. Atwood writes that a few pieces of evidence were acknowledged in the original police documents, but never explained. In addition to the bloodied book found in Nancy's bed, Kinnear's corpse was discovered wearing a shirt belonging to McDermott.

12. Atwood's Afterword contextualizes the novel historically; if one wishes to research her primary sources, or attempt to understand the methodology of her scholarship, it is possible, in large part, to do so.

13. My chapter on Pauline Hopkins's *Of One Blood; Or, the Hidden Self* as well as my introduction discuss in more depth Freud's rejection of his seduction theory. Also, some psychiatric literature reports Mary Reynolds' case as occurring in 1811 in Pennsylvania, not 1816 in New York, as Atwood cites. All accounts, however, leave no question that they are discussing the same Mary Reynolds.

14. When I use Dora without quotation marks, I am referring to the fictional Dora in *Alias Grace*. I use quotation marks around Freud's patient, "Dora" since that is a pseudonym or alias.

15. Freud understood that something untoward occurred between "Dora" and Herr K, but he considered her partially, if not totally, responsible for her abuse, and did *not* view her as a victim of sexual trauma.

16. Simon Jordan bears some resemblance to George Eliot's physician, Mr. Lydgate in *Middlemarch*, and in this dialogue he is paired with Lydia, the Governor' daughter. Nina Auerbach writes that "Simon is the sort of doctor Charlotte Brontë and

George Eliot exposed so shrewdly: enlightened, humane, gentle to women, but with an unplumbed sexual conservatism that borders on violence" (Rev. 3).

17. I am not implying that this phenomenon is unique to psychiatry or psychology; my research was limited to these fields of study.

18. Recently, scholars are taking a renewed interest in the old case of Mary Reynolds. Since a contemporary diagnosis of multiple personality disorder includes a past history of trauma ninety-seven percent of the time (Carlson), and none is reported in the Reynolds case or in documentation of other early cases of MPD, present researchers have been prompted to review her case. They find that she and her family were victims of religious persecution so severe that the Irish family felt forced to leave England when Mary was eight year old; sources disagree as to their destination, but it was either Pennsylvania or New York (Carlson). *Alias Grace*'s Dr. Joseph Workman (who actually was the Asylum's medical director during Grace's second "visit") informs Simon that he believes "religious fanaticism . . . to be fully as prolific an exciting cause of insanity as intemperance" (*AG* 48).

19. Simon is a very complex, multi-faceted character. The problem I am addressing in a few of the reviews is that the critics seem to expect him to have a contemporary knowledge base, and then are annoyed with him for his bumbling. (See especially Le Clair and Prose.) His misguided attempts at directing Grace's associations are problematic because they do just that—attempt to direct her thoughts; I attribute that to his patriarchal need for dominance rather than a lack of professional knowledge.

20. Regarding Braid's work on hypnosis, Atwood writes the following note in her Afterword:

> Mesmerism was discredited as a reputable scientific procedure early in the century, but was widely practised by questionable showmen in the 1840s [such as Jeremiah]. As James Braid's "Neuro-hypnotism," which did away with the idea of a "magnetic fluid," mesmerism began a return to respectability, and by the 1850s had gained some following among European doctors, although not yet the wide acceptance as a psychiatric technique that it was to achieve in the last decades of the century. (464)

21. Atwood reports that "the fate of Mary Whitney has a parallel in the medical records of Dr. Langstaff of Richmond Hill" (*AG* Afterword 464). But definitive documentation of her existence has not been uncovered.

22. Laycock also noted cases of hysteria in men, which he attributed to homosexuality. (See Janet Oppenheim, *Shattered Nerves: Doctors, Patients, and Depression in Victorian England*. New York: Oxford UP, 1991: 143.)

23. Jean-Marcot Charcot, whom I also discuss earlier is an exception in that he was widely known. Although not a household name, Dr. Binswanger, who both in the novel and in his actual life directed a sanatorium in Switzerland, was a well-known colleague of Freud's. In Atwood's novel, he has the fictional distinction of recommending Simon to Verringer's committee as an expert "on cerebral diseases . . . nervous afflictions and . . . amnesia" (*AG* 78).

24. Charlotte Perkins Gilman, "The Yellow Wallpaper" 1892 (New York: The Feminist Press at The City U of New York, 1973) 16; all further reference to this text are to this edition and will be cited in the text as "YW."

Additionally and crucially, in my extensive research for this chapter on the nineteenth-century mental health system, I discovered *only* information/ documentation/clinical vignettes concerning white women. Women of color are invisible in the scholarship; minority women and depression is a large topic beyond the scope of this chapter, but certainly an important one for future research.

25. I do not mean to simplify the complex relationship between Gilman's narrator and her entrapped self. The former certainly wants to emancipate the latter, but she is also ready to tie her up with rope if she tries to get out. Gilbert and Gubar discuss the dynamic of "doubles" in "The Yellow Wallpaper" in chapter two of *The Madwoman in the Attic*.

26. The portion of Gilman's narrative that is included in Geller and Harris's *Women of the Asylums* is excerpted from *The Living of Charlotte Perkins Gilman* (Gilman 1935).

All of the twenty-six authors included in *Women of the Asylum* write personal and poignant stories. Remarkably, they also transcend their individual accounts to lobby for political and legislative reforms, all of which originate in the urgent need for women's rights. Offering thoughtful suggestions as to how their ideas can be implemented, they seek long-sighted changes, from which another generation of women, not their own, will benefit; they also have more immediate demands, including more humane treatment, better food, more bathing privileges, and fewer rats.

27. For an in-depth description of Weir Mitchell's "rest cure," see Ammons, *CS* chapter 3.

28. In fact, collusion among husbands, doctors, and judges to insure the security of patriarchy was widespread. Legislation decreed that if a woman was declared "insane" by the state, her children and financial estate automatically and permanently reverted to her husband. Frequent (ab)use of the asylums involved the cooperation of judges who, along with one or two doctor(s), signed the forms (for a fee), often without setting eyes upon the woman; this procedure allowed men to institutionalize their wives indefinitely in order to steal their property (see Geller and Harris).

29. Aubrey, who is "of one blood" with Reuel and Dianthe is black, but he was raised as white and continues to believe that he is. Unquestionably, he represents the sadism of the dominant culture; also, he and Dianthe portray the lethal consequences of being deprived of one's ancestry and heritage.

30. From a completely different perspective, *The Handmaid's Tale* (Atwood 1986), like *Alias Grace* and "The Yellow Wallpaper," also deals with the sexual/cultural politics of women's imprisonment and institutionalization.

CHAPTER SEVEN

1. An exception would be Corky's sexual molestation by his mother, *if*, in fact, that occurred. (I discuss this possibility in my chapter on Oates's novel.) Still, I do not

consider this point important here for two reasons: first, Corky's trauma is undoubtedly attributable to his father's murder and its aftermath; and second, the language regarding that incest is so encrypted that, in my view, it would be irresponsible to read it as having definitely taken place.

2. I have not included Hopkins's Dianthe or Atwood's Grace in this group. While I would agree that both women are furious, their anger is not manifested as such. Grace's is veiled in ambiguity, Dianthe's in symptoms of hysteria.

3. Even Silko's Leah Blue is not an exception; she exploits the land and certainly is representative of Destroyer culture, but she does not derive sexual pleasure by inflicting or observing pain.

4. In fact, in this experimental novel, the reader knows for certain only that Megan is *accused* of terrorist activities including the murder of her lover in a Munich hotel room.

5. See Toni Cade Bambara's *The Salt Eaters*; Djuana Barnes's *Nightwood*; Willa Cather's *Sapphira and the Slave Girl*; Sarah Winnemucca Hopkins's *Life Among the Piutes: Their Wrongs and Claims*; South American writer, Luisa Valenzuela's *Black Novel* (written in Spanish and available in translation); and Anzia Yezierska's *Bread Givers*.

6. For example, in the Preface to her second book, *Like Subjects, Love Objects: Essays on Recognition and Sexual Difference* (1995), Jessica Benjamin tries to address the limitations of her earlier work. Despite her willingness to acknowledge the fact that *Bonds of Love* ignores issues of racial and cultural differences, and completely neglects sexual development in lesbians and homosexuals, *Like Subjects* (which is a collection of revised essays written prior to the publication of *Bonds*) does not address or correct her admitted gaps. Though her third book, *Shadow of the Other: Intersubjectivity and Gender in Psychoanalysis* (1998), engages the subject of sexual orientation, it remains silent on race.

Works Cited

Abel, Elizabeth, Barbara Christian and Helene Moglen, eds. *Female Subjects in Black and White: Race, Psychoanalysis, Feminism.* Berkeley: U California P, 1997.

Acocella, Joan. "The Politics of Hysteria." *The New Yorker.* April 6, 1998: 64–79.

Adorno, Theodor. "Aesthetic Theory." *Critical Theory Since 1965.* Eds. Hazard Adams and Leroy Searle. Tallahassee: UP of Florida, 1986. 231–237.

Allen, Paula Gunn. *The Sacred Hoop: Recovering the Feminine in American Indian Traditions.* Boston: Beacon Press, 1992.

Allison, Dorothy. *Two or Three Things I Know for Sure.* New York: Dutton, 1995.

———. *Skin: Talking about Sex, Class and Literature.* Ithaca: Firebrand, 1994.

———. *Bastard out of Carolina.* New York: Plume, 1992.

American Psychiatric Association. *Diagnostic and Statistical Manual of Mental Disorders* 3rd. ed. Washington DC: American Psychiatric Association, 1987.

Ammons, Elizabeth. *Conflicting Stories: American Women Writers at the Turn into the Twentieth Century.* New York: Oxford UP, 1991.

———. "*Winona,* Bakhtin, and Hopkins in the Twenty-first Century." Afterword. Gruesser 211–219.

Angelou, Maya. *I Know Why the Caged Bird Sings.* New York: Bantam, 1969.

Anzaldúa, Gloria. *Borderlands/La Frontera: The New Mestiza.* San Francisco: Aunt Lute Books, 1987.

Aparicio, Frances R. "On Multiculturalism and Privilege: A Latina Perspective." *American Quarterly* 46:4 (December 1994): 575–588.

Arnold, Ellen. "Listening to the Spirits: An Interview with Leslie Marmon Silko." *Studies in American Indian Literature* 10 (1998): 1–33.

Atwood, Margaret. *Alias Grace.* New York: Doubleday, 1996.

———. *The Handmaid's Tale.* Boston: Houghton Mifflin, 1986.

Auerbach, Nina. "The Housemaid's Tale." Rev. of *Alias Grace,* by Margaret Atwood. *The Women's Review of Books* April, 1997: 1–3.

———. "Magi and Maidens: The Romance of the Victorian Freud." *Writing and Sexual Difference.* Ed. Elizabeth Abel. Chicago: U of Chicago P, 1982. 111–130.

Bakhtin, M.M. *The Dialogic Imagination.* Ed. Michael Holquist. Austin: U of Texas P, 1981.

Barthes, Roland. *The Pleasure of the Text.* Trans. Richard Miller. New York: Farrar, 1975.

Barzun, Jacques. *A Stroll with William James.* New York: Harper, 1983.

Baym, Nina. *Woman's Fiction: A Guide to Novels by and about Women in America, 1820–1870.* Ithaca: Cornell UP, 1978.

Bellow, Saul. *Herzog.* Greenwich: Fawcett, 1961.

Bender, Eileen Teper. *Joyce Carol Oates: Artist in Residence.* Bloomington: Indiana UP, 1987.

Benjamin, Jessica. *Shadow of the Other: Intersubjectivity and Gender in Psychoanalysis.* New York: Routledge, 1998.

———. *Like Subjects, Love Objects: Essays on Recognition and Sexual Difference.* New Haven: Yale UP, 1995.

———. *The Bonds of Love: Psychoanalysis, Feminism and the Problem of Domination.* New York: Pantheon, 1988.

———. "A Desire of One's Own: Psychoanalytic Feminism and Intersubjective Space." De Lauretis, *FS/CS* 78–101.

Bernheimer, Charles and Claire Kahane, eds. *In Dora's Case: Freud—Hysteria—Feminism.* New York: Columbia UP, 1985.

Brennan, Teresa, ed. *Between Feminism and Psychoanalysis.* New York: Routledge, 1990.

Brooks, Peter. *Psychoanalysis and Storytelling.* The Bucknell Lectures in Literary Theory 10. Cambridge: Blackwell, 1994.

———. *Body Work: Objects of Desire in Modern Narrative.* Cambridge: Harvard UP, 1993.

———. *Reading For the Plot: Design and Intention in Narrative.* Cambridge: Harvard UP, 1984.

Brown, David W. "An Interview with Author Margaret Atwood." *Emailia Magazine* Nov. 1996: Online. Toronto: U of Toronto, Victoria College Campus, 16 March, 1997.

Brown, Laura S. "Not Outside the Range: One Feminist Perspective on Psychic Trauma." Caruth, *Explorations* 100–112.

Butler, Octavia. *Kindred.* Boston: Beacon P, 1979.

Carby, Hazel V. *Reconstructing Womanhood: The Emergence of the Afro-American Woman Novelist.* New York: Oxford UP, 1987

———. "'On the Threshold of Woman's Era': Lynching, Empire, and Sexuality in Black Feminist Theory." Gates, *RWD* 301–316.

Cardinal, Marie. *The Words To Say It.* 1975. Trans. Pat Goodheart. Cambridge: Van Vactor and Goodheart, 1996.

———. *In Other Words.* Trans. Amy Cooper. Bloomington: Indiana UP, 1977.

Carlson, E. T. "Multiple Personality and Hypnosis: The First One Hundred Years." *International Journal of the History of Behavioral Sciences* 25 (1989): 315–322. Abstract. *Medline* 1966–March 1997. CD-ROM. Ovid.

Carroll, James. "He Could Not Tell a Lie." Rev. of *What I Lived For,* by Joyce Carol Oates. *The New York Times Book Review* 16 Oct. 1994: 7.

Caruth, Cathy. *Unclaimed Experience: Trauma, Narrative, and History.* Baltimore: Johns Hopkins UP, 1996.

———. ed. *Trauma: Explorations in Memory.* Baltimore: Johns Hopkins UP, 1995.

Chesnutt, Charles. *The House Behind the Cedars.* 1900. New York: Penguin, 1993.

Chodorow, Nancy. *Feminism and Psychoanalytic Theory.* New Haven: Yale UP, 1989.

Chopin, Kate. *The Awakening.* 1899. New York: Bantam, 1981.

Christian, Barbara. "Trajectories of Self-Definition: Placing Contemporary Afro-American Women's Fiction." Pryse and Spillers 233–248.

Clatterbaugh, Kenneth. *Contemporary Perspectives on Masculinity.* Boulder: Westview, 1990.

Collier, George A. *Basta! Land and the Zapatista Rebellion in Chiapas.* Oakland: A Food First Book, 1994.

Collins, Patricia Hill. *Black Feminist Thought: Knowledge, Consciousness, and the Politics of Empowerment.* Perspectives on Gender Ser. 2. New York: Routledge, 1990.

Coltelli, Laura. *Winged Words: American Indian Writers Speak.* Lincoln: U of Nebraska P, 1990.

Cook-Lynn, Elizabeth. *Why I Can't Read Wallace Stegner and Other Essays.* Madison: U of Wisconsin P, 1996.

Cooper, Anna Julia. *A Voice From the South.* 1892. The Schomburg Library of Nineteenth-Century Black Women Writers Ser. Ed. Henry Louis Gates, Jr. New York: Oxford UP, 1988.

Crabtree, Adam. *From Mesmer to Freud: Magnetic Sleep and the Roots of Psychological Healing.* New Haven: Yale UP, 1993.

Cudjoe, Selwyn R. "Maya Angelou and the Autobiographical Statement." *Black Women Writers (1950–1980): A Critical Evaluation.* Ed. Mari Evans. New York: Anchor Books, 1984.

Culbertson, Roberta. "Embodied Memory, Transcendence, and Telling: Recounting Trauma, Re-establishing the Self." *New Literary History* 26 (1995): 169–195.

Daly, Patricia Ellen Martin, ed. *Envisioning the New Adam: Empathic Portraits of Men by American Women Writers.* Contributions in Women's Studies Ser. 149. Westport: Greenwood, 1995.

Darling, Marsha. "In the Realm of Responsibility: An Interview with Toni Morrison." *Women's Review of Books.* March 1988.

Davis, Allison. *Leadership, Love, and Aggression.* San Diego: Harcourt, Brace, Jovanovich, 1983.

Davis, Angela Y. *If They Come In The Morning.* New York: Signet, 1971.

De Lauretis, Teresa, ed. *Feminist Studies/Critical Studies.* Theories of Contemporary Culture Ser. 8. Center for Twentieth Century Studies. Bloomington: Indiana UP, 1986.

———. *Alice Doesn't: Feminism, Semiotics, Cinema.* Bloomington: Indiana UP, 1984.

Dickens, Charles. *Oliver Twist.* 1838. Rutland: Everyman, 1994.

Dimen, Muriel. "Power, Sexuality, and Intimacy." *Gender/Body/Knowledge: Feminist Reconstructions of Being and Knowing.* Eds. Alison M. Jaggar and Susan R. Bordo. New Brunswick: Rutgers UP, 1992. 34–51.

Doane, Mary Ann. *The Desire to Desire: The Woman's Film of the 1940's.* Theories of Representation and Difference Ser. Ed. Teresa de Lauretis. Bloomington: Indiana UP, 1987.

Dreiser, Theodore. *Sister Carrie.* 1900. New York: Signet, 1961.

Du Bois, W. E. B. *The Souls of Black Folk.* 1903. New York: Bantam. 1989.

duCille, Ann. "The Occult of True Black Womanhood: Critical Demeanor and Black Feminist Studies." Abel 21–56.

———. *Skin Trade.* Cambridge: Harvard UP, 1996.

———. *The Coupling Convention: Sex, Text, and Tradition in Black Women's Fiction.* New York: Oxford UP, 1993.

Ehrenreich, Barbara, and Deirdre English. *Complaints and Disorders: The Sexual Politics of Sickness.* Old Westbury: The Feminist Press, 1973.

Ellenberger, Henri R. *The Discovery of the Unconscious: The History and Evolution of Dynamic Psychiatry.* New York: Basic, 1970.

Elliot, Emory. *Columbia Literary History of the United States.* New York: Columbia UP, 1988.

Elliot, Patricia. *From Mastery to Analysis: Theories of Gender in Psychoanalytic Feminism.* Reading Women Writing Ser. Ithaca: Cornell UP, 1991.

Evans, Mari, ed. *Black Women Writers (1950–1980): A Critical Evaluation.* New York: Anchor, 1984.

Fanon, Frantz. *Black Skin, White Masks.* New York: Grove Press, 1967.

Felman, Shoshana, ed. *Literature and Psychoanalysis: The Question of Reading, Otherwise.* 1977. Reissued. Baltimore: Johns Hopkins UP, 1982.

———. and Dori Laub. *Testimony: Crises of Witnessing in Literature, Psychoanalysis, and History.* New York: Routledge, 1992.

Fetterley, Judith. "Reading about Reading: 'A Jury of Her Peers,' 'The Murders in the Rue Morgue,' and 'The Yellow Wallpaper.'" *Gender and Reading: Essays on Readers, Texts, and Contexts.* Ed. Elizabeth A. Flynn. Baltimore: Johns Hopkins UP, 1986. 147–164.

———. *The Resisting Reader: A Feminist Approach to American Fiction.* Bloomington: Indiana UP, 1978.

Flax, Jane. *Disputed Subjects: Essays on Psychoanalysis, Politics and Philosophy.* New York: Routledge, 1993.

Fleischner, Jennifer. *Mastering Slavery: Memory, Family, and Identity in Women's Slave Narratives.* New York: NYU Press, 1996.

Fox-Genovese, Elizabeth. "'To Write My Self': The Autobiographies of Afro-American Women." *Feminist Issues in Literary Scholarship.* Ed. Shari Benstock. Bloomington: Indiana UP, 1987. 161–180.

Frankenberg, Ruth. *The Social Construction of Whiteness: White Women, Race Matters.* Minneapolis: U of Minnesota P, 1993.

Freud, Sigmund. "Female Sexuality." 1931. *Sexuality and the Psychology of Love.* 184–201.

———. *Civilization and its Discontents.* 1930. Trans. James Strachey. New York: Norton, 1961.

———. "Some Psychical Consequences of the Anatomical Distinction Between the Sexes." 1925. Gay 670–678.

———. *An Autobiographical Study.* 1925. Trans. James Strachey. New York: Norton, 1963.

———. *The Ego and the Id.* 1923. Trans. Joan Riviere. Ed. James Strachey. New York: Norton, 1960.

———. "Medusa's Head." 1922. *Sexuality and the Psychology of Love.* 202–203.

———. *Beyond the Pleasure Principle.* 1920. Trans. James Strachey. New York: Norton, 1961.

———. "A Child is Being Beaten." 1919. *Sexuality and the Psychology of Love.* 97–122.

———. "Leonardo da Vinci and a Memory of his Childhood." 1909–1910. Gay 443–479.

———. *Fragment of an Analysis of a Case of Hysteria:* ("Dora"). 1905. n. trans. Ed. Philip Rieff. New York: Collier, 1969.

———. *Three Essays on the Theory of Sexuality.* 1905. Trans. James Strachey. New York: Basic, 1975.

———. "The Aetiology of Hysteria." 1896. Gay 96–111.

——— and Joseph Breuer. *Studies on Hysteria.* 1895. Trans. and ed. James Strachey. New York: Basic, n.d.

———. *Sexuality and the Psychology of Love.* n. trans. Ed. Philip Rieff. New York: Collier, 1963.

Frosh, Stephen. *Sexual Difference: Masculinity and Psychoanalysis.* London: Routledge, 1994.

Fryer, Judith. *Felicitous Space: The Imaginative Structures of Willa Cather and Edith Wharton.* Chapel Hill: U of North Carolina P, 1986.

Gates, Henry Louis Jr., ed. *Reading Black, Reading Feminist: A Critical Anthology.* New York: Meridian, 1990.

———, ed. *"Race," Writing, and Difference.* Chicago: U of Chicago P, 1986.

Gay, Peter, ed. *The Freud Reader.* New York: Norton, 1989.

Geller, Jeffrey L. and Maxine Harris. *Women of the Asylum: Voices from Behind the Walls, 1840–1945.* New York: Anchor, 1994.

Gilbert, Susan M. and Sandra Gubar. *The Madwoman in the Attic: The Woman Writer and the Nineteenth-Century Literary Imagination.* New Haven: Yale UP, 1979.

Gillman, Susan. "Pauline Hopkins and the Occult: African-American Revisions of Nineteenth-Century Sciences. *American Literary History* 8 (1996): 57–82.

Gilman, Charlotte Perkins. "The Yellow Wallpaper." 1892. New York: Feminist P at CUNY, 1973.

Glasgow, Ellen. *Barren Ground.* 1933. New York: Harcourt, 1985.

Goldberg, David Theo, ed. *Multiculturalism: A Critical Reader.* Malden, MA: Blackwell, 1997.

Goldstein, Rebecca. *The Dark Sister.* New York: Viking, 1991.

Gordon, Mary. *Good Boys and Dead Girls.* New York: Penguin, 1991.

Greene, Gayle. "Feminist Fiction and the Uses of Memory." *The Second Signs Reader: Feminist Scholarship, 1983–1996.* Eds. Ruth-Ellen B. Joeres and Barbara Laslett. Chicago: U of Chicago P, 1996. 184–215.

Greusser, John Cullen, ed. *The Unruly Voice: Rediscovering Pauline Elizabeth Hopkins.* Chicago: U of Illinois P, 1996.

Gutierrez, Ramon A. "Ethnic Studies: Its Evolution in American Colleges and Universities." Goldberg 157–167.

Haaken, Janice. "The Recovery of Memory, Fantasy, and Desire: Feminist Approaches to Sexual Abuse and Psychic Trauma." *Signs: Journal of Women in Culture and Society* 21 (1996): 1069–1094.

Habegger, Alfred. *Gender, Fantasy and Realism in American Realism.* New York: Columbia UP, 1982.

Hawthorne, Nathaniel. *The Scarlet Letter.* 1850. New York: Signet, 1959.

Henderson, Mae G. "The Stories of O(Dessa): Stories of Complicity and Resistance." Abel 285–304.

———. "Speaking in Tongues: Dialogics, Dialectics, and the Black Woman Writer's Literary Tradition." Wall 16–37.

Herman, Judith. *Trauma and Recovery: The Aftermath of Violence—from Domestic Abuse to Political Terror.* New York: Basic, 1997.

Higginbotham, Evelyn Brooks. *Righteous Discontent: The Women's Movement in the Black Baptist Church, 1880–1920.* Cambridge: Harvard UP, 1993.

Hirsch, Bernard A. "'The Telling which Continues': Oral Tradition and the Written Word in Leslie Marmon Silko's *Storyteller.*" *"Yellow Woman."* Ed. Melody Graulich. New Brunswick: Rutgers UP, 1993; 151–183.

Hirsch, Marianne. *The Mother/Daughter Plot: Narrative, Psychoanalysis, Feminism.* Bloomington: Indiana UP, 1989.

Hitchcock, Peter. *Dialogics of the Oppressed.* Minneapolis: U of Minnesota P, 1993.

Hoff, Paul. "Mesmerism: A Forerunner of Psychotherapy." *Nervenartz* 60 (1989): 732–739. no trans. Abstract. *PsycLIT* 1984–March 18, 1997. CD-ROM. Ovid.

Holquist, Michael. *Dialogism: Bakhtin and his World.* New York: Routledge, 1990.

hooks, bell. *Feminist Theory: From Margin to Center.* Boston: South End Press, 1984.

Hopkins, Pauline E. *Of One Blood; Or, the Hidden Self.* 1902–1903. *The Magazine Novels of Pauline E. Hopkins.* The Schomburg Library of Nineteenth-Century Black Women Writers Ser. Ed. Henry Louis Gates, Jr. New York: Oxford UP, 1988.

———. *Contending Forces: A Romance Illustrative of Negro Life North and South.* 1900. The Schomburg Library of Nineteenth-Century Black Women Writers Ser. Ed. Henry Louis Gates, Jr. New York: Oxford, UP, 1988.

———. "The Mystery Within Us." 1900. *Short Fiction by Black Women, 1900–1920.* Ed. Elizabeth Ammons. The Schomburg Library of Nineteenth-Century Black Women Writers Ser. Ed. Henry Louis Gates, Jr. New York: Oxford UP, 1991 21–26.

Horvitz, Deborah. "Nameless Ghosts: Possession and Dispossession in *Beloved.*" *Studies in American Fiction* 17 (1989): 157–167.

Howells, William Dean. *The Rise of Silas Lapham.* 1885. New York: Penguin, 1983.

Irigaray, Luce. *An Ethics of Sexual Difference.* Trans. Carolyn Burke and Gillian C. Gill. Ithaca: Cornell UP, 1984.

James, Henry. *The Portrait of a Lady.* 1881. New York: Bantam, 1983.

———. *Roderick Hudson.* 1876. New York: Harper Torchbooks, 1960.

James, William. *William James: The Essential Writings.* Ed. Bruce W. Wilshire. The Essential Writings of the Great Philosophers Ser. New York: Harper, 1971.

———. "The Hidden Self." 1896. *The Works of William James: Essays in Psychology.* Cambridge: Harvard UP, 1983, 247–268.

———. *William James on Exceptional Mental States: The 1896 Lowell Lectures.* Ed. Eugene Taylor. New York: Scribner's, 1982.

Jardine, Alice A. *Gynesis: Configurations of Woman and Modernity.* Ithaca: Cornell UP, 1985.

Johnson, James Weldon. *The Autobiography of an Ex-Colored Man.* 1912. New York: Penguin, 1990.

Jones, Gayl. *Eva's Man.* Boston: Beacon, 1976.

———. *Corregidora.* Boston: Beacon, 1975.

———. "About My Work." Evans 233–235.

Joplin, Patricia Klindienst. "The Voice of the Shuttle is Ours." *Stanford Literature Review* 1 (1984): 25–53.

Kahane, Claire. *Passions of the Voice: Hysteria, Narrative, and the Figure of the Speaking Woman 1850–1915.* Baltimore: Johns Hopkins UP, 1995.

Kanzer, Mark. "The Inconstant 'Principles of Constancy.'" *Journal of the American Psychoanalytic Association* 3 (1983): 843–865. Abstract. *PsycLIT* 1984–March 18, 1997. CD-ROM. Ovid.

Kaplan, Amy. *The Social Construction of American Realism.* Chicago: U of Chicago P, 1988.

Kassanoff, Jennie A. "'Fate Has Linked Us Together': Blood, Gender, and the Politics of Representation in Pauline Hopkins's *Of One Blood.*" Greusser 158–181.

Kingston, Maxine Hong. *The Woman Warrior: Memoirs of a Girlhood Among Ghosts.* New York: Vintage, 1975.

Kolodny, Annette. "Dancing through the Minefield." *Feminist Studies* 6 (1980): 1–25

Kravis, N. M. "James Braid's Psychophysiology: A Turning Point in the History of Dynamic Psychiatry." *American Journal of Psychiatry* 145 (1988): 1191–1206. Abstract. *PsycLIT* 1984–March 18, 1997. CD-ROM. Ovid.

Lanser, Susan S. "Feminist Criticism, 'The Yellow Wallpaper,' and the Politics of Color in America." *Feminist Studies* 15 (1989): 415–441.

Larsen, Nella. *Quicksand.* 1928. American Women Writers Ser. New Brunswick: Rutgers UP, 1986.

Le Clair, Tom. "Quilty Verdict." Rev. of *Alias Grace,* by Margaret Atwood. *The Nation* 9 Dec. 1996: Online.

Lewis, R.W.B. *Edith Wharton: A Biography.* New York: Harper, 1975.

Lewis, Sinclair. *Babbitt.* 1922. New York: Signet, 1992.

Lunbeck, Elizabeth. *The Psychiatric Persuasion: Knowledge, Gender, and Power in Modern America.* Princeton: Princeton UP, 1994.

Mantel, Hilary. "Murder and Memory." Rev. of *Alias Grace,* by Margaret Atwood. *The New York Review of Books* 19 Dec. 1996: 4–9.

Marcos, Subcomandante. *Shadows of Tender Fury: The Letters and Communiques of Subcomandante Marcos and the Zapatista Army of National Liberation.* Trans. Frank Bardacke, Leslie López, and the Watsonville, California Human Rights Committee. New York: Monthly Review Press, 1995.

Masson, Jeffrey. *The Assault on Truth: Freud's Suppression of the Seduction Theory.* New York: Farrar, Straus & Giroux, 1984.

McDowell, Deborah E. "'The Changing Same': Generational Connections and Black Women Novelists." Gates *RB, RF*: 91–115.

McLaren, Peter. "White Terror and Oppositional Agency: Towards a Critical Multiculturalism." Goldberg 45–74.

Meyers, Diana Tietjens. *Subjection and Subjectivity: Psychoanalytic Feminism and Moral Philosophy.* Thinking Gender Ser. New York: Routledge, 1994.

Milazzo, Lee, ed. *Conversations with Joyce Carol Oates.* Jackson: UP of Mississippi, 1989.

Miller, Laura. "Blood and Laundry": Interview with Margaret Atwood. *Salon Magazine* Jan. 1997: Online. 19 Feb. 1997.

Moi, Toril. "Patriarchal Thought and the Drive for Knowledge." Brennan, 189–205.

———. *Sexual/Textual Politics.* London: Methuen. 1985.

Moodie, Susanna. *Letters of Life and Duty: The Correspondence of Susanna and John Moodie.* Ed. Ballstadt, Hopkins, and Peterman. Toronto: U of Toronto P, 1993.

———. *Letters of a Lifetime.* Ed. Ballstadt, Hopkins, and Peterman. Toronto: U of Toronto P, 1985.

———. *Life in the Clearings.* 1853. Ed. Robert L. McDougall. Toronto: Macmillan of Canada. 1959.

Morrison, Toni. *Playing in the Dark: Whiteness and the Literary Imagination.* Cambridge: Harvard UP, 1992.

———. "Unspeakable Things Unspoken: The Afro-American Presence in American-Literature." *Michigan Quarterly Review* 28.1 (Winter 1989): 1–34.

———. *Beloved.* New York: Knopf, 1987.

———. *The Bluest Eye.* New York: Washington Square, 1970.

Mulvey, Laura. *Visual and Other Pleasures.* Bloomington: Indiana UP, 1989.

Nica-Udangiu, St. "J. Moreau de Tours (1804–1884)." *Neurologia, Psihiatria, Neurochirurgia* 29 (1984): 77–80. n. trans. Abstract. *PsycLIT* 1984–March 18, 1997. CD-Rom. Ovid.

Oates, Joyce Carol. *What I Lived For.* New York: Dutton, 1994.

Osagie, Iyunolu. "Is Morrison Also Among the Prophets?: 'Psychoanalytic' Strategies in *Beloved.*" *African American Review* 28 (1994): 423–440.

Otten, Thomas J. "Pauline Hopkins and the Hidden Self of Race." *English Literary History* 59 (1992): 227–256.

Perry, C. "Theorizing about Hypnosis in either/or terms." *International Journal of Experimental Hypnosis* 40 (1992): 238–252. Abstract. *Medline* 1966–March 1997. CD-ROM. Ovid.

Perry, Donna. *BackTalk: Women Writers Speak Out.* New Brunswick: Rutgers UP, 1993.

Personal Narratives Group, ed. *Interpreting Women's Lives: Feminist Theory and Personal Narratives.* Bloomington: Indiana UP, 1989.

Peterson, Carla. "Unsettled Frontiers: Race, History, and Romance in Pauline Hopkins's *Contending Forces.*" *Famous Last Words: Changes in Gender and Narrative Closure.* Ed. Alison Booth. Charlottesville: UP of Virginia, 1993.

Phillips, Adam. *On Kissing, Tickling and Being Bored: Psychoanalytic Essays on the Unexamined Life.* Cambridge: Harvard UP, 1993.

Prose, Francine. "Death and the Maid." Rev. of *Alias Grace,* by Margaret Atwood. *The New York Times Book Review* 29 Dec. 1996: 6.

Pryse, Marjorie and Hortense J. Spillers, eds. *Conjuring: Black Women, Fiction, and Literary Tradition.* Bloomington: Indiana UP, 1985.

Rampersad, Arnold. "Psychology and Afro-American Biography." *Yale Review* 78.1 (Autumn 1988): 1–18.

———. *The Art and Imagination of W. E. B. Du Bois.* 1976. New York: Schocken, 1990.

Reviere, Susan L. *Memory of Childhood Trauma: A Clinician's Guide to the Literature.* New York: Guilford, 1996.

Richards, Graham. "James and Freud: Two Masters of Metaphor." *British Journal of Psychology* 82. (1991): 205–215.

Ringel, Cheryl. *Criminal Victimization 1996: Changes 1995–1996 with Trends 1993–1996.* Washington DC: US Dept. of Justice; Bureau of Justice Statistics 1997. Online. National Victim Center, Arlington, VA. www.nvc.com.

Ross, John. *Rebellion from the Roots: Indian Uprising in Chiapas.* Monroe, Maine: Common Courage, 1995.

Roth, Philip. *Portnoy's Complaint.* 1969. New York: Vintage, 1994.

Sanders, Judith. "Response to Almanac of the Dead." unp. 1994.

Scarry, Elaine. *The Body in Pain: The Making and Unmaking of the World.* New York: Oxford UP, 1985.

Schrager, Cynthia D. "Pauline Hopkins and William James: The New Psychology and the Politics of Race." Greusser 182–209.

Showalter, Elaine. *Hystories: Hysterical Epidemics and Modern Media.* New York: Columbia UP, 1997.

———. *Sister's Choice: Tradition and Change in American Women's Writing.* New York: Oxford UP, 1994.

———. Interview with Joyce Carol Oates. Milazzo.

———. *The Female Malady: Women, Madness, and English Culture, 1830–1980.* New York: Penguin, 1985.

———. ed. *Feminist Criticism: Essays on Women, Literature and Theory.* New York: Pantheon, 1985.

Silko, Leslie Marmon. *Gardens in the Dunes.* New York: Simon and Schuster, 1999.

———. *Yellow Woman and A Beauty of the Spirit: Essays on Native American Life Today.* New York: Simon and Schuster, 1996.

———. *Almanac of the Dead.* New York: Penguin, 1991.

Smith, Barbara. "The Truth That Never Hurts: Black Lesbians in Fiction in the 1980s." *Feminisms: An Anthology of Literary Theory and Criticism.* Eds. Robin R. Warhol and Diane Price Herndl. New Brunswick: Rutgers UP, 784–806.

———. "Toward a Black Feminist Criticism." Showalter, *Feminist Criticism* 168–185.

Snyder, William U. *Thomas Wolfe: Ulysses and Narcissus.* Athens: Ohio UP, 1971.

Sophocles. Oedipus Rex. n.d. Trans. David Grene. Chicago: U of Chicago P, 1942.

Spillers, Hortense J. "'All the Things You Could Be by Now If Sigmund Freud's Wife Was Your Mother': Psychoanalysis and Race." *Critical Inquiry* 22 (1996): 710–734.

———. "Cross-Currents, Discontinuities: Black Women's Fiction." Afterword. Pryse and Spillers 249–261.

Stiehm, Judith. "Diversity's Diversity." Goldberg 140–156.

Stoller, Robert J. *Pain and Passion: A Psychoanalyst Explores the World of S&M.* New York: Plenum, 1991.

———. *Perversion: The Erotic Form of Hatred.* London: Karnac, 1975.

———. *Sex and Gender: The Development of Masculinity and Femininity.* London: Karnac, 1974.

Sui Sin Far. *Mrs. Spring Fragrance.* Chicago: A. C. McClurg, 1912.

Sundquist, Eric J. *To Wake the Nations: Race in the Making of American Literature.* Cambridge: Harvard UP, 1993.

Tal, Kalí. *Worlds of Hurt: Reading the Literatures of Trauma.* Cambridge Studies in American Literature and Culture Ser. New York: Cambridge UP, 1996.

Tanner, Laura E. *Intimate Violence: Reading Rape and Torture in Twentieth-Century Fiction.* Bloomington: Indiana UP, 1994.

Tate, Claudia. *Psychoanalysis and Black Novels: Desire and the Protocols of Race.* New York: Oxford UP, 1998

———. *Black Women Writers at Work.* New York: Continuum, 1983.

———. "Allegories of Black Female Desire; or, Rereading Nineteenth-Century Sentimental Narratives of Black Female Authority." Wall 98–126.

———. "Pauline Hopkins: Our Literary Foremother." Pryse and Spillers 53–66.

Taylor, Eugene, ed. *William James on Exceptional Mental States: The 1896 Lowell Lectures.* New York: Scribner's 1982.

Tinterow, M.M. "Satanic Agency and Mesmerism Reviewed—James Braid." *American Journal of Clinical Hypnosis* 36.1 (1993): 3–6. Abstract. Medline 1966–March 1997. CD-ROM. Ovid.

Todorov, Tzvetan. *Mikhail Bakhtin: The Dialogical Principle.* Trans. Wlad Godzich. Theory and History of Literature Ser. Minneapolis: U of Minnesota Press, 1984.

Tompkins, Jane P. "Sentimental Power: *Uncle Tom's Cabin* and the Politics of Literary History." Showalter, *Feminist Criticism.* 81–103.

Tubach, Sally Patterson. *Memoirs of a Terrorist.* Albany: SUNY P, 1996.

TuSmith, Bonnie. "The Cultural Translator: Toward An Ethnic Womanist Pedagogy." *MELUS* 16:2 (Summer 1989–1990): 17–29.

Waites, Elizabeth A. *Trauma and Survival: Post-Traumatic and Dissociative Disorders in Women.* New York: Norton, 1993.

Walker, Alice. *The Color Purple.* New York: Washington Square, 1982.

———. *The Third Life of Grange Copeland.* New York: Harcourt Brace, 1970.

Wallace, Michele. "Race, Gender, and Psychoanalysis in Forties Film: Lost Boundaries, Home of the Brave, and The Quiet One." *Black American Cinema.* Ed. Manthia Diawara. American Film Institute Ser. New York: Routledge, 1993. 257–271.

———. "The Search for the 'Good Enough' Mammy: Multiculturalism, Popular Culture, and Psychoanalysis." Goldberg 259–268.

Walton, Jean. "Re-Placing Race in (White) Psychoanalytic Discourse: Founding Narratives of Feminism." Abel 223–251.

Wesley, Marilyn C. *Refusal and Transgression in Joyce Carol Oates' Fiction.* Contributions in Women's Studies Ser. Number 135. Westport: Greenwood, 1993.

———. "Father-Daughter Incest as Social Transgression: A Feminist Reading of Joyce Carol Oates." *Women's Studies: An Interdisciplinary Journal* 21 (1992): 251–263.

Wharton, Edith. *The House of Mirth.* 1905. New York: Scribner's, 1969.

Wiley, David. "Atwood at a Glance: Interview." *Minnesota Daily News*/U of Minnesota Feb. 1997: Online 9 March 97.

Winnicott, D. W. *Home is Where We Start From.* Hammondsworth: Penguin, 1987.

———. *Playing and Reality.* New York: Basic, 1971.

Wolfe, Thomas. *Look Homeward, Angel.* New York: Scribner's, 1929.

Wolff, Cynthia Griffin. *A Feast of Words: The Triumph of Edith Wharton.* New York: Oxford UP, 1977.

Wright, Elizabeth, ed. *Feminism and Psychoanalysis: A Critical Dictionary.* Cambridge: Blackwell 1996.

———. "Thoroughly postmodern feminist criticism." Brennan 141–152.

Yezierska, Anzia. *Bread Givers.* 1925. New York: Persea, 1975.

Index

Abel, Elizabeth, 8, 64
Accocella, Joan, 138n. 18
Adorno, Theodor, 19
Alias Grace, 22, 24, 81, 99–121, 127, 129, 131, 139n. 24, 148n. 2, 149nn. 10, 11
  abortion, 116
  intertextual dialogue in 24, 71, 108–111, 120–122
    among, *Alias Grace,* "The Yellow Wallpaper," and *Of One Blood,* 126–127
    with *Oliver Twist* 106, 107
  Irish question, 101–102, 104, 110, 149n. 5
  narrative form, 129
  sadomasochism, 100, 115, 122, 127–128
  See also Atwood, hysteria, mesmerism, Susanna Moodie
Allen, Paula Gunn, 31–32, 36, 141n. 16
Allison, Dorothy, 22, 39, 40, 44, 50, 54–55, 94
Almanac of the Dead, 25–37, 140nn. 5, 7, 141n. 14
  art and sadism, 29
  cannibalism in, 27, 32, 141n. 8
  capitalism, 27
  Freud in, 25–26, 29, 31–32, 140n. 3
  Marx in, 25, 27, 31, 36–37
  narrative form, 26
  repetition, 27, 30, 32
  sadomasochism, 25–29, 30–31, 34, 37
  Zapatista army (EZLN), 36
Ammons, Elizabeth, 3–4
  on *Of One Blood,* 22, 66, 72
  on "The Yellow Wallpaper," 64, 123
Anzaldúa, Gloria, 25, 34–35, 136n. 5, 140n. 4
Armstrong, Louise, 138n. 18
Arnold, Ellen, 26
Atwood, Margaret, 1, 19, 22–24, 81, 94, 99–101, 103–121, 128–129, 131
  The Handmaid's Tale, 144n. 13, 149n. 9, 151n. 30
  The Servant Girl, 100, 104–105, 107, 111, 121, 148n. 3
Auerbach, Nina, 64, 104, 114, 116

Babbitt, 22, 76–77, 88–90, 93
    See also What I Lived For
Backlash
  against feminism, 3, 15
  against Freud, 12–15
  against trauma research, 14, 15
  See also false memory syndrome
Bakhtin, M.M., 149n. 8
Bambara, Toni Cade, 151n. 5
Barnes, Djuana, 151n. 5
Barzun, Jacques, 63
Bastard out of Carolina, 5, 19, 23, 39–40, 43, 45, 51–52, 144n. 12, 16
  gospel music in, 44, 50
  narrative form, 40
  sadomasochism, 43–48, 132
  scopophilia, 45–46
  trauma, 39–40
  See also masochism
Baym, Nina, 6
Belenky, et.al, 144n. 9
Bellow, Saul, 76
Benjamin, Jessica, 8, 21, 42, 48, 58–59, 65, 68–69, 87, 98, 152n. 6
Bettleheim, Bruno, 10, 137n. 11
Binet, Alfred, 62, 67, 145n. 7
Binswanger, Ludwig, 150n. 23
Braid, James, 118–120, 150n. 20
Breuer, Josef, 63, 65, 72, 139n. 21

Brooks, Peter, 8, 19, 47, 91, 97–98, 142n. 5
Brown, Laura S, 11
Brownmiller, Susan, 146n. 10
Burke, Kenneth, 8
Butler, Judith, 8

Carby, Hazel, 7, (on *Contending Forces*) 66, 69
Cardinal, Marie, 10, 49, 137n. 11
Caruth, Cathy, 4, 11, 16–17, 30, 131
Cather, Willa, 144n. 13, 151n. 5
Charcot, Jean-Martin, 13–15, 62, 64, 118–119, 137n. 15, 150n. 23
  Salpêtrière Clinic, 13, 62, 64, 118–119, 146n. 12
Chesler, Phyllis, 8
Chestnutt, Charles, 76, 90
Chichén Itzá, 35
Chinese Exclusion Act, 122
Chodorow, Nancy, 8
Chopin, Kate, 77, 90
Christian, Barbara, 7, 53–54, 136n. 5
Clatterbaugh, Peter, 78–79, 81–82, 84–85, 87
Cochran, Jo, 136n. 5
Collins, Patricia Hill, 53–54, 144n. 19, 146n. 16
Cook-Lynn, Elizabeth, 36, 139n. 2
Cooper, Anna Julia, 70
Corregidora, 4, 19, 23, 39–40, 42, 45–50, 52–54, 66, 70–71, 132
  the blues, 44–45, 54
  on curiosity, 41
  narrative form, 40, 51
  psychoanalytic reading of, 53
  sadomasochism, 4, 39, 44–48, 51–55
  scopophilia in, 45–46
  sexual difference and epistemophilia, 40–41, 43
  and Sophocles's *Oedipus Rex,* 47, 49, 54, 55, 143n. 9, 144n. 18
  story as art, 40–42
  trauma, 39–40.
Crews, Frederick, 138n. 19

Daley, Patricia Ellen Martin, 147n. 3
Davis, Angela, 78
de Biran, Maine, 120
de Lauretis, Teresa, 47
de Puysegeur, Marquis, 120
de Tours, Moreau, 120
Derrida, Jacques, 8
Dickinson, Emily, 8, 99, 109, 121
Dimen, Muriel, 21
Dinnerstein, Dorothy, 8
Doane, Mary Ann, 90–91
Doyle, James, 148n. 7
Dreiser, Theodore, 22, 76, 88
  Sister Carrie, 81
Du Bois, W. E. B., 59–60
duCille, Ann, 84, 135n. 4

Eliot, George, 149n. 16
Elliot, Emory, 8, 88
Estrich, Susan, 146n. 10

False Memory Syndrome, 16, 138nn. 18, 19
Felman, Shoshana, 9, 11, 20, 73, 143n. 10
Fetterley, Judith, 6
Fiedler, Leslie, 8
Fisk Jubilee Singers, 67, 71, 127
Fitzgerald, F. Scott, 88
Flax, Jane, 8
Fleischner, Jennifer, 8
Freud, Sigmund, 2, 118, 120–121, 126
  in *Almanac of the Dead,* 26, 29
  on curiosity, 41–43
  "Dora," 111, 113
  double consciousness, 63
  epistemology and sexual difference, 41
  feminist revisions of, 8–9, 43, 148n. 13
  hysteria, 18, 146n. 12
  in *Of One Blood,* 61–63, 66–67, 71–72
  repetition compulsion, 21, 31–32
  scopophilia, 45
  seduction theory, 3, 12, 14
    backlash, 12, 13, 15
  sublimation, 92
  trauma, 30.
  See also psychoanalysis

Frosh, Stephen, 97, 148n. 7

Giddings, Paula, 136n. 5
Gilligan, Carol, 8, 11
Gilman, Charlotte Perkins, 1, 21–23, 72, 90, 94, 126
  "The Yellow Wallpaper," 101, 121–127, 132

on depression, 122–124
on race and class, 122–123
Gilmore, David, 148n. 7
Glasgow, Ellen, 22, 90
Goldberg, David Theo, 7–9
Gomez, Alma, 136n. 5
Gordon, Mary, 86
Grant, Beth, 136n. 5
Gulf War Syndrome, 12, 15

Haaken, Janice, 138n. 18
Habegger, Alfred, 76, 82–84, 89
Harper, Frances, E. W., 70
Harris, Trudier, 7
Hemingway, Ernest, 88
Henderson, Mae G., 8, 21
Herbart, J.F., 119–120
Herman, Judith, 3, 15, 40, 44, 48, 62–64, 90, 94
definition of trauma, 6
study of psychic trauma, 11–14
Hirsch, Bernard, 28, 141n. 16
Hirsch, Marianne, 135
Hopkins, Pauline, 94, 145n. 1, 146n. 14
Contending Forces, 65–66, 70–71, 144n. 13
"The Mystery Within Us," 64
See also Of One Blood
Howells, William Dean, 22, 76, 82, 88
Hull, Gloria, 136n. 5
Hurston, Zora Neale, 147n. 18
Hypnosis, 13, 32, 61, 116–119
See also mesmerism
Hysteria, 61–64
definition of, 62
and gender, 58
and race, 57–58, 72
sexual trauma as cause, 58
symptoms of, 23, 57, 62
and trauma, 70

Incest, 3–5, 11, 13–16, 19, 39, 55, 63–67, 69, 73, 96–97, 133, 148n. 15
Isabella Beeton's Book of Household Management, 109–110

Jacobs, Harriet, 70
James, Henry, 88
James, William, 13, 61–64, 67, 74, 118, 146n. 13
Lowell Lectures on Exceptional Mental States, 62, 64
Janet, Pierre, 13, 61, 63, 67, 118
Johnson, Barbara, 8
Johnson, James Weldon, 76
Jones, Gayl, 39–40, 47, 50–51, 53–55, 94

Kahane, Claire, 59, 71
Kaminer, Wendy, 138n. 18
Kimmel, Michael, 148n. 7
Kingston, Maxine Hong, 144n 13
Kolodny, Annette, 6

Lacan, Jacques, 8–9, 23, 77, 91–92, 108
Lanser, Susan S., 122, 133
Larsen, Nella, 71, 90
Laycock, Thomas, 120
Lewis, Sinclair, 22, 76, 88
See also Babbitt
Leys, Ruth, 138n. 18
Lorde, Audre, 53
Lunbeck, Elizabeth, 60, 64

Mackenzie Rebellion, 103–104
Mantel, Hilary, 114
Marcos, Subcommander. *See* Zapatista Army
Masculinity, theories of, 148n. 7
See also Clatterbaugh, Frosh, Stoller
Masochism, 4, 23, 143n. 7
McDowell, Deborah, 7, 53
Mena, Maria Christina, 144n. 13
Mesmerism
in *Alias Grace,* 112, 118–120, 150n. 20
F.A. Mesmer, 112
in *Of One Blood,* 61, 64–65, 67
See also hypnosis
Meyers, Diana Tietjens, 8
Miller, Jean Baker, 148n. 12
Mirikitani, Janice, 144n. 13
Mitchell, S. Weir
rest cure, 24, 126
Moi, Toril, 142n. 5
Moodie, Susanna, 100, 105–109, 111, 114, 149n. 4
Moraga, Cherrî, 136n. 5
Morrison, Toni, 147n. 18
Beloved, 5, 39, 70–71, 94, 115, 117
Playing in the Dark: Whiteness and the Literary Imagination, 10
Song of Solomon, 70
Multiculturalism, 2, 7–9

Mulvey, Laura, 43, 45, 47, 51

Nagler, Michael, 30
Narrative (or story)
  and art, 41–42
  and curiosity, 23, 41–43
  and healing, 6, 10, 18, 39–43, 47, 57, 59, 63, 65, 72, 134
  and psychotherapy, 26, 57, 60
  and race, 86
  and sadism, 18, 28, 47, 55, 94
Narrative form. *See* individual texts
Nathan, Debbie, 138n. 18
Naylor, Gloria, 147n. 18
  Linden Hills
"New psychology," 23, 58, 61, 117, 120

Oates, Joyce Carol, 94, 96, 98, 147n. 2
  as social critic, 77
Of One Blood, Or the Hidden Self, 5, 15, 21–23, 32, 48, 57–62, 64–74, 77, 101, 114, 117, 122, 127, 145nn. 6, 8, 151n. 29
  in conversation with *Alias Grace* and "The Yellow Wallpaper"
  as hysterical text, 59
  mysticism in, 59–60
  narrative form, 59, 72–73
  "passing," 68
  sadomasochism, 68–69, 71
  trauma, 70–71
Otten, Thomas, 67

Painter, Nell Irvin, 8
Phillips, Adam, 48, 142n. 4
Pleck, J.H., 148n. 7
Political trauma. *See* trauma
Postmodern realism. *See* realism
Poststructural realism. *See* realism
Psychic trauma. *See* trauma
Psychoanalysis and psychoanalytic theory, 17, 148n. 13
  and fiction, 18, 26
  "new psychology," 23, 58, 61, 117, 120
  and race, 9
  repetition compulsion, 21, 31–32
  scopophilia
    in *Bastard out of Carolina* and *Corregidora,* 45–46
  See Freud

Rampersad, Arnold, 8
Realism, 22–23, 26, 59, 72–73, 76, 82, 88–89, 93–95, 110, 114
  postmodern, 26, 76
  poststructural, 81, 104, 129
Reynolds, Mary
  the case of, 113, 149n. 13, 150n. 18
Roth, Philip, 76, 88, 134
Rubin, Lillian, 148n. 7

Sadism and trauma, 39, 40
Sadomasochism, 4–5, 11, 18, 22, 131–134, 142n. 1
  and art, 29, 128
    nineteenth-century paintings, 128
  and gender, 132
  political, 146n. 19
  and race, 132, 146nn. 16, 18
  in story, 47
Sanders, Judith, 35
  Saussure, Ferdinand de, 8, 23, 91–92
Savran, Michael, 148n. 7
Schrager, Cynthia, 61, 145n. 5
Scott, Patricia Bell, 136n. 5
Showalter, Elaine, 75, 138nn. 18, 19, 20, 147n. 2
Silko, Leslie, Marmon, 1, 4, 19, 22–23, 25, 77, 94, 116, 132
Sinclair, Upton, 22
Smith, Barbara, 7, 136n. 5
Social Darwinism, 88, 93
Spillers, Hortense J., 5, 7–10, 53, 137n. 12
Stoller, Robert J., 81–84, 86–89, 148n. 7
Styron, William, 88

Tal, Kalî, 5, 6, 11, 19, 139n. 23
Tanner, Laura, 45, 51, 94
Tate, Claudia, 5, 7–11, 136n. 5
Tavris, Carol, 138n. 18
Tompkins, Jane, 6
Trauma
  defined by Caruth, 30; Herman, 6; Shatan, 6; Tal, 5; Waites, 5
  personal, 11
  political, 11
  study of, 11–15
    backlash against, 14–15
  post traumatic stress disorder (PTSD), 12
  and race, 23
  See also individual texts

Trillings, Lionel, 8
Tsutakawa, Mayami, 136n. 5
Tubach, Sally Patterson, 133, 152n. 4

Valenzuela, Luisa, 151n. 5
Violence, reading of, 51, 94

Waites, Elizabeth, 5, 11
Walker, Alice, 147n. 18
  The Third Life of Grange Copeland, 133, 144n. 13
Wall, Cheryl, 7
Wallace, Michele, 8–9, 11, 15
Wellék, Rene, 76
  See also realism
Wells, Ida B., 70–71
Wesley, Marilyn, 93, 148n. 15
Wharton, Edith, 22, 55, 77, 90–144n. 13
What I Lived For
  and *Babbitt,* 88–89, 147n. 4
  capitalism, 81
  liberalism, 79–80
  narrative form, 22–23, 81, 83–85, 95
  racism in, 79–81, 83–84
  realism, 22, 87–89
  sadomasochism, 80, 96–97
Wiesel, Elie, 73
Wilson, Edmund, 8
Winnemucca, Sarah, 151n. 5
Winnicott, D.W., 41
Wolfe, Thomas, 76, 88
Wright, Elizabeth, 8, 17

"The Yellow Wallpaper," 6, 24, 64, 72, 90, 101, 121–123, 125–127, 151nn. 25, 28
  intertextual dialogue with *Of One Blood* and *Alias Grace,* 126
  masochism in, 64
  racism in, 80, 122–123
Yezierska, Anzia, 151n. 5

Zapatista Army (EZLN), 36–37, 141n. 18